NIGHTHAWK F-117
STEALTH FIGHTER

PAUL F. CRICKMORE

ALISON J. CRICKMORE

MOTORBOOKS
INTERNATIONAL

Dedication

This book is dedicated to our parents,
Percy, Sylvia, Neil, and Pauline
and to the memory of
Ben Rich, "Father of Stealth."

First published July 1999 as "F-117 Nighthawk"

© Paul Crickmore and Alison J. Crickmore, 1999, 2003

Motorbooks International titles are also available at discounts in bulk quantity for industrial or sales-promotional use. For details write to Special Sales Manager at Motorbooks International Wholesalers & Distributors, Galtier Plaza, Suite 200, 380 Jackson Street, St. Paul, MN 55101-3885 USA.

ISBN 0-7603-1512-4

Cover photos courtesy of Lockheed Martin

Frontispiece and Title Page photos by Paul Crickmore

Printed in Hong Kong

contents

acknowledgments

The material for this book came from two basic sources: open literature, including books, professional journals, and declassified technical reports; and first-hand accounts from pilots, engineers, and key personnel associated with Have Blue and Senior Trend.

Most of the information contained within these pages was pieced together during the course of numerous interviews. A number of people also contributed information on the provision that their anonymity be respected. We have to say that none of those who so generously gave up their time divulged secrets that could in any way compromise the interests of the United States or its allies.

Our special thanks go to Brigadier General Buster Glosson, Alan Brown, Hal Farley, Kenny Linn, Squadron Leader Dave Southwood and his wife, Deri, Paul Martin, Graham Wardell, Major Jerry and Nancy Leatherman, Colonel Mike Mahar, Colonel Greg Feest, Colonel Al Whitley, John Nichol, Gene Boesch, Bobby Wall, Jim "J. B." Brown, Tom Morgenfeld, Dave Ferguson, and Skip Anderson.

Our thanks also go to Stan Piet, Bill Crimmins, Michael Gordon, Bob Pepper, Denys Overholser, James Lutz, Lieutenant Tara Shamhart, Bob Murphy, Jim Goodall, Chris Pocock, Ellan Bendall, Jay Miller, Malcolm English, Deny Lombard, Mike Badrocke, Ron Lindke, Bob Dorr, Paul Tilzey, Bernie Mearns, Tony Pennicooke, James Hepburn, Lieutenant Colonel Andrew Papp, Sergeant Wells Wilcox, Alan Warnes, and also our editor, Mike Haenggi.

We also thank our friends for their encouragement and continued support: Karen and Alberto, Paul and Helen, Gilly and Mike, Kevin and Jane, and Debbie and Phil.

From the earliest days of biplane fighters that attacked with the sun at their backs, one adage has always held true for the combat pilot: You cannot destroy what you cannot see. With the advent of radar and "fire-and-forget missiles," however, fighter pilots could no longer rely on the fallacies of the human eye to avoid detection. Even the craftiest of veteran fliers acknowledged the need for rapid advancements in detection-avoidance technology. Thus began the long and arduous process of developing a plane that could evade the newest, long-range target acquisition and missile guidance systems.

As at every point in military history, our scientists and industry leaders were up to the task. Their answer was the now well-known F-117 Stealth Fighter, affectionately named the Nighthawk by the men and women who fly her. The F-117 is the world's first pure stealth fighter. Its black, alien geometry defies conventional notions that to be effective, jet fighters should be sleek and fast. Nevertheless, despite its awkward appearance, the F-117 has unilaterally altered warfare, both in the air and on the ground, by defying the efforts of sophisticated air defenses to acquire, track, and engage it. Whether you are flying it or trying to defend against it, the F-117 is the preeminent weapons system for destroying the most highly defended and difficult-to-hit targets. Thus, the F-117 became the backbone of the Gulf War air campaign.

January 17, 1991, the first night of the Gulf War, served notice on the world that the F-117 was a dominant force capable of changing the tide of a war. At the beginning of hostilities, Iraq defended Baghdad with a threat array (anti-aircraft batteries and surface-to-air missiles) that was twice as dense as Eastern Europe during the Cold War and four times as dense as that mustered by Hanoi during the Vietnam War. Striking targets in Baghdad meant attacking one of the most heavily defended cities in the world. Due to its stealth attributes and consequent ability to avoid detection, the F-117 was the only aircraft allowed to go there.

Despite the impressive defensive gauntlet at Iraq's disposal, the success of the F-117 during the Gulf War was staggering. Critical air defense targets that would have taken repeated raids from large numbers of conventional aircraft were destroyed by a single F-117 strike. Specifically, during the first two weeks of the war, against the full array of Iraqi defenses, 36 F-117s destroyed more than 60

General Buster Glosson visits one of his 14th Air Division, Fighter Wings.
Gen. Buster Glosson

percent of the strategic targets without losing a single aircraft. By comparison, the remaining 40 percent of the strategic targets required six battle groups (which destroyed 8 percent) and 1,000 land-based, nonstealth aircraft (32 percent). The F-117 thus enabled the Coalition to destroy critical strategic targets and to unravel the Iraqi air defense system. The air-to-ground success of the F-117, coupled with the air-to-air dominance of the F-15C, permitted nonstealth Coalition aircraft to conduct the relentless interdiction that precipitated the collapse of the Iraqi field army and saved countless Coalition lives.

This book provides a complete history, complemented with photographs that have never been published before, of one of the greatest achievements in aviation since General Chuck Yeager broke the sound barrier over the deserts of California—the evolution of the F-117. Paul and Alison Crickmore trace the F-117 from its inception as one of the most covert military projects (code names: Have Blue and Senior Trend) through its greatest success, namely, its awesome and somewhat mind-boggling, accomplishments during the Gulf War. Their historical narrative is also laced with compelling eyewitness accounts of the birth, development, and combat successes of this technological marvel. For instance, the Crickmores provide anecdotal accounts of Denys Overholser and Bill Schroeder converting the low observable idea into engineering equations and computer designs; Ben Rich driving the bureaucracy of both Lockheed and the U.S. Air Force to undertake the unconventional; Bill Park and Ken Dyson recounting their initial test flights of the Have Blue; Colonel Bob Jackson and Colonel Jim Allen providing the leadership for the first F-117 combat fighting unit; and Colonel Greg Feest describing the first combat mission of the Gulf War.

By artfully recounting the creation and combat employment of the F-117 through the eyes of the people integrally involved at each milestone, the Crickmores have produced a historically accurate work that is second to none. In sum, their development of the F-117 Stealth Fighter from an idea to a feared force used to influence the political actions of nation states is a must-read for the informed citizen, as well as the political and military leaders of tomorrow.

General Buster Glosson
Architect of the Gulf War air campaign

chapter one

BLACK AND BLUE

During the air war over Vietnam, the most lethal threat facing U.S. air elements was radar-directed surface-to-air missiles (SAMs) and anti-aircraft artillery (AAA). It was extremely disruptive, often resulting in attack aircraft missing targets in order to evade SAMs or dodge AAA. As the war progressed the threat increased, and by the latter stages less than half the aircraft involved in major U.S. air strikes were tasked with hitting the primary targets. Most were involved in support activities, tanking, combat air patrols (CAPs), or the suppression of enemy air defenses.

During the 1973 Yom Kippur War, the Israeli Air Force lost 109 aircraft in just 18 days, virtually all falling victim to radar-guided SAM or AAA batteries. This occurred despite the Israeli Air Force being equipped with the most advanced attack aircraft of the day, employing up-to-date electronic counter measures (ECMs), and its pilots being as highly trained and professional as any serving in the U.S. Air Force.

During the Cold War, the Soviet Union had developed a highly sophisticated, integrated defense network, consisting of long- and medium-range surveillance radars that provided initial intercept or ground controlled intercept information to an outstanding fleet of high-performance fighters. Belts of radar-directed SAM and AAA batteries then provided an additional defensive ring around key targets. U.S. planners estimated that if the Israeli loss ratio were extrapolated into a NATO/Warsaw Pact scenario, NATO air forces would be decimated in just over two weeks. Clearly, what was needed was a fundamental rethink on how to redress this imbalance.

In 1974 Ken Perko in the Tactical Technology Office at the Defense Advanced Research Projects Agency (DARPA) requested submissions from Northrop, McDonnell Douglas, General Dynamics, Fairchild, and Grumman addressing two considerations:

1. What were the signature thresholds that an aircraft would need to achieve to become essentially undetectable at an operationally useful range?
2. Did those companies possess the capabilities to design and produce an aircraft with those necessary low signatures?

Fairchild and Grumman declined the invitation to participate, while General Dynamics emphasized the continued need for electronic countermeasures and provided little substantive technical content regarding signature reduction. The submissions from McDonnell Douglas and Northrop, however, demonstrated a grasp of the problem, together with a degree of technical capability for developing an aircraft with a reduced signature. Consequently, both companies were awarded contracts worth approximately $100,000 each during the closing months of 1974 to conduct further studies. These studies, classified confidential, also involved radar experts from the Hughes Aircraft Company whose role would also be to identify and verify appropriate radar cross-section (RCS) thresholds. By early 1975, McDonnell Douglas had identified likely RCS thresholds that could produce an operational advantage; these were later confirmed by Hughes. In the spring, these values were established by DARPA as goals for the program. DARPA then challenged the study participants to find ways of achieving them. The stage was set for the development of the first true stealth aircraft, but Lockheed was nowhere in sight.

Early in phase 1 of the XST program, it became apparent that the models undergoing tests had RCS values considerably lower than the Styrofoam mounting poles. Special mounting devices and improved testing were developed to overcome the problem. *Lockheed Martin*

In addition to being the first of only two pilots to fly Have Blue, Bill Park (in flight suit) also conducted carrier trials in the U-2R and was the second pilot to fly the A-12. *Lockheed Martin*

On January 17, 1975, Kelly Johnson's protégé, Ben Rich, became president of Lockheed's legendary Skunk Works. Rich had joined the company as an entry-level engineer in 1954 and began working on the U-2. Five years later, he and Dave Campbell were principal propulsion engineers on Project Gusto, a series of design submissions that would evolve into the A-12, YF-12, and later the SR-71.

Rich couldn't have inherited such an undertaking at a worse time. After Vietnam, defense spending was about as low as a snake's naval in a wagon rut. Lockheed was also still suffering from a bribery scandal from the previous year. Executives admitted paying millions of dollars in bribes over more than a decade in order to secure contracts (principally for the F-104 Starfighter) from key officials and politicians in The Netherlands, West Germany, Italy, and Japan. To make matters worse, Lockheed's attempt to re-enter the commercial airliner market with its L-1011 Tristar failed, plunging the company into financial turmoil. In 1972, Congress reluctantly helped bail out the company with loan guarantees of $250 million; however, losses continued to accumulate, and by late 1974 they had reached a staggering $2 billion.

It was into this corporate caldron that 50-year-old Ben Rich stepped, "hat in hand, with a fresh shoeshine, and a brave smile." He knew his task was to get new business fast and fill as much of the 300,000 square feet of production and assembly space in the two enormous hangars at Burbank, California, as possible. One possible route out of the morass, as proposed by the corporate accountants, was to unload some of the highly experienced, higher-salaried people and downsize the workforce (already cut from 6,000 workers in 1970 to just 1,500). On top of all this, there were several powerful enemies of the Skunk Works on Lockheed's board, including the vice president Gra-

ham Whipple who resented the high level of autonomy and independence granted to this small elite group. Given half an excuse, they would have gleefully shut them down.

Rich's first course of action was to convince General David Jones, the Air Force chief of staff, of the need to re-open the U-2 production line. This game plan was without precedent; never in its history had the U.S. Air Force restarted a production line for any aircraft in its inventory, let alone one whose tooling had been placed in storage six years earlier. During that meeting Gen. Jones indicated that he was "favorably disposed" to the idea, but Rich was under no illusions. To secure the long-term future of the Skunk Works, a substantial project involving revolutionary technologies was needed.

Lockheed hadn't been one of the five original companies approached by the DARPA team, simply because it hadn't produced a fighter for nearly 10 years. It was while networking his contacts at the Pentagon and at Wright-Patterson Air Force Base that Ed Martin, Lockheed California Companies director for science and engineering, was made aware of the study. He and Rich then briefed Kelly, who in turn obtained a letter from the Central Intelligence Agency (CIA), granting the Skunk Works permission to discuss with DARPA the low-observable characteristics of the A-12 and D-21 drone. Rich and Martin then presented the results to Ken Perko and Dr. George Heilmeier, the head of DARPA, and formally requested entry into the competition. Heilmeier,

Major Norman 'Ken' Dyson was nominated and recruited into the Have Blue program while serving as the Director of the F-15 Joint Test Force. *U.S. Air Force*

however, explained that two $100,000 contracts had already been awarded to two companies, and there was no more cash available. After a lot of arguing, Rich convinced the DARPA boss to allow Lockheed into the competition without a government contract—a move that ultimately paid a handsome dividend. Lockheed was given access to technical reports already provided to the other participants. Lockheed's new president, Larry Kitchen, supported Rich by helping him secure the necessary capital for the project.

In February 1975, Dick Scherrer joined Ed Martin from Lockheed's "White World," Advanced Concepts Department. He made inquiries within the Skunk Works to unearth any theoretical foundations on which he could base a low-RCS design. His investigations drew a blank; but then, he was introduced to Denys Overholser.

Overholser joined the Skunk Works from Boeing in 1964. He recalls, "When I left Boeing even as a young engineer, I was rated within the top 20 percent of their engineering staff. When I came to the Skunk Works, I ranked myself within the bottom 1 percent of their engineers. It frightened me

Lockheed C-5 Galaxies were used to transport both Have Blue aircraft and later F-117As from Burbank to Area 51. *U.S. Air Force*

so much, that I thought if these people find out what I don't know, they'll fire me. So I worked like a dog, and in return, they tolerated and trained me. I was one of the 120 design engineers that worked on the SR-71 and was a radome specialist, designing things that were transparent to radar. When Dick Scherrer asked me, 'How do we shape something to make it invisible to radar?' I said, 'Well, it's simple, you just make it out of flat surfaces, and you tilt those flat surfaces over, sweeping the edges away from the radar view angle, and that way you basically cause the energy to reflect away from the radar, thus limiting the magnitude of the return.'"

The framework for such radical thinking had its roots in discussions that Overholser had had years earlier with his boss, Bill Schroeder. Schroeder, a brilliant mathematician, had been employed by Kelly to resolve analytical problems, and he had trained Overholser. During the course of discussing the mathematics and physics of optical scattering, the two concluded that detectable signatures could be minimized using a shape composed of the smallest number of properly oriented flat panels. In addition, Overholser's boss believed that he could develop and resolve a mathematical equation capable of calculating analytically the reflection from a triangular flat panel. This in turn could be applied in a calculation relating to RCS.

With input from Overholser, Dick Scherrer drew a preliminary low-RCS shape based upon a faceted delta wing. By April, Overholser had hired his ex-boss

Bill Schroeder out of retirement, and they set about completing solutions to RCS equations that would enable the group to eventually predict results. Dick Scherrer recruited Kenneth Watson in as senior lead aircraft designer, tasked to site all systems inside the "Shell" that he and Overholser were designing.

As the design effort ratcheted up and Schroeder's mathematical computations became available, Overholser and his team of two engineers used these to write the computer program that could evaluate the RCS of prospective design submissions nominated by Scherrer and his group of preliminary design engineers. Overholser and his team worked night and day and in just five weeks produced an RCS prediction program known as "Echo 1," a truly remarkable achievement and one in the best traditions of the Skunk Works. As tests proceeded, it was determined that the edge contributions calculated by Echo 1 weren't exactly correct due to a phenomenon known as "diffraction."

Shortly after developing Echo 1, Overholser became aware of a publication entitled *Method of Edge Waves in the Physical Theory of Diffraction*, published in an unclassified technical paper in the Soviet Union in 1962 by Pyotr Ufimtsev, chief scientist at the Moscow Institute of Radio Engineering. The paper had been translated by Air Force Systems Command's Foreign Technology Division in 1971, and Overholser was able to incorporate elements of its theory into a refined version of the Echo 1 program. Overholser notes,

Area 51 is probably the best known "secret" base in Western military aviation circles. Situated approximately 100 miles northwest of Las Vegas, its exceptional remoteness and security restrictions (it is close to a large nuclear weapons test facility) made it the perfect site for Black World flight test operations. It was recommended to Kelly Johnson by Tony LeVier for the U-2 program and was subsequently used by the CIA and Lockheed during the Oxcart and Tagboard programs (A-12 and M-21/D-21). It was also used for flight testing the SR-71 and the Red Hat program, to mention but a few. *James Goodall*

"With the Echo 1 program, we were then able to iterate and rapidly look at over 20 designs and know which of those designs was the optimum, from a radar cross-section standpoint. Those same designs were then reviewed by Structures, Aero, and the other disciplines. We then made decisions as to what was the optimum useable design."

The faceted delta-wing design had more than its share of skeptics within the Skunk Works (some in aerodynamics referred to the shape as the "Hopeless Diamond"). Even the great Kelly Johnson had more than a few misgivings, betting a quarter with Ben Rich that, "Our old D-21 drone has a lower cross-section than that goddamn diamond."

To help ensure success for Lockheed in the competition, Warren Gilmour determined the necessary signature thresholds that would satisfy DARPA's objectives. With $25,000 procured from the Lockheed board, two one-third scale, wooden models of the Hopeless Diamond were built. One was used by the aerodynamists in wind tunnel tests; the other was coated with metal foil to provide a conductive surface and used to measure RCS in Lockheed's anechoic chamber. The first series of tests were conducted in June 1975, and they demonstrated that the RCS "spikes" matched precisely those predicted by Echo 1. Overholser recalls, "Well, this elevated me from the village idiot to the village expert, and I couldn't do anything wrong. I thought, oh my word, now I have to be careful what I say."

The model was moved outdoors to a radar test range near Palmdale on the Mojave Desert. Owned by McDonnell Douglas, the Grey Butte Range boasted improved capabilities, enabling the team to measure lower RCS values. Yet again, these test results conformed well with Echo 1 predictions, cre-

ating greater levels of confidence in both the computer program and the faceted design concept—a concept that reduced RCS values below those achieved by the D-21 by several orders of magnitude. As Ben Rich recalls, "September 14, 1975, [is] a date etched forever in my memory, because it was about the only time I ever won a quarter from Kelly Johnson. He grudgingly flipped me the quarter and said, 'Don't spend it, until you see the dammed thing fly.'"

Leo Celniker was brought in from the White World as chief engineer, and Dick Cantrell, the Skunk Works senior aerodynamicist, accepted responsibility for the aerodynamics and flight control effort. To improve the vehicles lift-to-drag ratio, the section outboard the engine inlets was thinned, resulting in the semblance of wings, which were eventually extended outward, changing the planform from the original diamond shape, to a notched-out delta. The trailing edge sweep was increased to 48 degrees to ensure that the signature spike, associated with the trailing edge, fell outside the frontal sector, to minimize "nose-on" detection. Tail surfaces that cantered inboard were also added.

Two proposals were submitted to DARPA from Lockheed. One included the predicted and measured signature data for the Hopeless Diamond; the other provided the predicted data for an air vehicle of flyable configuration. This came about in response to DARPA issuing proposals to the three competitors for what was to become known as the Experimental Survivable Testbed (XST) program, which was informally requested in the late summer of 1975. Responses were due in August or September, wherein the signature goals were those laid down in the earlier 1974–1975 directive.

Northrop's XST entry was similar in appearance to that of Lockheed's; however, its design was developed from a computer program called GEN-SCAT, which also had its origins in mathematical equations associated with the physics of optics. Like Lockheed, Northrop also used the Grey Butte Range to test and evaluate its design and computer modeling. By the summer of 1975, it too had reliable indications that its design would achieve the RCS goals set earlier.

Having been the first to determine what the RCS thresholds for the competition were likely to be, McDonnell Douglas, however, was unable to design an aircraft that could achieve anything like those goals. With RCS results coming from both Lockheed and Northrop verging on the revolutionary, Ken Perko called a meeting within DARPA to determine the program's future direction. It was decided that the program should be developed further into a full-scale, flight test demonstration, consisting of two phases. Phase 1 would culminate in a ground RCS evaluation of large-scale models. Following this, one contractor would be selected to proceed with phase 2, the construction and flight testing of two demonstration vehicles. The estimated cost for the XST program was $36 million, and this would be split between the successful contractor, a reluctant Air Force, and DARPA (with the latter contributing marginally more and thereby retaining program management control). By August 1975, funding arrangements were completed, and on November 1, 1975, Lockheed and Northrop were awarded contracts of $1.5 million each to conduct phase 1 of the XST program. The two companies were each given just four months to complete the full-scale, wooden test models, which would then be evaluated in a "high-noon shoot-out" at the Air Force's Radar Target Scatter (RATSCAT) test range located at White Sands, New Mexico.

It was already apparent that the RCS results achieved by both Lockheed and Northrop were unlike anything obtained before, and it would therefore be necessary to develop a new, low-signature pylon to ensure that returns from the pylon did not impinge upon results from the test models. Consequently, $187,000 was allocated to Lockheed for the purpose of building a 40-foot mounting pole with a radar return 10 decibels lower than the XST model. For this purpose, Denys Overholser designed a double-wedge pylon that was delivered to RATSCAT in January 1976 and was used by both contractor's models. It was initially tested by a 50,000-watt megatron state-of-the-art transmitter. Overholser remembers, "John Cashen, who was Northrop's stealth engineer, was in the control room when they fired up the radar, and I overheard their program manager whisper to John, 'Jesus, if they can do that with a frigging pole, what can they do with their damn model?'"

In March 1976, the Lockheed model was hauled by truck to RATSCAT, and the testing began. Throughout the tests the competing contractors and their models were kept in isolation from one another, billeted in temporary quarters, affording each independent access to the range. In early April 1976, Lockheed received word that it had officially won phase 1 of the competition.

Recognizing the outstanding results also achieved by Northrop, DARPA urged the team to remain together. Shortly thereafter, DARPA initiated studies for a Battlefield Surveillance Aircraft, Experimental (BSAX), which eventuated into Tacit Blue, the highly successful flight demonstration program that provided vital data for the subsequent B-2 bomber program.

Have Blue

Phase 2 of the XST program became known as the Have Blue program and was initiated on April 26, 1976. The Skunk Works was authorized to proceed with the design, construction, and flight testing of two technology demonstrator aircraft. To build Have Blue, Ben Rich needed to raise $10.4

million and recalls, "One can't imagine what goes through your mind when you have to ask the board of directors to invest $10.4 million at a time when the corporation was considering bankruptcy." Contract negotiations were completed two months later, and a first flight was scheduled for December 1977.

There were three objectives to the Have Blue program:

1. To validate in flight the four low observability signatures identified earlier in the program (radar, infrared, acoustic, and visual).
2. To demonstrate acceptable performance and flying qualities.
3. To demonstrate modeling capabilities that accurately predict low observable characteristics of an aircraft in flight.

Back at Burbank, Norm Nelson provided continuity as program manager of Have Blue. Leo Celniker, whose expertise was pitched more in the advanced design area, now worked on possible military extensions of the design (eventually turning Have Blue into the F-117). Denys Overholser maintained his position as general radar cross-section analyst and was therefore not "program" specific. He remembers, "It was incredible. As the program proceeded, all sorts of little things came up, like the precision of calculators used by the engineers. They found that they couldn't calculate the geometry of the airplane as their calculators only went to seven digits of precision. In the end they had to use Hewlett Packard calculators with eleven digits of precision!"

Alan Brown, became the chief technical engineer, while Ed "Baldy" Baldwin—the Skunk Works most experienced structural engineer—headed airframe design. Elmer Gath covered propulsion installation and reported to Baldwin. Bill Taylor was responsible for systems design, and he had Herb Ermer on hydraulics and Chuck Sturdevant on fuel systems working under him. Avionics was not a major issue on Have Blue, but flight controls came under Bob Loschke. Dick Cantrell was in charge of flight sciences for the Skunk Works, and so aerodynamics and propulsion performance continued under his purview.

Radar-absorbent materials (RAMs) for the program were developed within a Lockheed laboratory. The lab had been set up specifically for the development of RAM by Kelly Johnson back in the late 1950s. Two principal contributors for Have Blue were Mel George, head of the lab, and Ed Lovick, who did much of the material design. Both had been heavily involved in the design of the SR-71. Manufacturing was placed under the direction of Bob Murphy, and the entire engineering, fabrication, and assembly of Have Blue was carried out in legendary Building 82 (birthplace of the F-104, U-2, and A-12).

Just three assembly tools were used on the project: wing, forward fuselage, aft fuselage. The subassemblies were all made on a tooling plate left over from where the main frames for the C-5 galaxy had been machined. Templates were laid on the plate and subassemblies were built by hand. Some of the key players in the manufacturing effort were Ron Olsen and G. James, aft fuselage; G. Holquist, Mike Kammerer, K. Paton, and Fritz Fyre, wings; Jim Dry, C. Lee, and G. Davis, fuselage; Bob Murphy, cockpit; Red McDaris, instrumentation; John Stanley, fuel plumbing; Bill Patterson, tank seal; Steve Vaughn and I. Piquit, test rig; Ben Dehaven, paint; Dick Madison, landing gear; and Jack Greenley, night foreman.

Top Secret

In early 1977, the government realized what a major breakthrough had been achieved in VLO technology and what a radical impact the successful deployment of such techniques could have on national defense. Subsequently, program security migrated from the White World minimum security classification of "confidential," into the Black World, where the program became top secret, "special access required" (SAR).

To reduce time, costs, and risk in this revolutionary project, a Tactical Air Command major named Jack Twigg was cleared into the program and became the system program officer (SPO) whose remit was to procure wherever possible "tried and tested," "off-the-shelf" pieces of equipment that would then be delivered into Building 82, via circuitous, covert routes in order to retain tight security.

The two Have Blue aircraft were single-seat, subsonic machines, each powered by two 2,950-pound-thrust, General Electric J85-GE-4A nonafterburning engines. The power units were government-furnished equipment (GFE), and Twigg acquired six for the program from the U.S. Navy's North American T-2B Buckeye trainer stores. The only engine modification made was a coating applied to the spinners.

Have Blue was 47.25 feet long, 7.54 feet high, and had a span of 22.5 feet. Its modified delta wing planform, with a sweep of 72.5 degrees, created a wing area of 386 square feet. No flaps, speed brakes, or high-lift devices were incorporated into the structure, which was built mainly from an aluminum alloy, using steel and titanium in the hot areas. Aerodynamic control was achieved by ailerons, located inboard on the wings, and by two all-moveable fins at the tail. The fins had a leading-edge sweepback of some 35 degrees and were canted inboard about 30 degrees. Flight control actuators were the same as those used on the F-111. A small side stick controller (YF-16 stock) and conventional rudder pedals enabled the pilot to operate the control surfaces.

The external shape evolved from VLO and controllability considerations, the fallout from which is a relaxed static stability (RSS) aircraft that required a quadruple redundant fly-by-wire (FBW) flight control system to provide normal handling qualities throughout the flight envelope. The FBW system provided stability augmentation and was made by Lear-Seigler (also F-16 stock). Indeed, the aircraft was so dependent on this system that mechanical backup was not possible.

During the course of aerodynamic tests conducted by the Skunk Works on free-flight models, it was determined that the large leading edge wing sweep produced considerable nose-up pitch moments, actually causing pitch departure when a 17-degree angle of attack was exceeded. To prevent such events occurring on the two Have Blue aircraft, elevon "nose-down" pitch control was augmented by a large, two-position flap on the trailing edge of the exhaust deck. Called the "platypus," it automatically deflected downward, whenever a 13-degree angle-of-attack was exceeded. The platypus flap then retracted automatically after the pilot reduced the aircraft's angle of attack.

The forward retracting undercarriage was the same as that found on the Northrop F-5 Freedom Fighter. Equipped with main gear antiskid braking, nosewheel steering was only installed on the second Have Blue aircraft (HB1002) to improve ground handling. Forward gear retraction ensured reliable emergency extension; it also meant that takeoff and landing would always occur when the center of gravity (CG) was furthest aft due to the location of the gear (CG would shift with the gear as it retracted forward). The heads-up dis-

This old satellite shot of Area 51 was taken during September 1968. Since the collapse of the Soviet Union and that nation's subsequent need for hard currency, it is now possible to purchase satellite imagery of the location from them! *James Goodall collection*

play was an adopted version fitted in the F/A-18 Hornet. The inertial navigation system was to be found in B-52s, and the pilot sat in an F-16 ejection seat.

Externally, the two Have Blue aircraft differed from one another. The prototype HB1001 was equipped with a large flight test nose boom that included pitot-static pressure sources, angle of attack sensors, and side slip veins. A flight path accelerometer, was also located inside the probe at the angle of attack vein position. Additionally, HB1001 had a drag chute, unstealthily mounted, in an external box on top of the fuselage. This was because its career would not only demonstrate VLO technology, it would also

validate loads/flutter, performance, handling qualities, and stability and control test data. Its sister ship, HB1002, was designated as the RCS test vehicle. Gross weight of the aircraft ranged from 9,200 to 12,500 pounds; zero fuel weight was 8,950 pounds with 3,500 pounds of fuel being carried in fuselage and wing tanks.

The requirement to maintain VLO considerations beyond all others was absolute; despite this, the aircraft was a +3g, -1g highly maneuverable platform. The overriding VLO restrictions demanded new approaches to preserve efficient propulsion system performance. Each inlet duct was equipped with

VLO requirements also resulted in the design of a unique exhaust system. To prevent radar energy from penetrating to and reflecting back from the turbine face, the tailpipe was transitioned from a round duct to a 17 to 1 flattened, slot convergent nozzle. The trailing edge of each nozzle terminated at a 54-degree scarf angle that corresponded to the airframe aft closure. Veins interposed and angled within the slot then helped straighten the exhaust flow back to the aircraft's longitudinal axis (although some thrust vector "toe in" remained). Bypass air was also passed over the tailpipe to cool the aft fuselage structure and thereby reduce the infrared signature.

Adding a New Test Pilot

One day in 1976, the director of the F-15 Joint Test Force, Major Norman "Ken" Dyson, landed his F-15 back at Edwards Air Force Base, having just completed another test sortie. He was passed a message from Colonel Joe Guthery, the test wing commander at Edwards, instructing him to report to the commanding general's office, General Tom Stafford. On entering the office he was told to close the door. Gen. Stafford began telling Dyson that he had been recommended by both the wing and deputy wing commander, Larry McClain, for a highly classified flight test job.

The general continued that he was unable to discuss further details and that if Dyson decided to volunteer for the job, there was no going back. Dyson recalls, "I thought about it for not very long and I said, 'Well, I'd like to do that General,' and he put me to work. He told me about this unbelievable machine that would fly and be practically invisible to radar. The Skunk Works was working on it and did I know my way there? I didn't, so he gave me directions and told me that I was to report in civilian clothes, not to acknowledge any military affiliation, or tell the guards that I was there for classified reasons. I did the things instructed, and I went down and got briefed on the program. I recall being somewhat surprised, looking at the old ramshackle buildings that the Skunk Works guys were working in at Burbank Airport. I was met by a great guy, Norm Nelson, who was the Lockheed manager for the Have Blue plane."

Bill Park was Lockheed's chief test pilot on Have Blue, and he and Dyson worked closely together to prepare the aircraft for its first flight. Dyson remembers, "Bill and I prepared to fly Have Blue by working with the engineers as its design and construction came along. Sometimes we worked singly, sometimes together, with the engineers to understand their part of the airplane. When we had suggestions or questions for the guys, we would discuss them and see where we went from there. We also spent many hours in the simulator out at Lockheed's Rye Canyon facility. We did most of the simulating late at night so people didn't see us and wonder what was going on. It was all done in a very secure (from a classification point of view) environment. We would fly it, crash it, debrief it, then improve the control system, and fly some more until we had a pretty good control system developed. We continued flight system development in flight test. Bill and I also went on to develop the first flight profile and contingencies."

Building and Testing

The production schedule for HB1001 envisaged completion of the final assembly stage at the end of August, with ground testing continuing until mid-October. Roll-out was initially planned for October 24, after which the aircraft was due to be crated and flown to the test area. Following reassembly, Lockheed planned its first flight for Thursday, December 1, 1977.

Mathematical genius and extremely personable, Denys Overholser was the power-house behind the Echo 1 development team. In just five weeks, the team had a computer program that facilitated a technological breakthrough. *Lockheed Martin*

a flat, RCS treated grid whose porosity was matched for cruise flight. While great for cruise, they were too restricting at takeoff when additional airflow was needed. As a result, blow-in doors were mounted on the upper fuselage surface to provide airflow augmentation for takeoff. Concern that the inlet grids would create engine performance problems proved groundless. The grids actually helped straighten the vortex-disturbed inlet airflow generated by the highly swept-wing leading edges (a phenomena made more acute at high angles of attack).

Aviation legend Clarence L. "Kelly" Johnson joined Lockheed on August 21, 1933, as a tool designer. Founder of the Skunk Works, he and his team were responsible for producing the XP-80, America's first jet aircraft, and the F-104, U-2, A-12, YF-12, and SR-71. Highly skeptical of Have Blue, he later conceded that Ben Rich and his team had developed a winner. *Lockheed Martin*

On Thursday, September 1, 1977, Lockheed became embroiled in a four-month machinist strike. The Have Blue prototype was completed by Bob Murphy and some 18 managers whom he split into two groups. The teams started work the day after the strike began and each group worked 12 hours a day, 7 days a week. When they began, the aft fuselage had hardly been started, the fuselage structure in the assembly jig was about 60 percent complete, and none of the hydraulics or fuel plumbing had been mocked up.

Over the next six weeks, Have Blue slowly came together. The boom and stub fin assembly joined the forward fuselage in the final assembly area on September 14, the aft fuselage structure was taken from the jig on September 24, and the wing assembly joined the other components in the final assembly area on October 1, 1977. During final assembly—contrary to earlier reports—a partial iron-coat of paint was applied, and on October 17, HB1001 completed the final assembly stage and began ground tests.

During the first week of ground tests, flight instrumentation was calibrated. Then between October 24 and 28, the prototype was made ready for

a shakedown—an event that was completed on November 3. The next day fuel-flow tests were completed. Then, very late on Friday night, two semi-tractor-trailer units were drawn up parallel and parked immediately outside the doors of Building 82. A camouflage net was thrown over the top of both trailers and an air vehicle was towed into the intervening space. It looked more at home on a *Star Wars* set. Engine runs were then performed, and despite a local resident phoning to complain about the noise, Have Blue remained "in the black."

Over the next eight days, the iron-coat paint job was completed, and during the weekend of November 12 and 13, Alan Brown and Ben Dehaven gave the aircraft a final coat of paint. This ingenious camouflage pattern, devised by Brown, consisted of three colors each in three different tones and applied in such a way that it hid the faceting from any casual uncleared "onlookers." Have Blue 1001 was then disassembled, crated, and loaded overnight into the cavernous belly of a C-5 Galaxy. On the morning of Wednesday, November 16, during the early rush hour at Burbank Airport, people strained as the "aluminum cloud," complete with its valuable cargo, seemingly clawed itself into the air and disappeared from view. The prototype was disgorged from the C-5 at Area 51, where it was reassembled and readied for a final series of preflight tests. Bob Murphy's team at this remote site consisted of Fritz Frye, Jim Dry, John Stanley, Dick Madison, Red McDaris, Mike Kammerer, and Bill Patterson. Keith Beswick was the chief flight test engineer; Dick Miller was his assistant.

Another series of engine tests were conducted on Friday, November 25, during the course of which "Murph" stood on the top of the fuselage to check for top fuel leaks. Bill Park was at the controls, and shortly into the test Murphy shouted to Park to shut everything down as heat from the engine was rippling the fuselage skin above the tailpipes. This hadn't been detected back at Burbank as the engine runs had been conducted at night to maintain security. Murphy quickly identified the problem: Heat shields hadn't been installed to protect the outer skin of the aft fuselage section.

To solve this problem, bulkhead rings were enlarged to accommodate the heat shields, which in turn meant installing stiffener rings to reinforce the bulkheads. Murphy sent Bill Patterson, manager of the sheet metal shop, back to Burbank to manufacture the stiffener rings while he prepared to install the heat shields. They soon found there were no stand-off brackets with which to attach the heat shields to the bulkhead rings. Murphy recalls, "I went to Chris Fylling, a great engineer that Baldy had detached to the team. I asked him to give me a quick sketch of what was needed and an idea of the material necessary. He told me a simple Z bracket could be used and that mild steel would be the best material. As I had no mild steel, I asked him what his filing cabinet was made of. Mild steel, came the reply. I then asked if we could use it for the brackets. He said it should work just fine. As we were at full stretch, I asked him if he would mind cutting it up and making the bracket. He agreed and got right on it. When everybody arrived on Monday morning, we were

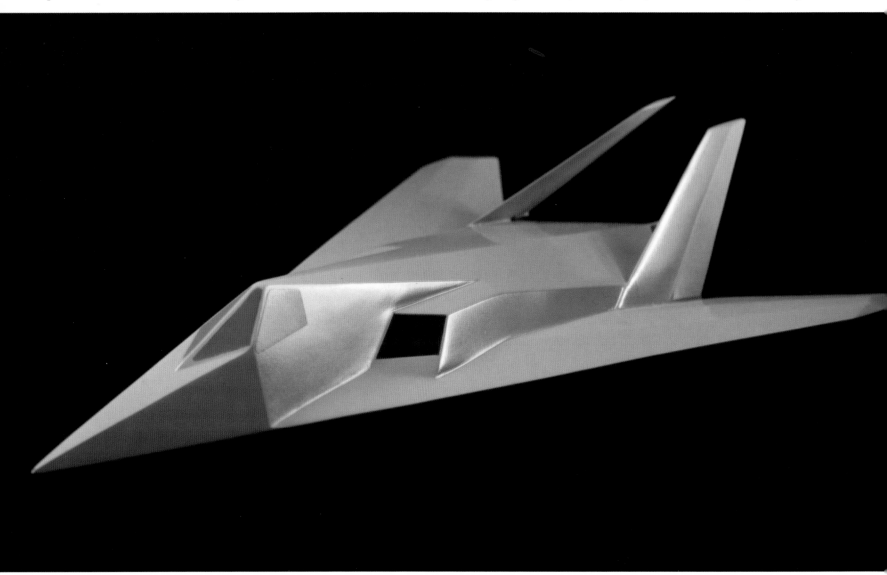

This early model of Have Blue, depicts the extreme nose-to-wingtip leading-edge sweep and highly faceted surfaces, which came to typify the design. Also of note is what appears to be conventional rudders, rather than the all-moving tails that would be adopted on the actual aircraft. *Lockheed Martin*

This small scale model of Have Blue is undergoing RCS tests in Lockheed's anechoic chamber at Rye Canyon. *Lockheed Martin*

ready for engine runs. These we carried out in the hangar, using a surplus army track vehicle to hold the ship back!"

Next came taxi tests. In preparation for the first, Mike Kammerer stood on top of the fuselage to fuel the aircraft, while Red McDaris was busy checking out the instrumentation package located in a bay in the underside. Murphy had just closed the computer access door and was busy installing the screws when fuel began dripping onto McDaris' head. With a few well chosen words, McDaris told Kammerer that he'd better stop spilling fuel on him or else there'd be trouble. Kammerer replied that he hadn't spilled any fuel, at which Murph thought, "Oh, Oh," and lowered the door to which the computer was attached and discovered the problem. A loose screw in the hinge behind the computer had punched a hole in one of the fuselage tanks. Since it was 11:30 at night and the team had been working since 5:00 in the morning, Keith Beswick told them to just drain that tank and fix it after the taxi tests—which is precisely what was done. Four low- and high-speed taxi tests

were conducted. A small problem arose during the third taxi test when the brakes overheated, causing the wheel fuse plugs to melt. Following the fourth taxi test, Have Blue 1001 was cleared to fly.

The prototype was made ready for its first flight during the night of Wednesday, November 30. When the test team arrived early the next morning, however, fuel in the fuselage tank had migrated to the wing tanks. With Bill Park sitting in the cockpit ready to go and Lockheed's corporate Jetstar carrying Ben Rich, Kelly Johnson, and the secretary of the Air Force in the circuit, John Stanley hooked up a pump under the aircraft and handed a hose up to Bob Murphy. Murphy remembers, "I undid the fuel cap, took the cap off the end of the hose, and we started pumping fuel from the wings back into the fuselage tank. When the tank was full, I told John to shut off the pump. As I started to put the cap back on the hose, it burped and blew the cap off, which then proceeded to fall right into the fuselage fuel tank! I couldn't reach into the tank to retrieve the cap as the opening was too small. I then tried

The external differences between the two Have Blue aircraft are immediately apparent. Note HB1001's large test instrumentation noseboom; the camouflage pattern; and external box, located on top of the aft fuselage, which housed the drag chute. *Lockheed Martin*

reaching it with a mechanical finger; however, this wasn't long enough. Bill Park then started yelling to me, asking what was causing the delay. I told him not to worry; I was worrying enough for both of us! Just then, I saw a large broom next to Mike Kammerer; he handed it to me. The hose cap lay upside down in the tank, it was a male plug, hollow on the inside. My Irish luck was with me; the broom handle fitted perfectly inside the cap. I lifted it out, put the cap back on the fuel tank, and told Bill to start the engines!"

Unaware of how close the flight had come to being postponed, Bill Park was airborne in HB1001 just after 7 A.M. In spite of a strong head wind, the take-off run was long and the climb-out sluggish, due to the aircraft's low lift-to-drag ratio and thrust-to-weight ratio. Additional power loss was associated with the inlet grids and the engine exhausts. The gear remained extended to avoid retraction problems, and the flight was completed satisfactorily.

The first five sorties in aircraft number one were completed by Bill Park, who was chased on each occasion by Dyson in a T-38. On January 17, 1978, Dyson had his first flight in HB1001 and was chased by Park. There after the two pilots more or less alternated between chase duties and flying the proto-type. During this phase-of-flight testing, aircraft number one's FBW computers were fine tuned, thereby improving the vehicle's handling characteristics. Many of these characteristics had been accurately predicted during some 1,500 hours of wind tunnel testing. For example, how the lack of directional stability due to the highly swept wing increased with increasing angle of attack. The

rolling, pitching, and yawing moments produced by the inboard-canted twin tail units were also predicted here. The aircraft's unique slotted exhaust nozzles did produce some discrepancies in relation to the aircraft's predicted lateral/directional characteristics. Directional stability was less than that predicted, and above 0.65 Mach, the aircraft became directionally unstable. Side forces, due to side slip, were less than half the predicted values; however, these problems were rectified by changing yaw gain in the flight control system.

On May 4, 1978, Park conducted 24 flights on HB1001 and Dyson 12. The aircraft had virtually completed all its flight test objectives. Park planned to fly early that morning, and on his way to breakfast he was stopped by Larry McClain, who asked if the paramedic could be scrubbed from that day's test flight schedule as he was needed at the base clinic. Park later recalled, "I told him, 'I'd rather you didn't do that, Colonel. We're not entirely out of the woods yet with Have Blue, and I'd just feel better knowing that paramedic is standing by if I happen to need him.' As it turned out, I had just saved my own life."

Have Blue Crashes

Alan Brown was standing on top of Area 51's control tower as Bill Park was returning. "The test in which 1001 was lost, was partially related to visual camouflage," says Brown. "The aircraft had a 'shades of gray' scheme to minimize its threshold of detection and was being flown in company with an all-white Northrop T-38 chase aircraft for comparative testing. I was performing

Have Blue 1002 was the RCS test vehicle and was flown throughout its life by Lieutenant Colonel Ken Dyson. Note the conventionally shaped undercarriage doors. These were redesigned for the Senior Trend program, a result of RCS measurements taken during the flight test program. *Lockheed Martin*

this assessment, and if I remember correctly, Bill came in fairly slowly, around about 113 knots. When he was about 3 or 4 feet off the ground, the moveable platypus actuated downward automatically, causing the aircraft to pitch forward rapidly. It hit the runway hard on the starboard landing gear, causing it to bend the wheel out of alignment. The aircraft then followed an 'S-shaped' weaving track along the runway as Bill tried to control it. Eventually he must have decided that he couldn't stop it successfully and, I must admit to my surprise, took off again under full power."

In the T-38, Larry McClain was in the front seat and Ken Dyson was in the back. Dyson recalls what he saw: "The test flight had just been completed and Bill was coming in for his landing. I was watching as we slid by in the T-38, and Bill slowed down to touch. I was looking out of the canopy. Have Blue was slightly behind the T-38, and it was making a nice stable approach. Just before touchdown the airplane pitched up, violently, way nose high. It seemed it slammed down on the ground real hard, and then the next thing I knew, Bill was on the go, announcing that he decided it was necessary to go around. He raised the gear on the go around, and when he tried to extend it on approach, only one of the mains and the nose wheel came down. We were all working on ways to get it down. Bill tried hitting the runway hard on two wheels several times in order to shake the third wheel loose, but it wouldn't budge.

"All this time, gas was being consumed (we didn't land the airplane generally with very much fuel), so I queried the control room about their next action. Their answer was, 'We'll have to eject if we can't get that gear down.' So as the gas was further consumed, I suggested he climb up to 10,000 feet for ejection, just to give him more time in case of a problem. He started climbing, but the engine started flaming out, from lack of fuel, so he ejected. We flew circles around him in our chase airplane, and the helicopter also orbited about him. We could see he was in trouble as he was coming down, he looked unconscious. The chopper landed close by shortly after he landed and the paramedic got to him. He had swallowed a lot of the desert and was unconscious, but they were able to get him to hospital where he was given the proper care. He later recovered fine, but having received [a] concussion, it was decreed that he would not fly test airplanes anymore." After this incident, Ben Rich named Park as Lockheed's chief pilot.

Have Blue 1002 was substantially complete but not ready for flight. Further modifications were carried out on the basis of lessons learned on the aircraft's recently departed stablemate. This included a rebuild of the aft fuselage by a team led by Lockheed's Henry Combs. The moveable platypus on the prototype tended to warp, causing both undesirable shape changes and gaps to open up. Several approaches to the problem were looked at before an

This is one of the first shots of Have Blue in flight to be released. The use of a wide-angle lens accentuated the leading-edge sweep of the vehicle. Note the slot into which the forward-folding, blade antenna retracts. *Lockheed Martin*

acceptable design was agreed upon. Additional work was also conducted by Bob Loschke's team on the flight control system.

Gen. Stafford directed that another Air Force pilot join the program as backup pilot. Consequently Russ Eastor, an instructor at the Air Force Test Pilot School at Edwards Air Force Base joined the team. Ray Gowdy was also recruited in as a backup pilot from Lockheed. Both provided superb support for the remainder of the Have Blue program, but neither would actually fly the aircraft. All flights on aircraft number two would be made by Lieutenant Colonel Ken Dyson. Dyson remembers, "There seemed to be a lot of people in the team uptight before this flight compared to before, flying airplane one.

We all realized how important it was to do this and do it well, as we only had this one remaining test vehicle left."

Early on the morning of the July 20, 1978, all was at last ready for HB1002 to take to the air. Here's Dyson's account:

The unstick was about 125 knots, and the climb speed likewise was slow around 250 knots. Russ and Ray were in the chase T-38s for that first flight, which lasted only four-tenths of an hour. We flew with less fuel onboard so that it wouldn't be heavy in case I needed to land immediately after takeoff. The flight consisted of basic aircraft airworthiness, systems checks, flying quality checks, flight control system evaluation, and

of course, it was a fully instrumented data collecting flight. We wanted to make sure that everything was right with the bird. We did not fly too high or go too fast, I guess about 20,000 feet and 250 knots. The airplane performed just fine, we had a nominal flight, and we were all pleased to get the bird back on the ground and through its maintenance recovery and preparation. I do recall the dinky brakes we had on that airplane, and on airplane number one. It was designed that way and it was all the brake we could stick in the wheel. After every flight, at the end of the landing roll, the brakes would just be glowing cherry red! Sometimes our maintenance crew were waiting with cooling fans to put on them to keep them from melting down. I don't recall that there were any write-ups on that first flight; I believe the call sign was Bandit 1-1.

We flew three flights to check the airplane out: flight control systems, the hydraulics, the engine and the data-collecting system, to make sure that we had a good airplane. Then on the 9th August 1978, we began to take the first airborne RCS measurements. Earlier flights on airplane one were associated with airworthiness testing. In fact, as far as I'm aware, it was the first time anyone had ever attempted to measure the RCS of a manned airplane in flight. I flew against a ground-based facility and on these first series of tests they wanted to check-out the cross-section of the airplane nose-on, that's with a look angle of zero. To achieve this I climbed to a predetermined altitude and maintained a heading that would take me right over the radar test site. When I reached the test point, I configured the airplane in a descent, making sure my speed, angle of attack, and rate of descent were exactly correct. I had to keep control movements to a minimum in order to provide accurate test data, so I switched in the autopilot. Well, as soon as I did that, the nose went right and the wing rolled slightly left.

I later learned that Ben Rich, who was watching the test in the radar control room went crazy, asking, "What does that goddamn Air Force pilot think he is doing? Is he deliberately side-slipping the airplane to screw-up our test results?" I decided to switch off the autopilot and fly manually, something we'd planned not to do, because the test engineers didn't think a man could achieve the necessary tight parameters. Well it seemed to work pretty good, and after that, I flew all the tests manually. We never did resolve the problem with the autopilot. Virtually every flight in airplane two was associated with RCS measurements, and if we weren't measuring radar returns, we would be flying the airplane against operational systems to see if they could see us. To my knowledge, none did.

By 29 June '79, we had flown against every system operationally that we could think of and we had measured the airplane every possible way; actual in-flight measurements, to see what the airplane really looked like. That day, shortly after takeoff, I noted that one of the hydraulics systems was acting a bit strange. The pressure was oscillating somewhat and going down, so I air aborted directly back and had the guys work on it. On 10 July, we flew again and the airplane was okay. The next day I got airborne and had the chase airplane look me over; everything was okay, so I flew outbound to get to a point to run against an F-15 Eagle to see how it performed against us. I was just short of the designated turn point, when I noticed the same hydraulic system begin to oscillate, again in the downward direction. I thought well, that's the end of this flight and turned back. I started to tell test control about my problem, when I got a fire light. After pulling the power back and telling them of my troubles, I shut the engine down. All this was in short

order. I had the airplane pointed towards home plate and configured at the right speed for single engine operation (it was not a good performer on a single engine, not much thrust, and a lot of drag). I was coming home somewhere between 20,000 and 25,000 feet. Shortly after that the remaining hydraulic system began to oscillate in a downward direction, and I knew that was not good for our unstable machine. Just about the time the remaining hydraulic system went to 0, the plane pitched violently down, something like 7 negative gs. It then pitched up; the pitch rates were just eye watering, something only an unstable machine could do. I was somewhere around 225 knots and above 20,000 feet, and the airplane was tossing me up and down and actually got as near vertical nose down and near vertical nose up. I began to try and reach for the ejection seat ring that was between my legs. I got my hand on it and pulled. The canopy blew off, the seat went out, and I found myself floating under a chute at about 20,000 feet. I had noted my take-off time, and while hanging in my chute I noted that 10 minutes had elapsed from takeoff. I watched the unstable machine flip-flop slowly it seemed, as it descended vertically below me and I saw it hit the ground and erupt into a ball of fire. It still had a lot of gas onboard. It took me quite a while to make my parachute descend down to the desert floor. After landing (that was my first and only jump to date) I again noted the time. I had been in the parachute for 10 minutes.

As Ken slowly descended by chute, the pilot of the F-15—with whom he had planned to conduct further tests—began orbiting above. Colonel Norm Suits, the director of the F-15 Joint Test Force, saw the stricken Have Blue aircraft impact the ground and shortly afterward spotted two unauthorized cross-country vehicles heading toward the crash site. Although the vehicle's occupants were probably intent on performing their public duty and offer help and assistance to any survivors, the highly classified nature of the program and the materials used in its construction couldn't be compromised. Acting on his own initiative, Suits began a series of extremely low passes at the vehicles to deter their drivers from closing on the wreckage. Just how low these passes were can only be judged from the fact that he succeeded in his objective!

Dyson continues: "I stood up, but my back was hurting, so I got back down and used my survival radio to talk to the rescue chopper. Those guys put me on a stretcher, carried me to the chopper, and took me to the hospital for some treatment. I was in the hospital for just one night and was then released. I was flying again within a couple of weeks, but my back was still sore. Eventually the docs figured that I'd sustained three vertebrae compression fractures—no wonder my back was sore!"

The cause of the crash was determined to be an engine exhaust clamp, which had become loose, allowing hot exhaust gases to enter the right engine compartment. This had triggered the fire warning light, and as the temperature built up, first the left and then the right hydraulic lines failed, which in turn caused a complete loss of control. Dyson believes that the aircraft didn't actually catch fire, but that the hot gases in the engine compartment illuminated the fire light.

Fortunately the program was within two or three sorties of its planned completion, which officially ended in December 1979. Having achieved all its test objectives, the Have Blue program can be categorized as a stunning success. The next step was to determine how the demonstrated technology could be integrated into an operational weapons platform.

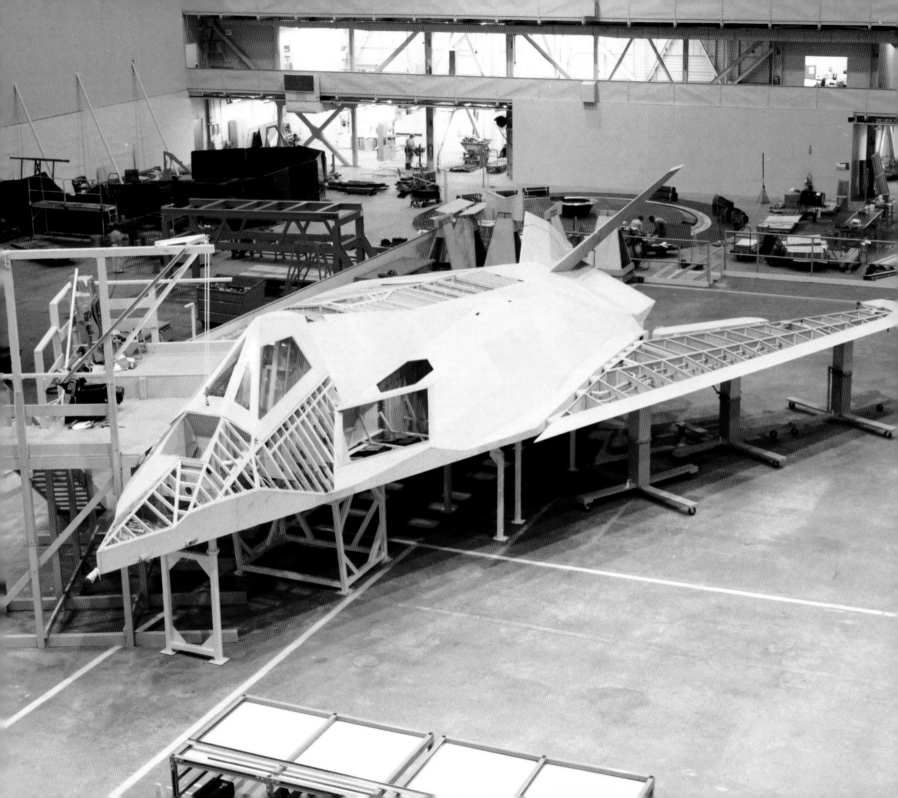

chapter two

SKUNK WORKS MAGIC

Technical

In June 1977 the Air Force set up a special project office (SPO) in the Pentagon. Its objective: to exploit low-observable technology then being demonstrated in phase 1 of the XST program. The small team, commanded by Colonel Dave Williams and consisting of Majors Jerry Baber, Joe Ralston, Ken Staten, and Bob Swarts, reported directly to the deputy chief of staff for research and development, Lieutenant General Alton D. Slay.

In addition to initiating conceptual studies into a manned strike aircraft program, referred to as the Advanced Technology Aircraft (ATA) program, the team also identified the need to develop, in parallel with the XST program, methods of locating, tracking, and striking targets in a way commensurate with maintaining a VLO profile. In response to a request for further information from Gen. Slay, a nine-point document was provided to the SPO from the vice commander of Air Force Systems Command. The document outlined various stealth-driven programs that would comply with such criteria (one particular line item referred to the development of a FLIR turret).

Two sets of preliminary requirements for the ATA were developed: ATA "A," a single-seat attack aircraft with a 5,000-pound payload and 400-nautical mile range, and ATA "B," a two-seat bomber with a 10,000-pound payload and 1,000-nautical mile range. An $11.1 million concept definition contract was awarded to the Skunk Works on October 10, 1977, for a one-year study based on the two sets of requirements. The engine selection process began on January 17, 1978, and 11 days later a wind tunnel program was inaugurated with test results from the Ames Research Center being made available on August 16 that same year.

To achieve the required range, while remaining within other stated parameters, it became necessary to reduce the proposed payload of ATA "B" to 7,500 pounds. As assimilation of the two proposals continued, it became increasingly apparent that ATA "B" (despite being strongly favored by Strategic Air Command following cancellation by the Carter administration of the B-1A) was in the upper right corner of what was at that time considered realistically achievable. Consequently, in the summer of 1978, Air Force officials decided to terminate further studies involving ATA "B" and instead opted to move forward with ATA "A" into full-scale development (FSD).

Covert funds were established, and key individuals serving on the House Appropriations Committee, the House Armed Services Committee, the Senate Appropriations Committee, and the Senate Armed Services Committee were briefed on the program. On November 1, 1978, production was authorized, the program was given the code name "Senior Trend," and Lockheed was awarded a $340 million contract to cover the cost of building five full-scale development aircraft, plus provide spares, support, and flight testing (this amount did not include the cost of purchasing the aircraft's General Electric engines).

Personalities

The initial Skunk Works Senior Trend management team consisted of Norm Nelson, former Have Blue program manager, who, shortly after taking up the appointment was promoted to vice president of engineering with the

Construction of a wooden mock-up began on January 1, 1979, and was completed 11 months later on December 3. Functional engineers then used the assembly to determine where to situate various aircraft subsystems, a job that now uses software technology. *Lockheed Martin*

Bob Murphy joined Lockheed as a flight test mechanic in 1952. Progressing up the ladder, he was division manager for Lockheed Advanced Development Projects (ADP) by 1962, responsible for all composite manufacturing for the A-12, D-21, YF-12, and SR-71. In 1964 he was the plant manager for Palmdale, became deputy director of operations in 1969, and director of operations in 1980. *Lockheed Martin*

vacant slot subsequently being filled by English-born Alan Brown. Bill Taylor was in charge of systems design (electrical, fuel, hydraulics, avionics installation, flight controls installation, and the environmental control system). Ed Baldwin was in charge of structural design and propulsion installation. Dick Cantrell was in charge of flight sciences and monitored aerodynamic design and propulsion performance calculation. Bob Loschke designed the flight control system together with Lockheed's Fritz Schenk and the Lear-Siegler company (as with Have Blue, this drew heavily on the design used in the YF-16). Bill Zeltner was in charge of all avionics development, and his team of 350

engineers became the largest individual design and development group on the program. Once again, Bob Murphy was designated director of manufacturing.

Changes were also implemented within the Air Force. Development of Senior Trend and other low-observable programs was transferred from the SPO commanded by Colonel Dave Williams at the Pentagon to a newly established SPO under Aeronautical Systems Division, located at Wright-Patterson Air Force Base in Ohio. Known initially as the Classified Aeronautical Systems Program Office (later redesignated the Directorate of Low Observables), its first director was Colonel David B. Englund. Jerry Baber also transferred across

The unique configuration of the faceted air data probes is readily apparent. Total pressure is measured from a single orifice at the top of each probe. Orifices on the left and right cheek of each front facet measures differential pressure to determine angle of sideslip (beta). Angle of attack (alpha) is resolved by the differential pressure taken from ports situated in the upper and lower front facets, while static pressure measurements are collected from four small orifices located on each probe's side facet further downstream. **Paul Crickmore**

from the Pentagon, and Colonel Eldred D. (Don) Merkl became the Air Force's first Senior Trend program manager.

The production time scales for this revolutionary aircraft program were tight. Its first flight was planned for July 1980, hence the last three digits of the prototype's serial number, 780. Initial Operational Capability (IOC) was to be achieved in March 1982, and the planned production run was 20 aircraft.

On January 1, 1979, construction of a full-scale wooden mock-up began. Eleven months later, on December 3, the assembly was completed, and functional engineers then used this representation to determine where to situate various aircraft subsystems (such activities have now been superseded by advances in computer software). Construction of FSD1, the prototype F-117A, (Aircraft 780) commenced at Burbank in November 1979.

The Theory

The F-117A Nighthawk is a survivable interdictor; the determinant in achieving this goal has been the development of VLO techniques. To confound the principal detection medium—radar—design focused on producing a low radar cross-section (RCS). The reduction of an aircraft's RCS to levels that would provide an explicit operational advantage had been the holy grail for military aircraft designers since the latter stages of World War II.

Development work in this area so far had, by and large, been focused around producing materials capable of absorbing to varying degrees incident radiation. The characteristics of this radar absorbent, or radar attenuating, material (RAM) addressed three areas of signal attenuation, namely that of specular reflections (reflections normal to the surface), attenuation of radiation that travels along the surface of the material, and the reduction of edge returns. The two former areas are tackled to varying degrees of effectiveness by multilayers of

absorbent materials. RAM produces either electric or magnetic losses. Magnetic materials are more concentrated in the effect they achieve but are heavy. The required thicknesses of RAM increase as frequency is reduced. Therefore there is a tendency to use magnetic materials to reduce high-frequency returns and electric materials to deal with lower frequencies. With care larger electrical absorbers for lower frequencies can be made integral parts of an aircraft's structure, known as Radar Absorbing Structure (RAS). The frequency range covered by these materials is 100:1, similar to a good hi-fi system, which likewise, has both woofers and tweeters to cover both low and high frequencies.

RAM for high frequencies usually has very small iron particles imbedded in a nonconductive plastic such as polyurethane. The particles are typically 3/10 microns (millionths of a meter) in diameter, about 1/10 the thickness of a human hair. The overall thickness of the coating may vary from 1/2 to 2 millimeters. The material works in two ways: either as a specular absorber or as a traveling wave absorber. In the specular mode, energy strikes the coated surface and is partially absorbed and partially reflected. In the traveling wave mode, the wave strikes the surface at a grazing angle and travels along the surface with continuous attenuation. Specular material works best at a particular frequency related to its thickness. It is possible to produce multilayer RAM, which will produce peak performance at several specific frequencies. Lockheed utilized RAM coatings on both the A-12, YF-12, and SR-71. Wedges of asbestos (to cope with high airframe temperatures) and composite framed the Blackbird's outer planform (fuselage chine and wing leading and trailing edges), which proved highly effective in reducing edge returns. Little was understood about shaping as a means of reducing RCS, beyond using a blended body, fuselage chines, together with tail units cantered inboard, to facilitate low side-look signatures.

Although the use of RAM certainly achieved a reduction in RCS, this was not enough to gain "an explicit operational advantage." That could be achieved only when designers were able to build a shape both capable of performing an operational mission and producing an RCS lower by several orders of magnitude than any current conventional aircraft. It was here that the odds were definitely stacked against the designers as perfectly demonstrated by the radar equation, which basically states that "detection range is proportional to the fourth root of the radar cross-section." That is to say, in order to reduce

Having considered and evaluated several methods of preventing ice encrustation of the air inlet grilles, a simple wiper blade used in conjunction with a de-icing jet proved to be the most effective, if not the most innovative or aesthetic. **Paul Crickmore**

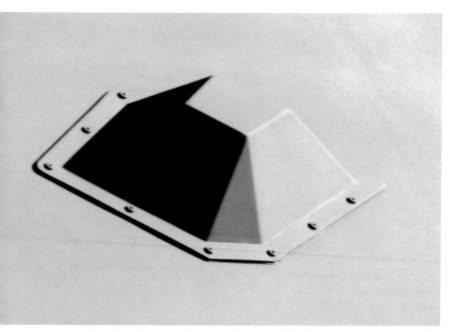

To enable air traffic control radar units to track F-117s during routine training sorties, a removable reflector is fastened to each side of the aircraft's fuselage. *Paul Crickmore*

the detection range by a factor of 10 in number, it is necessary to reduce the target aircraft's RCS by a factor of 10,000 or 40 dBs.

Radar Consideration

Having established the required RCS signature levels from various look angles, together with the overall shape required to meet those goals, it then becomes necessary to consider other aspects of the aircraft's design that will have an impact on RCS values. For a conventional jet aircraft, the next areas that warrant careful consideration are the air-intake and exhaust cavities. In the case of the inlet, radar energy will travel down this and then reflect back from the engine compressor face, rather like the beam from a lighthouse; predominantly, straight back to its source. By coating the inlet walls with RAM, some high-frequency returns can be dissipated; however, further signal dispersion will be achieved by redesigning a straight inlet duct into an S-shaped duct. By further introducing S-duct splitters into the design and also coating these with RAM, high-frequency radiated energy undergoes many more bounces, thereby further reducing reflected energy levels. The problem, however, is that although this design described above works well for dispersing high-frequency radiation, it actually amplifies returns from medium- to low-frequency radars.

The F-117A's inlet is positioned above the wing, and the inlet duct curves very slightly down to the compressor, thereby providing it with an element of shielding. Further reductions in RCS values are achieved by placing a grid over the inlet. The spacing in the grids is just 0.6 of an inch, and the top of the intake is angled back from the lower edge. The entire grid is then subjected to a further nose-aft sweep, applied to reflect radar energy away from the nose-on aspect. RAM is also applied to the grid so that the entire assembly functions as a shock absorber for any remaining energy that has not been reflected away from the unit. Any energy that does get past the "shock

absorber" is absorbed by a another coating of RAM inside the duct. Alan Brown likens the grid to, "The Roach Motel—the roaches go in, but they don't come out."

Because the F-117A is statically unstable, the requirement to provide accurate dynamic and static air data to the flight control system is a prerequisite. Alan Brown continues:

One possible approach to air data system design was to select a number of static holes at key positions around the airplane in such a way that the pressure measurements could be uniquely related to free stream total static pressures and angle of attack and angle of yaw. From these data, all the important air data information for operation of the flight control system could be inferred, including airspeed, Mach number, and altitude. While this system would in principle have a very low radar cross-section, we were compelled to abandon it, as we could not come up with a satisfactory anti- or de-icing system. In order for the system to work accurately, the flow path up to and somewhat beyond the static pressure holes

The main landing gear tires consist of two Goodyear 32x8.8 26-ply tubeless units. Early troublesome steel brakes have now been replaced by F-15E wheels fitted with carbon-carbon brakes, which have dramatically enhanced stop performance. *Paul Crickmore*

would have to maintain the original smoothness, and thus be completely free of ice at all times. As this was a fly-by-wire aircraft, it was calculated that a one-second loss of all data would be sufficient for the aircraft to lose control. The system was quadruply redundant, but in the event of an icing situation you had to assume that many static probes could be rendered inaccurate at one time.

This led us to revert to the more conventional pitot/static probe design, which was complicated by the necessity to measure both angle of attack and angle of yaw. We came up with a design of diamond cross-section, although recognizing that the cross-section shaping was only useful at air-to-air frequencies, because of dimension to wavelength ratio. Initially, we

tried to coat the tips of the probes with radar-absorbent material but had to give up because rain and hail erosion of the material would alter the characteristics of the pressure measurements. Also, we realized that we would have to employ anti-icing as opposed to de-icing because we could not afford the time taken for ice to build up before attempting to remove it. Even at that, the radar-absorbent material was a sufficiently good insulator that it could allow some ice buildup even in an anti-icing situation. The end result was that the probes were made with faceted copper tips which were heated at all times. Pitot pressure, alpha and beta, were measured right at the tips, and static pressure was measured a few inches downstream. With care, the radar cross-section was kept within budgeted limits.

The precision-guided munitions (PGM) originally prescribed for the F-117A at initial operational capability (IOC) was the GBU-10 laser-guided bomb, as seen on the aircraft's extended trapeze in the background. The weapon employed a 2,000-pound MK-84 body and a Paveway II guidance unit, which was fitted on the nose. *U.S. Air Force*

An ordinance specialist attaches one of the four forward canards to a GBU-10. The Paveway II guidance unit attempted to correct the weapons trajectory errors by utilizing full deflection commands to the canards. Such harsh control surface movements often led to overcorrection, resulting in a loss of energy and failure to achieve optimum trajectory. Net result: Even if the weapon reached its target, it often had a high angle of attack, low-impact velocity, and poor-impact angle. *U.S. Air Force*

A second PGM initiative produced the BLU-109 seen here on its handling dolly. The casing of this 2,000-pound weapon possesses an enhanced penetration capability. *U.S. Air Force*

Ice encrustation was never an issue with Have Blue, as it was purely a research aircraft and could therefore be flown in a selective manner. The F-117A however, is an all-weather aircraft, and so icing was a major issue. Extensive tests conducted early in the program determined where icing was liable to be a problem. When test pilot Dave Ferguson first saw the highly faceted, unconventional, "slab-sided" aircraft, he asked Dick Cantrell, the program's chief aerodynamicist, how airframe ice encrustation might effect the 117A's aerodynamics. Cantrell dryly replied, "Probably improve it."

In addition to the icing problems associated with the air data system, the other area of concern was the inlet grids. Alan Brown tells the story:

Initial testing showed that if we could keep any ice buildup to within the grid holes then differential pressure would drive the pieces of ice into the engine like French fries, and the engine could easily digest them. The problem would become difficult if the ice bridged across the front grids, thus stopping flow to the engines significantly. Several approaches were examined, some more grotesque than others. Firstly we looked at putting electronically conducting wires along the leading edges of the grid, much like a rear window defogger in an automobile. Despite trying different sizes and materials, we were unable to avoid an unacceptable increase in radar cross-section.

Another approach was based on an old technique for wing and tail leading edges. "Rubber boots" round the edges were inflated and deflated cyclically, to break the ice off as it formed. Now imagine molding very fine latex over edges surrounding more than 1,500 grid holes per inlet! We made some models with a small number of grid holes, but the difficulty of preserving the required engine inlet area coupled with the fragility of the system led to the abandonment of that approach. The clincher was probably the appearance of the latex system in operation—definitely in the Creature from the Black Lagoon category!

Russia had come up with unique approaches to ice removal from its Arctic icebreakers. One interesting technique involved charging capacitors which were attached to the inside of the hull. When they discharged, the bang dislodged the ice from outside the hull. We looked at variations on this theme for the inlet grids but were not successful in coming up with systems which would not damage the grids or cause too much flow constriction.

Finally we devised an old-fashioned windshield wiper. When not operating, it tucked away inside a box below the inlet without increasing the radar cross-section. In operation, it covers about 80 percent of the inlet area and keeps the ice in the "French fry" category so that it can be easily digested. Not too elegant, but it works.

An aircraft's cockpit, is also a major source of generating unwanted signal returns. To prevent radar energy reflecting back from numerous corner reflectors (not to mention the pilot's head, which in itself has a larger RCS than the entire aircraft), the F-117A's cockpit windows are metallicized. They work much like metallicized sunglasses, allowing the pilot to see out, but to all other intents, performing as a faceted panel in relation to electromagnetic radiation; they reflect energy away from its source.

The potential risks (both in terms of time and money) involved in developing an attack radar for the F-117A, with a commensurate, low probability of intercept, necessitated the installation of an infrared target acquisition system. Known as, Infrared Acquisition and Designation System (IRADS), and

The second element of the improved weapon was a Paveway III guidance section. Designated GBU-27, Jim Dunn flew the weapon's first accuracy test from Aircraft 783 on May 28, 1987. The inert weapon scored a direct hit on a 55-gallon barrel being used as a target, splitting it in half—the shape of things to come! Note the GBU-24 in the port weapons bay. *U.S. Air Force*

Canards attached, the GBU-27 completed certification testing in late 1988. Coupled with the F-117A's weapons delivery system, this dynamic duo demonstrated its unprecedented accuracy to the world during its operational debut in Desert Storm. *U.S. Air Force*

unique to the F-117A, its hardware consists of two external elements: a unit mounted in the upper nose section, known as the Forward-Looking Infrared (FLIR) unit, and a Downward-Looking Infrared (DLIR) unit located in the underside of the aircraft's nose section. Completely self-contained, the system enables the pilot to perform night time recognition and designation of his targets for his guided weapons without recourse to the telltale, electromagnetic radiation emissions associated with radar. Mounted in turrets, which in turn are located in commodious cavities, these units required apertures that were able to pass infrared and laser energy out and back but be opaque to radar.

Two materials were considered with which to build the covers, zinc selenide and zinc sulphide (ceranium was also in the offing, but manufacturing techniques were not mature enough at the time). Zinc selenide was evaluated and although it would pass the required enforced bands, it was not opaque to radar; therefore some form of metallicized screen would have to be

deposited on the transparency to achieve the required opacity. This in turn would limit infrared transmission, but it was hoped not to a debilitating level.

It had already been decided to procure major items "off-the-shelf" to reduce risk, however. The zinc selenide route consisted of literally growing the unit as a crystal, which took months. A message of maintainability was received loud and clear when a competent laboratory technician broke one of the windows during the first installation. The cost of one pair of windows: $650,000—ouch! Not surprisingly, that led to a rethink. As an interim solution, Alan Brown designed a high-tensile, fine-wire screen, which satisfied both radar, laser, and infrared requirements. It necessitated some work to ensure that the inside of the cavities didn't succumb to sonic fatigue, as they were to some extent, exposed to airflow; however, the success of Brown's design can be judged from the fact that these "interim" apertures were in use until the development of new screens on April 13, 1994.

All this led to a crash program to come up with a spray coating that was environmentally safe, satisfactorily bonded, and that preserved the required radar attenuation characteristics. We eventually installed what became the largest computer-controlled system in the country, if not the world. When you think of the faceted shape of the F-117A and imagine having to spray-paint around the corners while preserving the required thickness, you realize that the computer programming was not trivial. The machine had to be able to "walk round" a complete aircraft, applying multiple coats (the final thickness was much greater than conventional paint) and finish with a structurally sound, low-maintenance coating with absolutely the correct radar absorbing characteristics at all points on the vehicle.

An SUU-20 practice bomb and rocket dispenser belonging to the 410th Flight Test Squadron provides temporary housing for six practice bombs. It awaits removal of the static tags prior to a range sortie flown by Jim "J. B." Brown (Dagger 05) in Aircraft 831 in July 1997. *Paul Crickmore*

Other early problems were encountered relating to the maintenance of the aircraft's RAM. Here's Brown's recollections:

The trailing edge of the exhaust nozzle was comprised of multiple ceramic bricks which were loaded with radar-absorbing material. These in turn had to be attached by their leading edges to a high-temperature structural member and on their lower edges to a lower temperature radar-absorbing, nonmetallic, structural member. The combined requirements of structural rigidity, low cross-section, and compatible thermal expansions made this an extremely difficult design issue. Maintainability was also an extremely important feature, and a substantial part of the flight test program was devoted to steady improvements in all these areas. The internal shell of the nozzle itself was coated with a radar-absorbing material which had to be effective in its prime purpose, remain adhered in a heavily fatigue-inducing environment, and be compatible in thermal expansion, with the basic nozzle structural material. Well into the production program, we were still removing nozzles for recoating every 400 hours.

The coating applied over the rest of the aircraft was originally made up of 8-by-2-foot sheets glued on to the aircraft's surface like linoleum tiles. When I watched the first aircraft being coated and saw the number of people involved, I made a quick calculation and realized that it would cost about $750,000 dollars, just in labor to apply the material. We also found that it was very difficult to come up with an adhesive that was impervious to all fluids that an aircraft carries. In particular, hydraulic oil was very pervasive. Fluid would leak inside the aircraft, drip through the aircraft skin, dissolve the adhesive and drop out of the airplane maybe 6 feet away from where the original leak started. You can imagine the frustration of chasing

Other Considerations

In addition to producing a low RCS, the F-117A designers also paid good attention to reducing electromagnetic emissions and infrared radiation from the aircraft's hot parts. An important feature regarding design for low observability is that, in general, the design of an aircraft does not have to be compromised between the different observables. For example, if something is good for reducing radar returns, it can generally be made good for reducing infrared returns and vice versa; similarly this holds good for the other low observability disciplines. It was, for example, appropriate to shield the exhaust nozzle for both radar and infrared reasons. The high-aspect ratio nozzle design selected to minimize these returns also had the effect of increasing the surface area of the exhaust wake, which rapidly increased its cooling (good for both radar and infrared). This also increased the acoustic frequencies, thus attenuating sound from the aircraft more than from a circular nozzle.

One area of partial conflict, however, was the platypus bill–shaped shield behind the exhaust nozzle. This reduced direct radar reflections and infrared emissions from the exhaust nozzle at the expense of generating some infrared radiation from the shield itself. Yet because the vast majority of detectors and anti-aircraft weapons are located below the aircraft, it was elected to allow this radiation to be seen from above. Visual observability was also taken into account but considered secondary to the preceding disciplines. For example, engine smoke was treated by procuring engines that were not smokers. In addition, contrail suppression by chemical additives to the exhaust stream were also looked at but never actually implemented, as this only becomes an issue during daylight operations and therefore is no more important than visual camouflage.

Pictured at Lockheed's Helendale, California, test range, a one-quarter scale pole model is readied to undertake RCS evaluations. On June 21, 1990, a program to improve the durability and maintainability of the aircraft's RAM coating began. Three years later, the program had successfully developed a compound that addressed these problems—BX185. *Lockheed Martin*

Operational Analysis

An operational threat analysis was conducted. It was modeled on data and assumptions commensurate with a NATO/Soviet Warpack conflagration. Range specifications dictated basing the aircraft in theater, the fall out from which identified the principal radar types to be deceived in order to significantly enhance survivability. These were airborne intercept and SAM radars, which typically operate on a wavelength of between 3 and 10 centimeters.

Objects that are large compared to wavelength are sensitive to shape, reacting in a way similar to mirrors in the optical sense. When wavelengths become comparable to or larger than the dimensions of the object being illuminated, then the effects of shape diminish substantially, and there is much more interaction between components. A simple analogy is to think of the return at high frequencies (short wavelengths) being similar to that from shining a flashlight on the object; while the return at low frequencies (long wavelengths) is more like the response from striking a metal bell with a hammer.

It follows therefore, that at high frequencies, external surfaces should be designed to reflect energy away from the transmitter, avoiding where at all

possible, internal cavities, which become corner reflectors, focusing energy back to the source. At low frequencies, more effort is put into damping materials, for example, and into avoiding high-energy point sources on the aircraft, like sharp metal wing tips, which could act as focal points for energy return.

Working on the premise that all the RCS goals had been met, the aircraft would now be invisible to detection by attack radars. The next phase of the operational analysis considered optimum speed and altitude in order to achieve accurate weapon delivery. It was soon determined that flying at supersonic speed didn't enhance survivability. Indeed, flying at high subsonic speeds actually increased survivability by reducing a defender's ability of detecting the aircraft using infrared systems. It was therefore decided that the platform would be powered by nonafterburning engines, which also reduced airframe temperatures, further lowering its IR signature.

The improved Texas Instruments F-3 turret houses an IR seeker with much improved range and a longer life laser. *Paul Crickmore*

Flying at tree-top height and 500 knots doesn't leave much time to acquire the target. It also places the attacking aircraft within range of many more weapons systems. At the other extreme, maintaining a similar speed at 35,000 feet provides the aircraft with greater target acquisition time; but to be effective, weapon dispersal has to be much greater. Optimum weapon effectiveness was achieved by placing the aircraft at medium altitude, which, for a subsonic aircraft, touting such a modest performance envelope would be utter suicide unless it was stealthy.

The amount of "stealth" required to enhance survivability depends upon the "detection zone." Therefore, with the aircraft maintaining high subsonic speeds, a successful missile attack from the flank would require the weapon to undertake a tight high g turn, a maneuver still outside the envelope of most systems. From the rear, it is hoped the aircraft would have already hit its target and be returning home, thereby placing the missile in a catch-up situation.

Directly above and below the aircraft are zones of almost negligible importance. The aspect that presents the defender with the greatest chance of a successful intercept is the frontal zone, however. If the threshold of detection, by radar using wavelengths of between 3 and 10 centimeters, can be foiled to a point where the aircraft is just 1-minute flying time (about 10 miles) from the radar head, then there is a good chance of avoiding a successful intercept. Pulling all the strands together, an F-117A flying at an altitude of 12,000 feet and 500 knots will achieve that 1-minute detection goal parameter by being at its most "stealthy," head on, 25-degrees look down and 25-degrees look up.

The Airframe

The F-117A is 65 feet, 11 inches (20.08 meters) in length, 12 feet, 5 inches in height (3.78 meters), has a wingspan of 43 feet, 4 inches (13.2 meters), and a wing area of 913 square feet (84.8 square meters). Its planform

Engines equipping the F-117A were a version of the General Electric F404 turbo fan, which powered the McDonnell Douglas F/A-18. The variant used in the Nighthawk is designated the F404-GE-F1D2, and unlike that which powered the Hornet, it is not equipped with an afterburner. *U.S. Air Force*

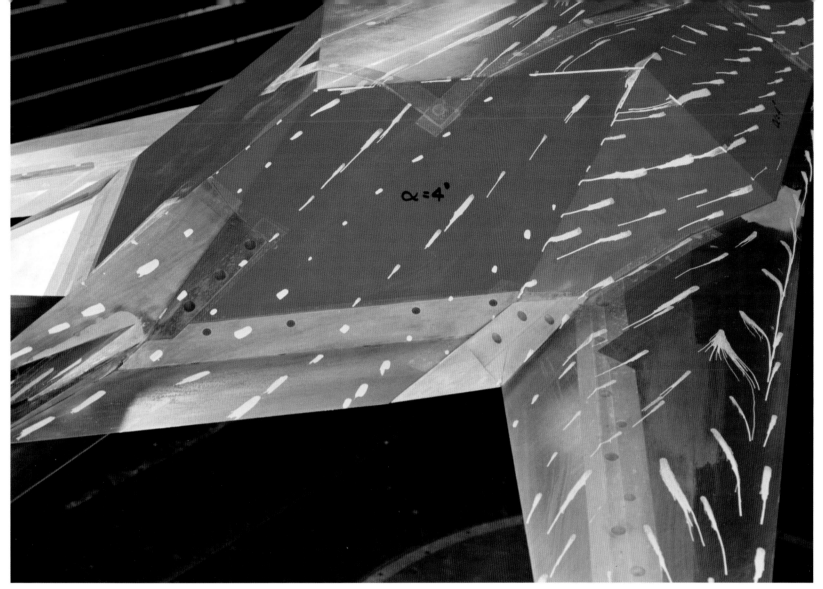

Buffeted up in the Lockheed wind tunnel, it can be noted that the F-117A model is ready for flow checks with a positive pitch angle set at 4 degrees. *Lockheed Martin*

is a modified delta with the wings mated to a broad lifting body. Low observability necessitated a leading-edge sweep, which is completely unbroken from nose to wingtip, of 67.3 degrees. The trailing edge of the delta is notched out for both low-observable considerations as well as to reduce wetted area. Another concession to low observability is the highly swept V-tail surfaces, the objective of which is to reduce the overall size of such surfaces while maintaining adequate control in the unstable pitch and yaw axis.

Powerplant

The F-117A Nighthawk is powered by two General Electric F404-GE F1D2 two-shaft, low-bypass-ratio turbofans. Its three-stage compressor fan has a bypass ratio of 0.34 and airflow through each engine is 142 pounds per second (64 kilograms). The high-pressure compressor is a seven-stage element with an overall pressure ratio of 25:1. The engine's combustion chamber is annular and is a single piece. The high-pressure turbine consists of a single-stage unit with air-cooled blades; similarly, the low-pressure turbine is also a single-stage unit. Maximum diameter of the engine is 34.8 inches (880 mil-

limeters), and it has a maximum sea level thrust rating of 10,800 pounds.

The engine gearbox drives the main fuel pump, the oil pump assembly, the engine alternator, and the power take-off (PTO) shaft, which powers the Airframe Mounted Accessory Drive (AMAD).

Each engine's ignition system contains one igniter plug and is powered by its respective engine alternator. In order for the alternator to produce enough power for the plug to cause engine ignition, the engine must be spun above 10 percent rpm. Once this has been achieved, the ignition system remains firing until engine power increases above 45 percent, after which it automatically cuts off (idle power is usually between 62 to 64 percent). In the event of a flame out, sensors within the engine detect a pressure drop, and as the engine winds down below 45 percent, the ignition system again cuts in and remains in operation until engine rpm drops below 10 percent, at which point the system becomes powerless.

Each engine is controlled by a throttle, mounted on the left console with detents at OFF, IDLE, and MIL. The off position terminates engine ignition and fuel flow. The idle position commands minimum Unified Fuel Control

(UFC) thrust and is used for all ground starts and air starts. From IDLE to MIL, the throttle controls the output of the engine.

Hydraulics

The F-117A's hydraulic system architecture is similar to that of the F-15. There are two pressurized hydraulic reservoirs in the aircraft: a flight reservoir and a utility reservoir, thereby providing a wide margin of redundancy. Pressure is provided by a flight pump and a utility pump, which are located on each AMAD. Each system is divided into an A side and a B side, creating a four-branch system. These are characterized as Flight A, Flight B, Utility A, and Utility B. The two flight pumps power the flight control system, with either pump capable of powering both Flight A and Flight B.

The two flight systems each power three separate control surfaces for survivability. This is further backed-up by Utility B. Utility A provides the muscle for all other hydro-powered equipment on the aircraft: air refueling door, nosewheel steering, auxiliary power unit exhaust door, wipers, landing gear, weapons bay doors, trapeze, and wheel brakes. Back up of the hydraulic system is provided by an emergency power unit, which powers a hydraulic pump that drives the flight system.

Fuel System

From the pilot's perspective, there are eight fuel tanks in the F-117A. There are two wing tanks, two forward transfer tanks, two aft transfer tanks, and two feed tanks. They are arranged as their names imply, with the feed

Aircraft 780 is lifted from the forward fuselage, final assembly jig (103 Jig). According to Bob Murphy (director of manufacturing), early production delays of the first FSD F-117As were caused by a shortage of 70-50 aluminium. This could have been alleviated had 70-75 been substituted. The 70-75 aluminum is more accessible but has slightly inferior fatigue characteristics. *Lockheed Martin*

Construction of all 60 F-117As took place within the Skunk Works facilities at Burbank. Machining was carried out at Plant C1, sheet metal fabrication at Building 82, and final assembly (seen above) at Buildings 309 and 310. *Lockheed Martin*

tanks being situated in the middle, between the forward and aft transfer tanks. Fuel is not used to trim the aircraft; this is achieved aerodynamically using control surface position. A controlled fuel burn sequence is used to maintain the center of gravity (CG), within limits. Again, a high level of redundancy is built into the fuel transfer system, with a combination of electronically powered transfer pumps and motive flow used, to move fuel from one tank to another. Wing tank fuel is transferred into the fuselage, then the forward and aft transfers push fuel into the feeds. Total fuel capacity is approximately 19,000 pounds or 2,800 U.S. gallons of JP-8.

Electrical System

The generators are the same as those used on the F/A-18. The AC equipment consists of a 115/200-volt, three-phase, 400-Hertz system, supplied by two 30/40-kilovolt amps, constant-speed generators, one mounted on each engine. DC power is then obtained from two converters. Emergency power is provided by a 5-KVA auxiliary generator, which is powered by the emergency power unit, driven by auxiliary power unit exhaust gases. In the event of a multiple generator and emergency power unit failure, batteries provide power to the flight control system for approximately 10 minutes, during which time

Ben Rich joined Lockheed in 1950 as a thermodynamicist; he helped design inlet ducts for the F-104, C-130, and a stainless steel fighter, the F-90 (which was later canceled). He joined the Skunk Works in December 1954 and worked on the U-2, the CL-400 (a proposed hydrogen-fueled bomber), the A-12, D-21 drone, YF-12, and SR-71. "The father of stealth," Rich died on January 5, 1995. *Lockheed Martin*

an immediate landing is essential, if a complete failure of the fly-by-wire, flight control system is to be avoided.

Avionics

Senior Trends' original avionics package was oriented around three Delco M362 F computers with 32-K words of 16-bit core memory, as used in the F-16. Interconnected via a dual redundant, MIL-STD-1553 data bus, the weapons delivery computer was the executive, providing overall control, as well as updating cockpit displays, performing weapon delivery calculations, and controlling data distribution. The navigation control computer performed all navigation and control functions, including inertial measurement, navigation and flight director steering, as well as position update, Tacan and Instrument Landing System (ILS) interface. The third computer provided control and data processing for a supplementary system and, in addition, provided back-up, should either of the other two computers fail.

The avionics package is highly integrated; once mission planning has been completed, details are fed into the Mission Data Planning System (MDPS). The data could then be loaded into the aircraft's data transfer module interface unit. As the Honeywell SPN-GEANS INS navigated the aircraft to the target area, the computer system cued the IR system to the target. Placing the crosshairs of his sensor display on the target at various off sets, the pilot refined the aiming point, laser designated the target, and consented for weapon release. The weapon delivery computer simultaneously performed relevant ballistic calculations, based upon the weapon to be dispatched, together with Inertial Navigation System (INS) and IR inputs. Weapons release then occurred via the stores management system at the appropriate time.

The Infrared Acquisition and Detection System (IRADS) is built by Texas Instruments (now Raytheon). As mentioned earlier, two turrets are mounted in "contour" to conform with set RCS criteria. The target is initially acquired by the FLIR unit located in the top turret. It is then tracked by a video camera and displayed on the IR targeting screen in the cockpit. As the "look angle" increases, the target is "handed-off" to the DLIR housed in the lower turret. Because the two turrets are identical (and interchangeable), the video picture received by the DLIR has to be inverted electronically when displayed to the pilot, thus enabling the image to remain topside up. Despite many initial problems, the system is capable of tracking the target throughout dive toss type deliveries, where it could be subjected to as many as three hand-offs and air loads of 4 g during loft maneuvers.

From 1984, the F-117's avionics architecture was the subject of a three-phase Offensive Capability Improvement Program (OCIP). Phase 1, the Weapons System Computational Subsystem (WSCS) upgrade program was initiated to replace the Delco M362Fs with IBM AP-102 MIL-STD-1750A computers. These new units boosted the capability to one million instructions per second, 16-bit CPU with 128-K words of 16-bit memory expandable to 256 K. It is a repackaged version of that used in the space shuttle.

There are the same number of AP-102s and they address the same disciplines as the Delcos; however, each now controls a dual redundant MIL-STD-1553 bus. Onboard systems are divided between buses 1 and 2 with the third computer and bus held as spares for growth. A unique high-speed bus was incorporated to enable direct communications between the three computers and the Expanded Data Transfer Module Interface Unit. Either of the three computers can now assume the identity of either of the others, and a number of new capabilities have been made possible, the first of these being the successful deployment of the GBU-27 laser-guided bomb together with the ability to perform dual-bay weapon deliveries.

Phase 2 of OCIP afforded greater situational awareness and reduced pilot workload by allowing a 4D flight management system to fly complex profiles automatically, providing speed and time-over-target (TOT) control. Also included in this phase was the installation of color multifunctional display indicators and a digital tactical situation display or moving map, a new data

Initially skeptical of the faceted "Hopeless Diamond" concept, Dick Cantrell, the Skunk Works senior aerodynamicist, worked within the incredibly tight design parameters to ensure that both Have Blue and the F-117A retained the smallest possible RCS yet remain aerodynamically viable. *Lockheed Martin*

Depicted is the pre-OCIP phase 3 F-117A flight simulator. The green-and-white multifunction display indicators (MDIs) flanking the centrally mounted IR sensor display were built by Texas Instruments and have since been replaced by color multifunctional display indicators (CMDIs). Air Force operating procedures require the left MDI/CMDI to display primary flight data information at all times. *Lockheed Martin*

A post-OCIP phase 3 F-117A cockpit—the clue being the active liquid crystal display, incorporated in the Heads-Up Display (HUD). The right CMDI can also display primary flight data; however, operational aircraft use this display for the Horizontial Situation Indicator (HSI), moving map, or access to status and maintenance pages. If attack mode is selected on the HUD, the display automatically cues the weapons arming page. *Lockheed Martin*

F-117As undertake depot maintenance at Air Force Plant 42, Site 7, Palmdale. Also located at Site 7 is the 410th Flight Test Squadron (the F-117A combined flight test squadron). *Lockheed Martin*

entry panel, a display processor, an auto throttle system, and a pilot-activated automatic recovery system (PAARS).

PAARS was installed as a result of the fatal F-117A accidents, where spatial disorientation was a contributing factor. Upon pilot command, the autopilot, even if not engaged, commands the flight-control system and auto throttles to fly a preprogrammed set of maneuvers, based upon entry attitude and airspeed, to recover the aircraft to straight and level flight.

OCIP phase 3 saw the replacement of the aging SPN-GEANS, INS system, with a new Honeywell H-423/E Ring Laser Gyro (RLG). The original acronym for this program was to be RNIP, which stands for ring laser gyro navigation improvement program. But the system was supplemented by a Rockwell-Collins Global Positioning System (GPS), thereby giving rise to the title RNIP plus. The new INS vastly reduces alignment time from 43 minutes for SPN-GEANS to just 9 minutes, and it considerably enhances overall reliability, increasing the mean time between failures from 400 to 2,000 hours.

As is apparent from this perspective, the F-117A is at it most stealthy head on, reflecting incident radiation away from the radar head. *Lockheed Martin*

The F-117 is capable of hauling a wide array of hardware, including the B61 nuclear weapon, the delivery of which requires a loft maneuver to ensure aircraft survivability. *Lockheed Martin*

The H-423 may not boost enhanced accuracy (still believed to be 0.12 nautical miles per hour); however, when used in association with GPS, the system represents a significant advance in navigational accuracy.

Environmental Control System (ECS)

The ECS air conditioning and pressurization functions to provide temperature-controlled, pressure-regulated air for heating, cooling, ventilating, canopy defogging, cockpit pressurization, canopy sealing, g-suit pressurization, fuel tank pressurization, and electronic equipment cooling. Engine bleed air is directed through a turbine compressor and air-to-air heat exchanges where it is cooled by ram air. Conditioned air enters the cockpit, having received signals from temperature sensors and from a manually operated control panel, to automatically control the cockpit temperature.

Air pressurization is provided by the pressurization system for control/operation of some of the ECS, canopy seal, g-suit, and fuel tanks. Pressure in the cockpit is controlled automatically according to a predetermined schedule. A cockpit pressure safety valve relieves pressure if ever the cockpit pressure exceeds ambient pressure by 5.4 psi. The canopy seal is inflated/deflated with the mechanical locking/unlocking of the canopy.

Oxygen System

A 5-liter liquid oxygen system provides breathing oxygen to a diluter demand oxygen regulator. The regulator provides for selections of normal diluted oxygen and 100 percent oxygen. Oxygen duration varies depending upon altitude, regulator settings, and usage. The emergency oxygen system consists of a high-pressure bottle and a regulator mounted on the side of the ejector seat and is activated automatically upon ejection or manually by tugging a green ring located on the left side of the seat.

FACETED SURFACE PRESSURE DISTRIBUTION

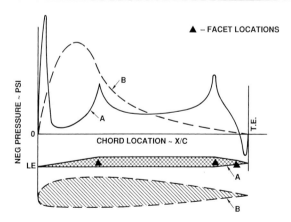

Pressure distribution over the surface of a conventional wing (B), compared to that of a faceted surface (A). The lift at the leading edge of the elevon, together with the pressure spike on the elevon's underside trailing edge, are particularly unhelpful and explain the need to beef up its attachment assembly. *Lockheed Martin*

UNAUGMENTED AIRFRAME CHARACTERISTICS
(CLEAN AIRCRAFT)

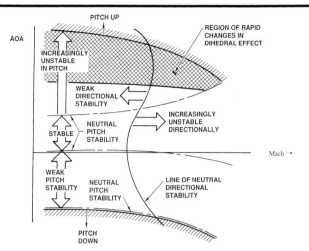

The cost of achieving low observability: This graph clearly illustrates the aerodynamic sacrifices made to achieve XST's ultimate goal. *Lockheed Martin*

Ejection Seat

The pilot of an F-117A sits in an ACES II ejection seat. This zero-speed, zero-altitude seat's mode of operation depends on the aircraft's speed and altitude. Seat ejection is initiated by pulling ejection handles on the side of the seat. This retracts the shoulder harness and locks the inertia reel, fires initiators for canopy jettison, and ignites the canopy-removal rockets. As the seat leaves the aircraft, lanyards fire two seat-ejection initiators. A rocket catapult propels the seat from the cockpit, and the emergency oxygen is activated. The recovery sequencer selects the correct recovery mode based on pitot sensor inputs and ignites the stabilization package and the trajectory divergence rocket. If the ejection sequence was initiated with the aircraft traveling above 250 KIAS, initiation of the drogue gun for seat stabilization occurs.

Ejection Sequence Times (at sea level)

| | Time (secs) | |
| | (Mode 1) | (Mode 2) |
Event	0-250 KIAS	250-650 KIAS
Catapult initiation	0.0	0.0
Drogue gun fired	N/A	0.17
Drogue chute inflated	N/A	0.38
Parachute fired	0.20	1.17
Seat/drogue separation	N/A	1.32
Seat/pilot separation	0.45	1.42
Recovery parachute inflated	1.80	2.80
Survival kit deployed	5.50	6.30

chapter three

FLIGHT TEST

Assembling the Team

In 1977, Lieutenant Colonel Dave Ferguson commanded the 6513th Test Squadron, a unit that had its administrative headquarters at Edwards Air Force Base. Equipped with F-4s and T-38s—which for the most part were also based at Edwards—the 6513th had a black side: Seven of its other aircraft most certainly couldn't be seen anywhere on the large, sprawling base. They were involved in a highly classified program known as "Red Hat," and their country of manufacture wasn't the United States. These aircraft, MiG-17s and MiG-21s, were based up at Area 51, and it was while carrying out his duties at "a remote test site," that Ferguson met Bill Park. At that time, Park was the director of flight operations for the Skunk Works, but he hadn't flown military jets since his involvement in Project Tagboard, the M-21/D-21 drone evaluations that had taken place nearly 10 years earlier. Park was gearing up to fly Have Blue, and Ferguson was asked to get him requalified. This was achieved in a T-38, and through this initial contact Ferguson flew the occasional T-38 chase sortie during the Have Blue program. In 1978, Park offered Ferguson a job on the Senior Trend Program, which he accepted following his retirement from the Air Force in 1979.

Tom Morgenfeld worked on the YF-18 project development team. He was extremely impressed with the aircraft's predicted capabilities and was convinced that it would provide the Navy with a first-rate, close-combat fighter. Such views were extremely unpopular among certain senior Navy figures, however, particularly at a time when Grumman was intent on populating the fleet attack/defense role solely with Tomcats. Here is what Morgenfeld recalls:

Sometime in mid-1979, I was relaxing after work with Dave Ferguson and Bill Park. Dave is a colleague with whom I'd worked on several joint USAF/USN test programs, and Bill was the chief test pilot at the Skunk Works. Dave and I

were still on active duty, but he had already submitted his retirement papers with the intention of going to work for Bill on a program that was, as yet, unknown to me. I had been having severe reservations about continuing my naval career, as it looked to me that my flying days were coming to an end. In fact, I had submitted a letter of resignation as a form of damage control until I could sort out where my career was really heading.

During our conversation Bill sympathized with me over my career dilemma, then asked if I would be interested in coming to work for Lockheed. I was floored, but accepted immediately. As it turned out, when Fergie hired in, he found out there was one more pilot position to be filled and mentioned my situation to Bill. As I was a known commodity and available at the time, Bill went ahead and offered me the job. Timing is everything, but imagine my surprise when I'd formally hired in and got to see what it was that I was supposed to fly!

In addition to contractor pilots, it had been decided that developmental together with category I and II, operational test and evaluation (OT&E) of the F-117A, would be conducted by a joint test force. Tactical Air Command (TAC), controlled testing and initially provided three pilots and two analysts. These numbers grew as preparations for the first operational squadron got underway. The third party involved in this "tripartite" force was Air Force Systems Command (AFSC), which provided three pilots, four engineers, and

To increase airflow to the engines during low-operating or off-limit speeds, two blow-in doors were cut into the aircraft's upper intake ducts (as seen in this photograph). These caused Hal Farley some consternation when they modulated half a dozen times, during his first flight, generating loud thumps. *Lockheed Martin*

approximately 40 aircraft maintenance personnel. It was in relation to AFSC's involvement in Senior Trend that in June 1979, Lieutenant Colonel Skip Anderson received a phone call from Colonel Larry McClain. Anderson had accumulated hundreds of hours flying F-4 Phantoms, which included 214 combat missions in Vietnam. At the time of the call, he had just taken command of the 435th Tactical Fighter Training Squadron (TFTS), 49th TFW, at Holloman Air Force Base in New Mexico. But having spent two years with Red Hat as the ops officer (1974–1976), Anderson knew McClain, who, after exchanging pleasantries, cut to the chase and offered him a job. He told Anderson that he couldn't talk about the program, but assured him that he would enjoy it. Knowing Larry McClain as he did, Anderson recalls "In the end, I couldn't resist, even without knowing what the job was. I borrowed a T-38 and flew out to Nevada for a day to talk with Larry. It was interesting because I had to hold out of sight for quite a while without much fuel. Later I learned it was because Ken Dyson was up in Have Blue. By the time I got back [to Area 51] full time in August, the second Have Blue had been lost."

Earlier that same year Park had phoned Harold "Hal" Farley, who at the time was working for Grumman flying F-14 Tomcats from Naval Air Station (NAS) Point Mugu in California. Park introduced himself, saying that he worked for Lockheed and was Farley interested in a job? "Bill was very abrupt on the phone and wouldn't give me any details," Farley says.

He just simply said, 'I'll get in touch with you later.' Well, I wasn't looking for a job. I was enjoying myself flying F-14s, but I didn't say no; I was just so surprised. Bill called back a few days later and invited me out to his house. His home was in Bel Air, one of the really exclusive suburbs of L.A. During the meeting I thought to myself, 'Gee, they must pay well at Lockheed.'

Bill discussed the job only to the extent that it would be flying airplanes and that he couldn't tell anymore. I went home to think it over, knowing that the Skunk Works was unsurpassed when it came to designing and building aircraft on the leading edge of technology. I decided it was an opportunity of a lifetime that I couldn't pass up. I gave Bill a call and said I was definitely interested in the job. We discussed the total package. I was given an offer, which I accepted, and so I joined Lockheed. I had a top-secret clearance, but this program was Special Access, so for a few weeks I was in the penalty box, waiting for the clearance to come through. When it finally did, I went to the Lockheed Burbank plant; there I was met and escorted into the conference room, upstairs in Building 3-11, by Norm Nelson, who, I discovered, was the program manager. Once inside this large room, Norm showed me some large 3D drawings posted on the wall of an airplane. He asked me what I thought about it, and of course, when I saw it, I didn't know what to think. The vehicle was

faceted, with highly swept wings. I thought, my goodness, it must be very fast; but that turned out to be a bit of a joke! I then looked at it from a head-on view, and it had a bit of a lifting body aspect to it, so I thought maybe it's a re-entry vehicle. Finally Norm chuckled and told me what it was really for. I must admit I didn't really comprehend the significance of stealth at that time, but it was still an interesting thing to see such an unusual airplane.

Preflight Preparation

To prepare themselves for the first series of flights in the F-117A, Skip Anderson recalls, "We spent a lot of time with Bob Loschke in the Lockheed simulator out at Rye Canyon, working the control problems. The key effort became one of finding a set of gains which supported both up-and-away flight and an engine failure on takeoff. I recall we ran the sim off the runway a discouraging number of times. We also flew F-16s on a few occasions because it too was a fly-by-wire system, plus we practiced the F-117's early flight profiles in F-4s and T-38s. In my opinion, the F-16 was of little value to our preparation, because of the side stick and in the event Bob's simulator turned out to be quite accurate." In addition, the team contacted Calspan to provide a flight simulation based on aerodynamic data acquired through wind tunnel tests and Have Blue. Because the program was so highly classified, the data was delivered to Rogers Smith of Calspan by Farley, Ferguson, Morgenfeld, and Bob Loschke in a restaurant out at Newhall. During that meeting they discussed what they

This heavily enhanced shot, taken from a video camera, shows Tom Morgenfeld recovering Aircraft 782 onto a bed of foam, on January 27, 1982, following the loss of the nose wheel. *Lockheed Martin*

After arriving from Burbank, California, the FSD1 is seen here supported by hydraulic jacks in a hangar at Area 51 while undergoing final assembly. Note where the wings were detached for transportation. *Lockheed Martin*

wanted from Calspan; however Rogers couldn't be told what he would be simulating. All he was given to work from was a set of aerodynamic data.

The data supplied was basically that of the predicted flight characteristics of the F-117A in the landing pattern. In addition, the team requested that stability conditions were degraded by degrees and that simulation of various failures was also built into the program. Test data indicated that the aircraft was unstable in both pitch and yaw and was barely flyable without input from the fly-by-wire computers. During the planned first flight, ballast would be added in the nose, enabling the center of gravity (CG) to be positioned as far forward as possible, thereby providing a degree of positive pitch stability; the hope being that there would be enough yaw stability to ensure that the aircraft at least remained manageable. Rogers Smith took the information with him to Buffalo, New York, to create a simulation that would be programmed into the Lockheed/Calspan NT-33A. This aircraft enabled the predicted stability and control aspects of different aircraft to be artificially simulated, allowing pilots to familiarize themselves with the likely characteristics to be encountered prior to their first flights.

Some months later, Farley got a call from Rogers informing him that the simulation was ready. Dave Ferguson and Farley together with Major Russ Easter (an Air Force pilot who had been assigned to the program to monitor progress), flew up to Buffalo. Farley recalls, "I'm not sure whether Russ flew the NT-33 or not, but Dave and I took turns. I think we flew it three times apiece, varying the stability in pitch and yaw and performing takeoffs and landings and degrading the flight characteristics below the air data we had, in order to see if we could land it. It turned out to be a valuable learning process for us; the airplane was flyable in its degraded state and this gave us some confidence that even if the air data was wrong, we would be able to get it back on the ground safely."

In keeping with earlier Skunk Works "Black World" aircraft development projects, flight testing would be conducted at Area 51. On January 1, 1979, preparations at the remote site got underway in readiness to receive its latest guest. On January 16, 1981, a C-5 from Burbank touched down at Groom Lake, onboard was Aircraft 780, FSD 1—the combined test team at last had an aircraft.

Lieutenant Colonel Skip Anderson joined the Senior Trend program as its joint test force director, reporting in parallel to Colonel Pete Winters, commander of the AFFTC detachment–Detachment 5 at Area 51, and Colonel Don Merkl, program manager at the Special Program Office (SPO). (Don Merkl retired in August 1981, after which the position was filled by Colonel Richard Schofield. Anderson notes that communication to the SPO was difficult in the literal sense of the word, as secure speech devices were very poor at that time.

program, so several had to just wait at home. Once cleared, others spent time at the Skunk Works with designers and engineers and writing up the F-117A's maintenance manuals. When the prototype, Aircraft 780, was moved from Burbank to Area 51, they were integrated with Lockheed crews under Red McDaris. Lockheed was also having problems getting enough people cleared into the program, so this additional help was most welcome. Clearance problems eventually degenerated to such an extent that Al's group took over operation of one of the aircraft (Aircraft 783). This was a real tribute to the trust developed between Lockheed and the Air Force.

Politics

It wasn't the first time during a presidential election campaign that references to a highly classified program were released to the public to help secure votes. Even before Senior Trend had taken to the air, it provided some useful political ammunition when, on August 22, 1980, the following statement by then Secretary of Defense Harold Brown (under President Jimmy Carter) was released to the public:

I am announcing today a major technological advance of great military significance.

This so-called "stealth" technology enables the United States to build manned and unmanned aircraft that cannot be successfully intercepted with existing air defense systems. We have demonstrated to our satisfaction that the technology works.

This achievement will be a formidable instrument of peace. It promises to add a unique dimension to our tactical forces and the deterrent strength of our strategic forces. At the same time it will provide us capabilities that are wholly consistent with our pursuit of verifiable arms control agreements, in particular, with the provisions of SALT II.

For three years, we have successfully maintained the security of this program. This is because of the conscientious efforts of the relatively few people in the executive branch and the legislative branch who were briefed on the activity and of the contractors working on it.

However, in the last few months, the circle of people knowledgeable about the program has widened, partly because of the increased size of

Upon receiving his bachelor of science degree, Harold "Hal" C. Farley joined the U.S. Navy in 1959. After completing flight training, he was assigned to Attack Squadron 164 (VA-164), flying A-4Ds, from the USS *Oriskany*. After graduating from the U.S. Navy Test Pilot School at Patuxent River, he performed a variety of tests and evaluations on F-4s, F-8s, A-4s, A-6s, and the RA-5C before joining the Grumman Aircraft Company as an experimental test pilot. There he tested A-6s and F-14s. *Lockheed Martin*

The group of 40 Air Force maintenance NCOs assigned to AFFTC was formed to work with the designers on aircraft maintenance factors. Chief Master Sergeant (CMS) Al LeBlue headed the group. Senior Master Sergeant George Malone was in charge of the avionics shop, and Technical Sergeant Dwayne Coleman was the supply officer. Others were recruited by Skip Anderson and LeBlue during trips to several TAC fighter wings during the fall of 1979. This exceptional group was willing to move without knowing what they would be doing. They arrived in Las Vegas in the spring and summer of 1980. At the time it was taking between six to nine months to obtain security clearance into the

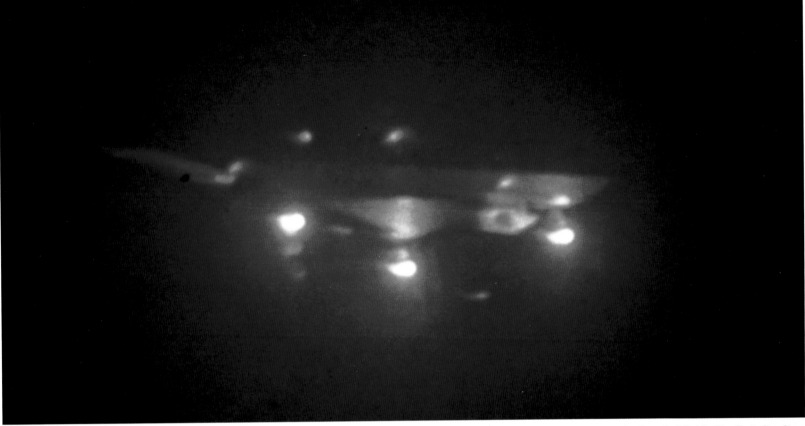

Until it was revealed to the public, the F-117 spent nearly seven and a half years flying almost exclusively at night from two remote desert airfields. The first site, Area 51, has attracted wild speculation: from a base for stealthy hypersonic aircraft to a storage and evaluation center for UFOs. Perhaps this shot of an F-117 on approach qualifies for an entry into the latter category. *Lockheed Martin*

Aircraft 780, or FSD1, is pictured inside a hangar at Area 51, displaying the names of the first two pilots to fly the aircraft. The remote desert home of the first five test and evaluation aircraft led to them being designated Scorpion 1 through 5. This was after the joint Lockheed/Air Force team adopted the Baja Scorpion as its symbol, after one of the venomous creatures found its way into the teams' office area. *Lockheed Martin*

To preserve the tightest level of security surrounding Senior Trend, attendance at the first flight was rigorously controlled. Several key insiders agreed not to attend, including Air Force Secretary Orr, General Burke (DCS/R&D), and Major General Larry Welch (TAC/DO). Those pictured above are some of the essential support personnel privileged to witness the historic event. *Lockheed Martin*

the effort, and partly because of the debate underway in the Congress on new bomber proposals. Regrettably, there have been several leaks about the stealth program in the last few days in the press and television news coverage.

In the face of these leaks, I believe that is not appropriate or credible for us to deny the existence of the program, and it is now important to correct some of the leaked information that misrepresented the administration's position on a new bomber program. The so-called stealth bomber was not a factor in our decision in 1977 to cancel the B-1; indeed, it was not yet in design.

I am gratified that, as yet, none of the most sensitive and significant classified information about the characteristics of this program has been disclosed. An important objective of the announcement today is to make clear the kinds of information that we intend scrupulously to protect at the highest security level. Dr. Perry, my undersecretary of defense for research and engineering and a chief architect of this program, will elaborate this point further.

In sum, we have developed a new technology of extraordinary military significance. We are vigorously applying this technology to develop a number of military aircraft, and these programs are showing very great promise.

We can take tremendous pride in this latest achievement of American technology. It can play a major role in strengthening our strategic and tactical forces without in any way endangering any of our arms control initiatives. And it can contribute to the maintenance of peace by posing a new and significant offset to the Soviet Union's attempt to gain military ascendancy by weight of numbers. I would now like to ask Bill Perry to give you some additional details on our stealth program.

William Perry then stated the following:

World War II demonstrated the decisive role that air power can play in military operations. It also demonstrated the potential of radar as a primary means of detecting aircraft and directing fire against them. On balance, though, the advantage clearly was with the aircraft. Subsequent to World War II, defensive missiles—both ground-launched and air-launched—were developed and "married" with radar fire control systems. This substantially increased the effectiveness of air defense systems, shifting the balance against aircraft. For the last few decades we have been working on techniques to defeat such air defense systems. At present, our military aircraft makes substantial use of electronic countermeasures (jamming) and flying low to place themselves in "ground clutter," both of which degrade the effectiveness of air defense radars. By these means we have maintained the effectiveness of our military aircraft in the face of radar-directed defensive missiles.

However, the Soviets continue to place very heavy emphasis on the development and deployment of air defense missiles in an attempt to offset the advantage we have in air power. They have built thousands of surface-to-air missile systems, they employ radars with high power and monopulse tracking circuits, which are very difficult to jam, and in the last few years they have developed air-to-air missiles guided by "look down" radars which are capable of tracking aircraft in "ground clutter."

Because of these developments and because of the importance we attach to maintaining our air superiority, we have for years been developing

Hal Farley exits the cockpit of the 780, having completed the first flight of an aircraft destined to revolutionize air warfare. He flew the first six flights of FSD1 and marked his retirement from Lockheed and test flying by completing his last Senior Trend flight, exactly 10 years from the first flight (on July 18, 1991). *Lockheed Martin*

All smiles, Hal Farley obliges with a short photo call, following the successful completion of the 780's first flight on July 18, 1981. *Lockheed Martin*

what we call "penetration" technology, the technology that degrades the effectiveness of radars and other sensors used by air defense systems. A particular emphasis has been on developing that technology which makes an aircraft "invisible" (a figure of speech) to radar. In the early 1960s, we applied a particular version of this technology to some of our reconnaissance aircraft. In the mid-1970s, we applied it to the cruise missiles then being developed (Tomahawk and Air Launched Cruise Missile [ALCM]). By the summer of 1977 it became clear that this technology could be considerably extended in its effectiveness and could be applied to a wide class of vehicles including manned aircraft. We concluded that it was possible to build aircraft so difficult to detect that they could not be successfully engaged by any existing air defense systems. Recognizing the great significance of such a development we took three related actions: First, we made roughly a tenfold increase in our investment to advance this technology; second, we initiated a number of very high-priority programs to apply this technology; and third, we gave the entire program extraordinary security protection, even to the point of classifying the very existence of such a program.

Initially we were able to limit knowledge of the program to a very few government officials in both the executive and legislative branches and succeeded in maintaining complete secrecy about the program. However, as the program increased in size—currently the annual funding is 100 times greater than when we decided to accelerate the program in 1977—it became necessary to brief more people. The existence of a stealth program has now become public knowledge. But even as we acknowledge the existence of the stealth program, we will draw a new security line to protect that information about the program which could facilitate a Soviet countermeasures program. We will continue to protect at the highest security level information about:

a. the specific techniques which we employ to reduce detectability

b. the degree of success of each of these techniques

c. characteristics of specific vehicles being developed

d. funds being applied to specific programs

e. schedules of specific programs

With those ground rules, I think you can see that I am extremely limited in what I can tell you about the program. I will say this. First, stealth technology does not involve a single technical approach, but rather a

During its first period of downtime, from August 6, 1981, to October 21, 1981, Aircraft 780 had larger fins fitted to improve directional stability and the earlier desert-camouflaged paint pattern replaced with an overall, low-visibility gray scheme. *Lockheed Martin*

Aircraft 784, the final FSD aircraft, successfully completed its first flight on April 10, 1982, nearly three months ahead of 783 which was delayed due to RCS preparation. The former is seen here, dropping a 2,000-pound GBU-27 LGB during separation trials. Note the weapon is released from the trapeze, which remains in the bomb bay, ensuring the aircraft retains the lowest possible RCS. In addition, note the underwing fairing and the smaller structure under the nose, both housing cameras to record weapon separation characteristics. *Lockheed Martin*

complex synthesis of many. Even if I were willing to describe it to you, I could not do it in a sentence or even a paragraph. Second, while we have made remarkable advances in the technology in the last three years, we have been building on excellent work done in our defense technology program over the last two decades. Third, this technology—theoretically at least—could be applied to any military vehicle which can be attacked by radar-directed fire. We are considering all such applications and are moving with some speed to develop those applications which are the most practical and which have the greatest military significance. Fourth, we have achieved excellent success on the program, including flight tests of a number of different vehicles.

Testing Senior Trend

In April 1980 the first production engine arrived at Burbank, and on September 2 the first engine run was conducted. The complex design and

engineering of the exhaust nozzle caused more than a few headaches, and on December 22, 1980, the first nozzle failure was experienced. This led to further delays with the first flight; however, on February 12, 1981, an improved nozzle was fitted that helped to eradicate at least some of the problems.

Preparations for the first flight became quite involved, as Hal Farley remembers:

The preflight briefing was a real predication. The Air Force is very heavy on formality, so we created the flight profile and the flight briefing around it and gave it to I don't know how many different levels of personnel. Finally, after everybody had their inputs, we had a flight profile that would last approximately an hour and ten minutes scheduled flying time. The unstick speed for the first flight was supposed to be somewhere around 170 knots, a relatively high speed. The flight profile itself called for the aircraft to climb with the gear extended. In fact, I had opted to leave the gear down for the entire flight; I didn't want any surprises. We

were then going to test the four probes on the front of the airplane, which are faceted on the ends to be stealthy. They provide the angle of attack and side slip information due to differential pressure, through very small ports on those facets.

There was not a high level of confidence at the time that the wind tunnel data had given accurate results, so we de-activated those probes in such a way that they would not be providing dynamic flight information to the flight-control computers. Instead other sensors would be used to supply information: accelerometers, rate giros, and so forth. So essentially we planned to take off and fly to 10,000 feet above ground level, and then activate the probes, just in case they gave us erroneous flight data information. We would then have plenty of room underneath us to turn them back off again, as we had switches in the cockpit that could control the input from the probes in pitch and yaw. I had extenders put on the switches so that I could quickly reach over and isolate these if there was a problem.

As the day for the first flight dawned, Skip Anderson recalls, "As the mission director, I was feeling the responsibility quite heavily. Fortunately, Dick Abrams had been through this a few times and was a steadying force and confidence builder. There was a bit of a hold due to winds very near our crosswind limit. In addition to the usual aerodynamic considerations about crosswinds, we had some concern about the drag chute, because it was housed ahead of the fins and deployed between them. High-speed taxi tests revealed no problems, but of course, these were accomplished within tight cross-wind constraints."

A day forever etched upon Hal Farley's memory will be the day of that historic first flight.

The day was June 18, 1981, and my call sign, was Bandit 0-1 (it was later changed to Bandit 1-17 for the rest of the project). I began to roll at 0605 hours. We got airborne a little earlier than expected, and after rotation the plane immediately lifted off, so we were a few knots below the target speed, but that was not a problem. As I accelerated, the plane started to yaw, not rapidly, but very slowly. First 2 degrees off to the right, then 3 degrees left, followed by a larger yaw to the right. In each instance I applied opposite rudder, but the plane didn't seem to respond right away. I applied more rudder, then the plane started slowly yawing to the left and building up side slip to the left. I realized that this was not working out exactly as we expected; it was quite loose in yaw. Another rudder input to the right, and I realized that things were getting bigger. In other words, I was creating more of a problem with the rudder input. I didn't like what was happening,

On April 1, 1984, the weapons system computational subsystem (WSCS) upgrade was authorized. The expanded computational capacity brought about by replacing the three Delco M362Fs with three AP-102s enabled the weapons release capability to be increased from a single weapon per pass, to the use of both weapons. *Lockheed Martin*

so I reached down for the extended switch on the yaw access and turned on the probe. The computer started calculating control inputs, utilizing side slip from the probes, and the plane stiffened up immediately and felt quite normal at that point in time. I remember the test conductor Dick Broughton asked me what had happened. I guess they had seen what I had done on telemetry. Bob Loschke, who was the flight controls engineer, was quite concerned, but I explained to him that the side slip was excessive so I had turned it on. I proceeded on with the acceleration and climb out.

The next thing that happened that was unusual was a good solid loud thud in the airplane. That frightened me quite a lot. I reported it to the test conductor, and we had a little discussion over the radio. The engineers were scratching their heads, wondering what the sound was, but nobody could come up with a solution. The indications in the cockpit were solid. Obviously with a new plane you wonder if something had broken loose, but everything seemed to be fine and all the telemetry data looked good, so we continued with the flight. Shortly afterwards I got a canopy warning light. The significance of that is, it's a clamshell canopy, with no forward fixed windscreen, so if the canopy comes off, the pilot gets a real blast of air in his face. The question would then be whether the pilot could see to land the airplane. The prototype did not have a head-up display in it, so we put a fake combiner glass up where the display would have been, to deflect airflow should the canopy come off, that was the only protection that I had. I was still concerned about this red canopy light staring me in the face, and we had further discussions with the ground station. We came to the conclusion that it was a micro switch out of adjustment or too finely adjusted. As the canopy moved slightly, the micro switch had activated and turned the light on. We continued the flight. We then started getting a temperature buildup in the exhaust section. The exhaust is a long rectangular slit on each side of the tail. Heat had built up in the square corners during engine runs on the ground. We carried out modifications in the hope that we had solved the problem. Well, obviously, we had not, as we were still getting excessive temperatures in the

Only three pilots were to fly 780 in its "Desert Scheme" prior to the aircraft being stood down after flight number 10. The second pilot was Skip Anderson, who was also the first Air Force pilot to fly an F-117. Note the addition of Anderson to the left cockpit canopy frame. *Lockheed Martin*

On September, 6, 7, and 8, 1983, another program milestone was achieved when Dave Ferguson carried out three flights in Aircraft 781 and refueled Senior Trend for the first time from a KC-10 Extender. *Lockheed Martin*

tailpipes to the point where they were exceeding the limits that we had established for ourselves. Consequently Dick Burton called and said, 'We're getting out of limits; you're going to have to bring the plane back.' So we went into our abort profile, which was nothing more than just turning towards the downwind leg and setting up to make a landing. In the meantime, as I was making this turn around the field, I made some very small, abrupt, control inputs in pitch, yaw, and roll. These are known as MMLE (modified maximum likelihood estimator) inputs and were part of the planned profile. This enables the aerodynamicist to see what the plane does in response to these and then compare them to the predicted aerodynamic coefficiencies. It can then be determined if the simulation needs to be upgraded. In effect they measure what the airplane is like, as opposed to what the wind tunnel data predicted.

I flew a relatively wide landing pattern with a long straight in approach to the runway. Of course, in the case of all pilots' egos, you want to make a good landing, and certainly on the first flight of a new plane. There were a lot of people watching, and in fact, as it turns out, the plane was quite easy to land and it looked good. I landed about 15 minutes after take off. We flew early in the morning, just as good light

occurred, so that the desert air was smooth. The drag chute worked, and I rolled out. Despite being a short flight, it was a success, and we found out what we had needed to know. The directional stability of the plane was lower than we had predicted; therefore, we would need larger fins which, when fitted after 780's 10th flight, were 50 percent bigger than those we flew with on the first flight.

During that flight I was chased by two T-38s; primary chase was Dave Ferguson, and in the back was Pete Barnes, one of the Air Force pilots. The other chase aircraft was flown by Russ Easter, but I can't remember who was in his back seat.

It later turned out that the banging I had heard that had concerned me during the flight was the blow in doors, located on the top of the inlets, which provide additional air to the engines during taxiing or low-speed flight. They are spring loaded, and what happens is as you accelerate, the dynamic pressure inside the inlets builds up and slams the doors shut. We hadn't anticipated the resultant noise level!

The significance of this first flight was such that film footage shot during the sortie was edited at the test area into a one-minute sequence. It was then

From left to right, in check-out order, the first 11 original F-117, Lockheed, and Air Force test pilots: Hal Farley, Skip Anderson, Dave Ferguson, Tom Morgenfeld, Roger Moseley, Pete Barnes, Tom Abel, Denny Mangum, Dale Irving, John Beesley, and Paul Tackabury. Bob Riedenauer is not present. *U.S. Air Force*

flown by special courier aircraft to Andrews Air Force Base and taken to the White House, where it was viewed by President Ronald Reagan.

During the following five flights of Aircraft 780, Hal Farley retracted the landing gear and expanded the flight envelope out to 330 KEAS, +3 g and 10-degree angle of attack, completing initial airworthiness tests on July 25. Three days later, Skip Anderson became the first Air Force pilot to fly Senior Trend, in a flight lasting 1 hour and 2 minutes. He was airborne again on July 30 in a 1-hour, 18-minute flight:

My primary purpose was to conduct the initial pitot static calibration. I collected climb performance data up to about 20,000 feet and did some handling qualities evaluations to become familiar with the aircraft. I then descended to the pitot static tower fly-by racetrack pattern. The cleared airspeed envelope of the aircraft at this point was between 180 and 350 knots. To calibrate the airspeed/altimeter system, you fly past a tower at an altitude just above ground effect, about 60 feet. By that time you have to be trimmed, "hands-off," with both stick and throttles (I have never heard of anyone who actually took their hands off). You fly a series of passes, varying the speed by increments of 10 knots from the cleared minimum to cleared maximum airspeed. An engineer in the tower measures the exact height of the altimeter reading on the instrument panel and from this can

be extrapolated a calibration curve. Anyway, all went well. The aircraft flew like a dream, and I was hitting the test points with amazing grace. Then the sun came up over the ridge to the east and the plane began to oscillate in yaw, just a bit at first and then more and more. We had started the tests at medium speed and were stepping up to maximum, so we decided to examine the lower end of the envelope. The oscillations, however, continued to grow. When it hit a 5-degree swing, we chickened out and I landed.

In the desert, you do flight testing at first light in order to collect data in the smoothest possible air conditions. It turned out we had a serious problem with lack of directional power, and any small desert thermal was enough to excite the aircraft into a yaw oscillation. The term Wobblin' Gobblin was born by noon that day. It was obvious we had to increase the size of the tailfins, but the data showed enough margin to complete the air speed/altimeter calibration if we flew before the sun came up. We flew just a few more times and then stopped until a bigger tail could be built.

Dave Ferguson was the deputy chief pilot during the early days. He was airborne on his first F-117A flight at 0656 hours, on August 1, 1981. It was the 780's ninth sortie and Ferguson recalls, "It was a flying qualities mission; we were concerned that the directional stability of the plane was much lower than predicted. We knew we had to increase the size of the vertical fins, so they tufted the aircraft's vertical fins and the inboard portion of the fuselage in order to get a better idea of how the air was flowing around the back part of the plane. I had carried out standard performance and flying qualities maneuvers on the way up to 20,000 feet and about 420 knots. In all I flew the entire card and everything went well."

Ferguson's second flight (the 780's tenth) took place five days later and was delayed until 0856 hours, due to conflict with a "Red Hat" evaluation. It lasted just 48 minutes and was terminated early due to predicted satellite cov-

erage of Area 51. On landing, the aircraft was grounded to have a partial heat shield installed and interim tailfins fitted. These "quick-fix" larger units, provided greater surface area built onto the same structure. They solved many of the aircraft's directional stability problems, while further testing helped refine the design of units to be fitted on subsequent FSD aircraft.

The root cause of the stability problem is interesting and best described by Alan Brown: "The most obvious early change that had to be made to the F-117A configuration was to increase the fin and rudder areas. The inflight measurements of yaw stability indicated a lower value than had been predicted

Despite the F-117's operational environment being nighttime, Alan Brown, Senior Trend's program manager and low-observability guru, could scientifically prove that gray was the best low-observable paint scheme for the aircraft. However, General Screech, commander of Tactical Air Command, decreed that they should be painted black. This led to Ben Rich commenting, "In the Skunk Works, we work to the golden rule: He who has the gold, makes the rules." F-117's are black! *Lockheed Martin*

Viewed from the back seat of a T-38 chase aircraft, 780 undertakes a test evaluation during one of the first 10 sorties of its 137 total flights. *Lockheed Martin*

from analysis and wind tunnel results. It appeared on examination that the effects of the wind tunnel model mounting sting were to improve the local airflow, giving a false measure of the fin effectiveness. Even at that, one might still question why the aircraft was so marginal in yaw stability. The question was in fact asked of the aerodynamics group, and the answer given was that they were trying to keep the fin size down to help out the radar cross-section. In fact, the design of the fins from the RCS point of view was such that an increase in size at the same leading and trailing edge angles would, if anything, improve the aircraft survivability. The longer edges would lead to a narrower detectable spike, with a consequent decrease in radar dwell time. The moral of that incident was not lost on me. Trust your experts to do their own job, but don't let them help you in a subject where they have little knowledge!"

Having successfully completed its first maintenance check, Hal Farley conducted the 780's 11th test flight at 0802 hours on October 21, 1981. It was decided to qualify the aircraft for air refueling (AR) early in the program; the first such sortie was airborne at 0707 hours on November 17, 1981. Skip Anderson had an enormous amount of AR experience particularly in RF-4Cs in Southeast Asia. With typical modesty, he recalls, "I had never been near the

Between January 4 and February 3, 1984, Aircraft 780 had wing leading edge extensions added to improve its handling qualities. *Lockheed Martin*

envelope edges. Fortunately the AFFTC tanker test crew was the best. They had two boomers who had done the F-15, F-16, F-17, and A-10 tests. We used four F-4 sorties for practice, and the boomers talked me through all the positions. The corners of the envelope were amazingly extreme, especially 'up and in.' Anyway the F-117 was easier to refuel than the F-4. The only thing it lacked was the rapid-throttle response of the F-4. Attitudewise it would trim out and fly beautifully on the boom. For first contact, the plan was to start by applying some gentle pressure in all directions without engaging the boom. This was to ensure the flight controls didn't react to external forces. Everything worked perfectly and was straight forward." Flight duration was 2 hours, 12 minutes.

Once AR qualified, the test program further accelerated, as evidenced from a flight flown by Farley in the 780 just two days later, which lasted 2.8 hours. "We made the decision that if we got a test plane in the air with all instrumentation working, it was best to keep it there for as long as possible," he says. "So we frequently flew longer duration flights, doing tests until we got quite tired. It was later in the program that we started taking into consideration crew fatigue, but initially we did a lot of long flights. Later in the flutter program we had to demonstrate that there might be a problem ahead of the limit cycle, on the inboard aileron, during loaded rolling conditions. So we had a program where we needed to get down low to the ground for high Q (hydrodynamic pressure). So we flew from our base of operations out to the coast of California, off of Vandenberg Air Force Base. Using inflight tankers, we did a flutter program, investigating this limit cycle. We had shakers installed on the plane that would shake the various control surfaces on command by the pilot.

"My job was to get the plane at its limit speed, go into a maximum G rolling, pull out, and activate the shakers to measure the dynamic response of the flight control surfaces. Those flights were a lot of hard work, but they were quite satisfying, in that we felt we had accomplished a great deal. They were long too, in the neighborhood of three hours, including a long time over the water, refueling on the job, and then returning back to base. The problem was, from our base in the desert, the terrain level was well above sea level, so we couldn't get low enough over land to get the dynamic pressures that we needed for this test. For that reason, it was necessary to fly out over the ocean."

Two static tests models of the F-117A were constructed. The first, referred to as "Aircraft 779," was used for stress testing and its assembly began in March 1980. The following January the test program started, and on January 21, 1985, the specimen was stressed to failure. On June 12, 1991, following program completion, 779 was placed in storage at Tonopah. The midfuselage section and later the cockpit were transported to Palmdale, as mentioned previously, and components from other aircraft were then used to construct the "gate-guard" at the Lockheed Martin Skunk Works.

Construction of the fatigue test bed, "Aircraft 777," began in January 1985 and lasted seven months. On January 3, 1986, the test bed was moved from Burbank to Rye Canyon, where fatigue testing commenced in early 1987. The test vehicle reached its first, second, and third life cycles, on September 24, 1987; March 15, 1988; and July 29, 1988, respectively. By September the 777 had reached the equivalent of 20,500 hours of flight, and the tests were completed. The vehicle was then placed in storage at Palmdale, the wings later being sent to Tonopah to enable maintenance technicians to undergo advanced battle damage repair (ABDR) training. When Tonopah Test Range (TTR) closed, the wings were moved to Holloman for ABDR use. On August 23, 1994, they were once again returned to Palmdale. After receiving the go-ahead, the Skunk Works reunited the components of the 777 and prepared it for its final assignment, that of pole model at Holloman Air Force Base, where it arrived in July 1995 and can still be seen to this day.

Tom Morgenfeld remembers his first flight in the aircraft: "My first flight in the F-117 was on November 20, 1981. In fact I flew two flights that day, the 20th and 21st flights of Aircraft 780. The first flight of the day took off at 0713 hours and lasted for 0900 hours, and my second flight took off at 1355 hours and was 1.1 hours long. The call sign was, as usual, our personal call sign, mine being Bandit 101. At that stage of the program, we did not have the time to give pilots the luxury of a familiarization flight. All flights were data-gathering events due to the urgency of the program. My profile was a handling qualities investigation at various speeds and altitudes in both cruise and single-power approach configurations. By that time 780 had been fitted with the larger rudders; therefore, the handling qualities were quite good.

When the Detachment changed command from Roger Moseley to Paul Tackabury, on December 14, 1983, John Beesley was airborne for 1.1 hours, completing a memorable flyby at 1400 hours with the 782 patriotically adorned. *U.S. Air Force*

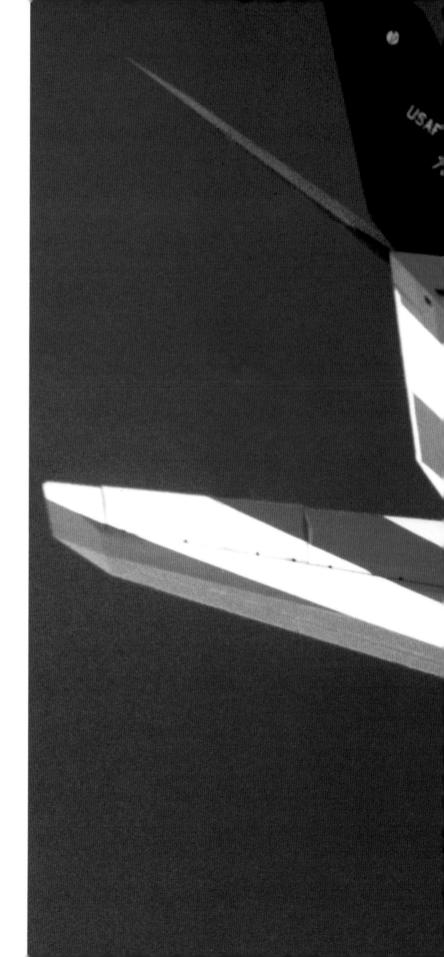

There was no real change from what I had prepared for except for a case of terminal goose bumps when I first taxied under the American flag (one of which was hung in each hangar) and out the door."

The myriad of work necessary to successfully navigate an aircraft through flight testing ensured the overall workload was fairly evenly split between the three primary Lockheed pilots. Each pilot was responsible for a particular flight discipline but would also participate in evaluations conducted by the others; so, for example, although Hal completed the first flight and initial air-worthiness testing on the F-117A and was primary pilot on flutter testing, he also carried out some weapons separation tests, engine icing, and loads work. Similarly, Tom Morgenfeld's primary responsibilities were avionics; weapons compatibility, separation and accuracy; icing trials; and autopilot development. In addition he was designated as the unit's instructor pilot, a job he still holds to this day—18 years later.

The second FSD aircraft, the 781, was flown for the first time by Dave Ferguson on September 24, 1981. After completing just four sorties, however, it underwent considerable rework, which included retrofitting larger interim tail units and a "production" nose section, which after further tests housed the IRADS units. In addition, an asymmetric, four-probe, production-configured, air data system was added. The reworked aircraft underwent a functional check flight conducted by Ferguson on December 1, 1981; however, shortly after takeoff, acoustic resonance in the empty IRADS bay caused the DLIR screen to fail, and the sortie was aborted after just 24 minutes. Following repair work, the 781 undertook another sortie two weeks later, before it was again grounded, following a flight on December 18, 1981. During its down time, sheets of BX210 RAM were applied, in readiness for the first airborne RCS tests of Senior Trend. On January 22, 1982, Ferguson completed a 30-minute functional check flight, and the following day, Lieutenant Colonel Roger Moseley was airborne at 0730 for three hours of RCS tests. It was only the fourth occasion that Moseley had flown the Senior Trend, and it is a tribute to both his piloting skills and the aircraft's handling characteristics, made possible by the outstanding flight control system, that such a critical undertaking was possible after a nominal amount of time on type. Aircraft 781 flew six more sorties, including one on February 6, 1982, of which, three were RCS evaluations flown by Moseley. The aircraft was then grounded yet again, until June 15, 1982, for the installation of two retractable trapeze units, to which its internally housed weapons were secured.

Aircraft 780 and 781 had Spartan, flight test-oriented cockpits, with no advanced displays or equipment. The third FSD aircraft, the 782, featured a fully configured avionics fit and cockpit. It was flown for the first time by Tom Morgenfeld on December 18, 1981; however, the flight was terminated after just 18 minutes due to a problem with the bleed air system, which caused high platypus temperatures immediately after takeoff. A couple of days later, a very successful second flight achieved all the first flight test goals. The aircraft's seventh flight occurred on January 27, 1982. Modified multipurpose display indicators (MDIs) had been installed, and Morgenfeld was to conduct a thorough airborne evaluation, as he recalls, "Of course, I thought it would be real easy, and the beautiful weather made it seem more like a pleasure ride than a test hop. Little did I know! Due to a maintenance error, the nose wheel fell off the airplane at take-off rotation. It took a couple of seconds to sort out the problem, as I had several people telling me of my plight simultaneously on the radio. I climbed to altitude while we all talked the problem over. There was

even some talk of a controlled ejection, which I summarily rejected. Instead, I just drilled around with my gear still down and completed my test objectives, while the fire crew foamed the runway. The landing went well and the airplane was back flying within days. I did have the machinists' union file a grievance against me, however, for grinding on a nose strut without having the proper job classification! All in good fun and in keeping with our close, team-oriented atmosphere."

The Real Thing

The first night flight of an F-117A was completed by Roger Moseley flying Aircraft 782 on March 22, 1982. He flew the same aircraft on April 19, 1982, successfully conducting the first night air refueling. Due to various delays, the fifth F-117A built, Aircraft 784, was the fourth to fly, an event that took place on April 10, 1982. The first operational aircraft due to be delivered to the Air Force (785), would also have had its first flight before Aircraft 783 had it not been written-off during the course of getting airborne on its maiden flight. It wasn't until July 7, 1982, that FSD 4 finally undertook its first flight with Tom Morgenfeld at the controls; it was planned that this would be the dedicated RCS test vehicle.

Low-observability airborne testing of the F-117A was exhaustive. On the 783's second flight, Morgenfeld carried out systems checks in readiness for more Air Force evaluations. Two days later, on July 14, 1982, TAC pilot Tom Abel verified those checks and the next day was airborne again at 0512 hours to conduct IR tests of Senior Trend with the help of an NKC-135. This 1.4-hour flight was followed up on July 16 by Pete Barnes, conducting a 2.6-hour flight with the same NKC-135. Between July 17 and 22, Air Force pilots conducted four more flights in the 783 against an F-4 to evaluate the IR threat from air-launched heat-seeking missiles. For the most part these one-and-a-half-hour flights were launched at around 0500 hours, before temperatures had an opportunity to rise. This gave the F-4 a distinct advantage, searching for the F-117A against the cold backdrop of a dawn sky. After systems checks and a pre-RCS, functional check flight, conducted by Hal Farley, on September 20, 1982, the 783 was in the thick of it again, with Air Force pilots flying no less than 21 RCS and IR sorties between September 21, 1982, and January 13, 1983. These included cued and uncued tests against the best U.S. detection systems available, and "Special Category" tests, flown against Soviet-made equipment, "acquired" through various means, by the United States. One particular test, flown by John Beesley on December 3, 1982, included taking RCS measurements while the aircraft's right bomb-bay door was open.

Paul Tackabury flew the 782 on December 17, 1982. During a 1.4-hour sortie, he successfully completed the first weapons release from an F-117A when he dropped an MK-106 practice bomb from its BDU-33 canister while in level flight.

Aircraft 783 continued to be the fleet's RCS workhorse throughout 1984, with analysis of the air-to-air threat continuing. On April 24, 1984, an F-16 made four radar passes against the aircraft while it was being flown by Morgenfeld. Two days later, an F-16 flew 13 radar passes against the 783, and by July 23, 1984, F-15s, F-14s, and an EF-111 had conducted similar threat tests against the aircraft. Thereafter, the 783 was used alternately between low-observability tests and evaluations and the integration of improvements made to the navigation and weapons delivery systems.

pilot Major William Aten (Bandit 164), thereby enabling the system to be evaluated from a front line pilot's perspective. In all, 34 sorties, totaling 45.4 hours, were flown, the last on December 12, 1985.

Those interviewed who were involved in this evaluation have stated that the system was remarkable and incredibly stealthy; however, it was not deployed operationally for reasons of cost and on the basis that, to date, Senior Trend as a concept, had not been tested under actual combat conditions. Stealth still had its doubting Thomases.

The F-117A's fuel system was originally designed to retain fuel in the wings for as long as possible. This was thought to significantly lower in-flight loads, as the aircraft's center of gravity was positioned further aft, thereby leading to an extended airframe life. As flight testing progressed, it was determined that the elevon control power was less than predicted, with the aircraft becoming progressively more difficult to manage at higher angles of attack when configured with high-aft CG settings. Therefore, to regain the loss of control power,

The highly classified nature of Senior Trend, particularly in the early days, ensured that the customary award of a wooden factory model to key program individuals and pilots was completely out of the question. As Senior Trend's chief Test Pilot, Hal Farley asked Dave Ferguson and Tom Morgenfeld to explore an alternative, innovative design, that could be used to covertly recognize significant achievements. This was the result: a hardwood, handcrafted, faceted block based upon the Rock of Gibraltar. This particular example was presented to Squadron Leader Dave Southwood (Royal Air Force). When Farley retired from the program, maintenance engineers presented him with a solid crystal version of the design. *Dave Southwood collection*

Aircraft 784, FSD 5, was the dedicated IRADS test and evaluation ship; consequently, its first 106 flights were made in association with successfully achieving this goal. It was placed in temporary storage on completion of a sortie flown by Roger Moseley on September 23, 1983. At the end of November 1984, the aircraft was dismantled and moved from Area 51 back to Burbank in the belly of a C-5. The operational shortcomings of an infrared targeting system with which to aim weapons (however accurately) was fully appreciated; therefore, the possibility of substituting this with a low observable radar system to conduct ground mapping and target acquisition offered a considerably enhanced mission capability. Consequently, while at Burbank, Aircraft 784 underwent modifications to install such a system. It was then returned, via C-5 again, to Area 51. At 0744 hours on August 13, 1985, Hal Farley conducted a thorough functional check flight, lasting 1.2 hours. Two days later, Don Cornell was forced to air abort the aircraft back to home plate after just 18 minutes of flight, due to a problem with the flight control system. It wasn't until September 4, 1985, that the 784 was again ready to take to the air. Making up for lost time, Dave Ferguson flew the aircraft twice that day, once at 0657 hours and again at 0911 hours, during which time, base line data of the new radar system was collected. Over the following four months, all aspects of the radar mapping and targeting system in the 784 was evaluated: RCS of the antenna and radome, the ability of the system to perform the ground mapping task, threat evaluation during system operation, system resolution including four sorties flown by 4450th Tactical Fighter Group (TFG)

The day of the first flight of the F-117. Key people from Area 51 are listed below.

#1	Tom Agnew	#11	Bill Howler/	#20	John Wall	#30	Mag
#2	Skip Anderson		Jim Whiting	#21	Don Merkle/Burton	#31	Hal
#3	Ben Rich	#12	Howard Fay	#22	Alan B.	#32	Cal Dias
#4	Dick Abrams	#13	Paul Rue Koff	#23	Iron Mike	#33	Rog
#5	Bill Fox	#14	Gary Decker	#24	Russ Rose	#34	Bill Park
#6	Don Allen	#15	Vern Weebe	#25	Jim Callan	#35	Snake Reeves
#7	Red	#16	Tommy Field	#26	Pete M.	#36	Dick Boyle
#8	George Bollinger	#17	Norm Nelson	#27	Bryan Dockworth	#37	Dan Bennett
#9	Rhett Clifton	#18	Pat	#28	Skip Holm	#38	Willy Oaks
#10	Dick Madison	#19	Keith	#29	R. Goodeg	#39	John Slicker

Aircraft 780 was grounded between December 21, 1983, and January 4, 1984, and wing leading edge extensions were added. During nine subsequent flights in this configuration, the modification was judged to be successful, having achieved the stated objectives; however, the Air Force decided not to modify the exterior of production aircraft. Instead, fuel sequencing was changed, and wing fuel was used first, thereby avoiding degraded elevon control suffered during high-alpha maneuvers and aft center of gravity conditions. Subsequently, the structural engineers decided that in any event, flying the aircraft in aft center of gravity conditions, made little difference, by way of increased airframe life.

At 1302 hours on September 25, 1985, Major John Beesley was airborne in Aircraft 781 to conduct a series of high alpha evaluations. Shortly into the sortie, and following a pull-up maneuver at 10,000 feet, the left fin completely failed. The incident, which was filmed by a chase aircraft, ended without further incident, as Beesley retained control of the aircraft and completed a successful recovery back at Area 51, 42 minutes after takeoff. Having saved a highly valuable aircraft, and in so doing demonstrating outstanding pilot skill, Beesley was secretly awarded a Distinguished Flying Cross.

In 1984, a Weapons System Computational Subsystem (WSCS) upgrade program was started to replace the three Delco M326F computers and the interconnecting databus, with three IBM, AP-102 computers and a unique, high-speed databus. This vastly increased onboard computational power, considerably augmenting the performance and capability of the aircraft's avionics package (see chapter 2 for details). Two aircraft were modified for testing. The first, Aircraft 782, received only the computer change. Having completed the radar evaluation and with that installation now removed, work began on January 9, 1986, to ready Aircraft 784 to join its stablemate. In addition to the computer upgrade, 784 also received a weapons bay improvement (WBI) upgrade. This would effectively double the aircraft's single-pass capability, by enabling it to perform dual-bay, weapon deliveries. To achieve this, extensive modifications were necessary in order to relocate the test instrumentation package from the bomb bay, into a modified fuel tank area. In all, the lay-up lasted 11 months; the aircraft then undertook two functional check flights, both conducted by Dave Ferguson on November 20 and 25, 1986. On February 12, 1987, at 12:46, Hal Farley flew the 784 on the first phase 1A flutter test, which would steadily expand the limit speed of dual bay operation from 400 KEAS to 500 KEAS. Once the operating envelope of this configuration had been thoroughly tested and validated, Ferguson completed a WSC/WBI avionics check flight on July 22, 1987. Over the next two years, nearly 200 flights in 784 were attributed to weapons evaluations and delivery profiles.

An additional aircraft was added to Detachment 5's test and evaluation program. Tom Morgenfeld undertook Aircraft 831's maiden flight on October 20, 1987. It was delivered to the Air Force on November 27, and having completed just 16 flights, it was returned to Lockheed in February 1988 to begin modification work as the testbed for phase 2 of the Offensive Capability Improvement Program (OCIP). Ironically it was Morgenfeld who again checked out 831, following completion of these modifications. The flight on December 1, 1988 was aborted after just 12 minutes, however. Undaunted, Morgenfeld was once again airborne at 0732 hours the next day, and following an functional check flight lasting 1.2 hours, 831 was decreed ready for business. These latest updates improved situational awareness and reduced pilot workload (see chapter 2 for details). The four-dimensional flight management system utilizes three spatial coordinates plus time on waypoint to an accuracy of +/- 1 sec. In addition, other advances included a digital tactical situation display, an improved autopilot and auto throttle, and PAARS, Pilot-Activated Attitude Recovery System. The latter was first tested by Steve Green on April 25, 1989.

Following a flight made on April 14, 1989, Aircraft 784 spent three months undergoing yet more modifications. This time composite rudders were installed, which maintained the basic planform, shape, and size of the metal units, but featured a completely redesigned structure with rudder posts "beefed up" to double their torsional stiffness. In addition, the outboard elevon-supporting backup structure was redesigned because of a wing/elevon oscillation problem identified during earlier testing. The resultant modification is referred to as the Brooklyn Bridge Assembly.

On July 18, 1989, Hal Farley was airborne at 0754 hours and 1.8 hours later had completed 784 functional check flight. Two days later an intensive aeroelastic stability flight test program began. Its purpose was to validate the operational envelope of the F-117A with the newly configured all-composite fin and the Brooklyn Bridge modification and to determine the effects of load oscillations applied to flight control surfaces at various speeds, attitudes, side slip angle, fuel, and store configurations, with the weapon bay door both closed and open during 1-g flight conditions. Test data points generated frequency and damping data for comparison with predicted values, which were then used to validate the design and generate the appropriate flight envelope restrictions.

Unlike earlier flutter tests—which depend on excitation of the control surfaces and adjoining structure, on stick and pedal raps, and later a stepper box, working through the flight control system—this program used an electronic flutter excitation system (FES) and an inertial exciter system (IES) to provide the required excitation to all test areas. Two small panels were located in the cockpit to enable the pilot to activate the relevant systems, having achieved the required flight conditions. Switches on the Lima panel controlled FES activation, allowing the pilot to select the mode of operation—Burst, Sweep, or Random—the amplitude of the oscillation, its frequency, together with the number of cycles of input. The Golf panel controlled the axis of excitation. The maximum surface-deflection angle achieved by the FES reached 2.25 degrees for the elevons and 4.05 degrees for the rudders, and the maximum force exerted by the IES was increased during tests from +/- 500 pounds to +/- 800 pounds.

The aircraft was equipped with accelerometers and strain gauges to provide information relating to vehicle and component response, and this data was recorded on the aircraft and transmitted via telemetry to a ground station for real-time monitoring and recording.

In a superb American Institute of Aeronautics and Astronautics paper written by Lieutenant Colonel Steve Green and Dennis Fernandez, the concluding paragraph reads, "As a result of this testing, the F-117A aircraft, incorporating the composite fin and Brooklyn Bridge and elevon free play modification, had its operational airspeed restrictions increased to 562 KEAS and Mach 0.90, the original aircraft specification values."

Area 51 had served as host for low-observability flight test operations since November 16, 1977. Now that certain elements of stealth had ventured out from the Black World, it was decided to move to a more amiable site: Palmdale, California. The change of address occurred on March 27, 1992, thus bringing to an end an association that had lasted nearly 15 years.

chapter four

TONOPAH YEARS

Formed on October 15, 1979, designated the 4450th Tactical Group, and referred to as A-unit, the Air Force's first operational F-117 unit was commanded by Colonel Robert "Burner" Jackson. Unlike White World units, he didn't report into a numbered Air Force but directly to the Tactical Air Command director of operations (DO) to preserve security. While work on aircraft number one, the 780, continued at Burbank, Bob Jackson began organizing a new covert operational base. It was decided it would be located at the Tonopah Test Range, located northwest of Nellis Air Force Base, Nevada. The base was a training establishment during World War II, and during the Cold War, the range witnessed drop tests of nuclear weapon configurations.

To convert the site into a fully operational base, a three-phase multimillion dollar construction program was launched. Phase 1 consisted of little more than peripheral work, which included the construction of 16 large mobile homes, purchased secondhand from the Chevron Oil Company, at the bargain basement price of just $1.5 million. Phase 2 and 3 completely transformed the base. The original 6,000-foot runway, built in 1954 by Sandia National Laboratories, was increased to 12,000 feet.

Maintenance facilities, a control tower, fuel and weapon storage areas, and permanent housing were also built. Individual aircraft hangars were also constructed and organized into parallel blocks, referred to as canyons. By early July 1982, the enormous construction program was completed. A security cover story for the Black World unit was provided by 20 Ling Tempo Vaught A-7Ds, including a small number of two-seat A-7Ks. These were based at Nellis Air Force Base and referred to as P-Unit. Other support elements of the 4450th were also given similar oblique short nicknames to further conceal their purpose. The 1880th Communication Squadron became C-Unit, Detachment 8 of the 25th Air Weather Squadron was D-Unit, and the 4450th Combat Support Group, E-Unit. The 4450th Test Squadron (established on June 11, 1981) was I-Unit and Detachment 1 of A-Unit, based at Tonopah was Q-Unit. In addition to providing the "avionics testing" cover story, the A-7s were used to maintain pilot proficiency until F-117As became available and were also used as chase aircraft.

Specialist Support Equipment

The unique characteristics of Senior Trend necessitated the construction of several pieces of atypical support equipment. On February 1, 1979, design of the first of three maintenance vans was started. These were delivered to the Air Force on September 21, 1981, June 17, 1982, and May 15, 1985.

On September 12, 1985, go-ahead was given for the production of two air transportable equipment vans, known as Elvira I and Elvira II. In addition to providing extra maintenance and support equipment, they also incorporated a complete avionics diagnostic system, which itself was upgraded in the two vans on October 4, 1991, and May 13, 1992, to reflect avionics changes on the F-117A fleet, brought about by the Offensive Capability Improvement Program (OCIP).

In March 1984, a contract was awarded for the construction of a Weapons System Trainer. This was accepted by the Air Force in November 1985 and was declared operational on January 1, 1986.

Aircraft 802 was flown for the first time by Dave Ferguson on March 7, 1984. It is depicted here, bathed in early evening sunlight, whilst flying over Half Dome in Yosemite Valley. *Lockheed Martin*

In addition to overseeing the construction program, Colonel Bob Jackson also set about recruiting the initial cadre of pilots, as Al Whitley, at that time a major, recalls:

My interview occurred in late 1980 at the Nellis Air Force Base Visiting Officers Quarters. Colonel Jackson had called me a few weeks earlier and said he would be visiting Nellis and wanted to know if we could meet and discuss a potential assignment. Since I was probably headed to the Army Command and Staff College the following summer, I was certainly interested in discussing any alternative that would keep me in the cockpit.

I had just completed the A-10 Fighter Weapons Instructor Course in August and had been reassigned to the 66th Fighter Weapons Squadron (FWS) [the A-10 Fighter Weapons School] as an instructor and assistant operations officer. Soon after I told my new squadron commander, Lieutenant Colonel Joel T. Hall [who retired as a brigadier general], about this opportunity. I learned that Col. Jackson had also approached another member of the 66th FWS, Major [retired as a colonel] Charlie Harr, who eventually became Bandit 151. While Charlie and I were both concerned about the problems Lt. Col. Hall faced replacing two instructors on short notice, he supported our decision to join the 4450th TG.

When the time came for the interview, I proceeded to the designated meeting place—Col. Jackson's room. When I knocked on the door, it opened slightly and Col. Jackson asked to see my identification card. I produced it, the door closed, and a few seconds later he opened the door and said, "Yes, you're Whitley, come in."

In the next few minutes, Col. Jackson told me very little about a program which would involve significant family separation, yet the opportunity to not only remain at Nellis Air Force Base for another full assignment, but

also the chance to fly the A-7 again. He didn't say much more other than I would have no opportunity to discuss it with my wife and that I had five minutes to make up my mind. With no hesitation, I said, "Sign me up." Col. Jackson said he'd be contacting me in the future on specifics. That was the end of the interview.

In the spring of 1981, Lieutenant Colonel [retired as a colonel] Jerry Fleming, our squadron commander, called me and a couple of the new members of the unit to our remote, secure location in Area 11 (or Lake

Photographs of the first three Royal Air Force pilots to fly the F-117—Colin Cruikshanks, Dave Southwood, and Graham Wardell—during their time with Senior Trend, remain locked in a Pentagon safe. Graham, pictured here, is now a test pilot for British Aerospace at Warton, Lancs, England, where he flies fast jets. *British Aerospace*

Following the November 10 revelation, the F-117 again returned to the gray shadows of the Black World. Its first public unveiling took place at Nellis Air Force Base on April 21, 1990. On that occasion, two aircraft, one carrying markings of the 37th TFW commander, the other carrying 415th and 416th Squadron markings on either side of the fin, attended a "meet the people" ceremony frequented by thousands. *U.S. Air Force*

Mead Base) of the Nellis Air Force Base complex. He showed me a photograph of the airplane and briefed me in on the real mission of the unit. Jerry seemed to really enjoy doing this for he got to see each individual's reaction to such a new, innovative concept in aviation. His favorite questions were "How fast do you think it will go?" and "What weapons do you think it employs?" Since the movie Star Wars was a big hit at the box office and the airplane had that "Darth Vader" look, my first thought was this must be a real fast machine. However, Jerry pointed out the relatively large frontal surface area and hinted speed was probably not its strongest attribute. When I did learn what the airplane was all about, it was somewhat hard to believe. I was genuinely excited and honored to be part of something that was on the "leading edge" of technology. I quickly added a new word to my vocabulary that would have a significant impact on the rest of my Air Force career—"stealth."

An AT-38B taxies past a security control point on its way out to the runway. Security at Tonopah was uncompromising. Two high barbed wire topped fences separated by a well lit highly monitored "dead zone" isolated the control tower, flight-line, hangars, and other sensitive areas from the rest of the base. *U.S. Air Force*

Lieutenant Colonels Bill Hepler, Sandy Sharpe (initially the unit plans officer), and Jerry Flemming were also open to any recommendations on potential candidates for the program; but it was Colonel Bob Jackson who carried out the majority of early recruiting, and it was he who selected Al Whitley out of his "pool of pilots" to become the first operational F-117 pilot. Shortly thereafter, Whitley and a few other pilots were sent to the Burbank "product-line" to become completely familiar with every facet of the aircraft. In addition they spent many hours in the static, cockpit procedures trainer.

To patrol the outer peripheries of the base at Tonopah, the security force operated UH-IN Hueys, and to commute to work, pilots, housed with their families at Nellis Air Force Base 190 miles away were transported in on Monday and back home on Friday by Boeing 727s, belonging to civil contractor Key Airlines. In addition, the 4450th operated three Mitsubishi MU-2 turboprop executive aircraft, used to shuttle small groups between Tonopah, Nellis, and Burbank.

The original plan was that the unit should achieve initial operational capability (IOC) 40 months after Aircraft 780's first flight, which was scheduled for July 1980. Therefore Q-Unit, nicknamed the "Goatsuckers," were expected to assume a limited operational role in November 1982. This was not achieved due to various design and manufacturing obstacles. In fact, the first production aircraft, number 785, didn't attempt to undertake its first flight until April 20, 1982. As with the previous FSD aircraft, airplane number one from lot 2 had been completed at Burbank and flown via C-5 Galaxy to Area 51. There it had been re-assembled, and following various ground checks, Lockheed test pilot Bob Riedenauer advanced the throttles and began his take-off run. The aircraft rotated as planned, but immediately after lift-off everything went horribly wrong. The nose yawed violently, it then pitched up, and completed a snap roll that left it on its back before impacting the ground. It was nothing short of a miracle that Riedenauer survived; Aircraft 785 was totally wrecked. A postaccident investigation established that the pitch and yaw rate gyro input to the flight control computer had been crosswired. The result: As the aircraft rotated, the computer's interpretation of events was that of an uncommanded yaw departure. Its "restorative" action was to apply rudder. This, however, caused real yaw departure, which to the computer, was perceived as pitch. A full-up elevons response was therefore communicated to the flight control surfaces, resulting in what so easily could have been a fatal accident. Riedenauer suffered two broken legs and other injuries that ended his test pilot career. Ground testing had failed to reveal the problem. Lockheed conducted an audit following the accident, which highlighted various corrective actions to improve production performance and quality. All recommendations were implemented, one of which included redesigning the gyro connectors to physically prevent misinstallation.

Various remains of the 785 were subsequently used to build a "gate-guard," which was mounted on a pole and is displayed outside Lockheed-Martin Skunk Works' Palmdale Plant. This consisted of the 785's right wing and aft fuselage, the nose was hand-built, the cockpit and midfuselage came from the static test bird the 779, and its left wing is the right wing from the 801 (lost on August 4, 1992), which was 90 percent rebuilt to fit the left side.

As the 785 was written off prior to being accepted by the Air Force, it was to be aircraft number three from lot 2, which would be first to enter the inventory. First flown by Hal Farley on July 20, five days after he had flown 786, Aircraft 787 was accepted by the Air Force on August 23 and was joined eleven days later by 786. In September, Detachment 1 of the 4450th was designated the 4452nd Test Squadron, and it was while the unit had a compliment of just two aircraft that another milestone was achieved. On the night of Friday, October 15, Major Al Whitley conducted his first Senior Trend flight and became the first operational pilot to fly the aircraft. A nighttime, preflight, high-speed ground run helped familiarize him with the locations of the controls. After a "pleasant flight" he was presented with a simple wood-and-brass plaque bearing the inscription "In Recognition of a Significant Event, Oct. 15 1982." Having been given his own personal designation "Bandit 150," it would be six years before he could tell his wife, Ann, what the "significant event" was all about.

The sporadic nature of the delivery schedule continued, and by the end of 1982, the unit still only boasted seven aircraft. Unlike the Senior Trend CTF at Area 51, all Tonopah's F-117 flight activity took place at night. Hangar doors were not opened until one hour after sunset, which put first scheduled takeoffs at about 7:00 P.M. in winter and 9:30 P.M. in summer. For the first year, flights were restricted to within the Nellis range complex, but as confidence grew,

Ben Rich takes to the podium during a ceremony held at Palmdale on July 12, 1990, marking the final F-117A delivery to the Air Force. At $42.6 million a copy, they represent incredible value for the money. *Lockheed Martin*

Jerry Leatherman undertakes the suit-up ritual at Tonopah. Note the positive/negative F-117 design on the neck scarf. *U.S. Air Force*

flights were cleared off the range. In the event of an unscheduled landing, however, pilots carried a signed letter from a senior Air Force general ordering the base commander to protect the aircraft. By the end of 1983, 12 F-117As had been accepted by the Air Force and were operating out of Tonopah.

Colonel James S. Allen had assumed command of the 4450th from Colonel Bob Jackson on May 17, 1982. By October 28, 1983, Senior Trend was deemed to have achieved limited initial operational capability (LIOC). There remained a number of issues that would need to be resolved if the aircraft were successfully deployed overseas and engaged in combat. These included spare parts shortages for IRADS; a weapons delivery accuracy below expectations due to minor errors within the weapon delivery software; decking aft of the jet exhaust outlets overheating, causing concern should long-range deployments become necessary; and lack of an automated mission planning system (AMPS), meaning time-consuming manual mission target planning, which dramatically impacted sortie rates. Finally, sheets of BX210 RAM tended to become detached, and it was difficult for the unit to analyze accurately what effect this was having on the aircraft's RCS.

By the end of 1982, the potential of Senior Trend was apparent to those cleared into the program, and the procurement plan increased to 57 aircraft (the final total was 59). The impact of this decision created the need for two additional squadrons. Consequently in July 1983, I-Unit "Nightstalkers" was activated to be followed in October 1985, by Z-Unit "Grim Reapers" (later redesignated the 4450th Test Squadron and the 4453rd Test and Evaluation Squadron, respectively). On June 15, 1984, Colonel Howell M. Estes III became the third commander of the 4450th, and on May 5, 1985, he led the unit successfully through its first Operational Readiness Inspection (ORI), earning in the process a rating of excellent. Tenure of the unit transferred again on December 6, 1985, to Colonel Michael W. Harris; it was to prove a period in which events on the world stage threatened to involve Senior Trend.

World Tension

The early to mid-1980s was a period of world tension. The Soviet Union had invaded Afghanistan, and Britain fought a war with Argentina, after the latter invaded the Falkland Islands. Relations between the hawks of the Reagan administration and a similarly hostile Kremlin, led by Brezhnev, Andropov, and Chenenko, were also at a low ebb. In Europe, Poland began to break out from the shackles of Communism, but it was the Middle East that was the cause of greatest concern.

Operation Eagle Claw, the attempted rescue by Delta Force of 53 U.S. embassy staff members held hostage by the Iranians, failed. This left eight would-be rescuers dead. Iraq attacked Iran, signaling the beginning of a bloody eight-year war. Israel invaded Lebanon in a bid to crush the PLO. This led to the United States becoming embroiled in peace-keeping duties in the region, which in turn triggered a backlash from various terrorist organizations, many of which were supported by Iran, Syria, or Libya. These attacks included two coordinated suicide bombs in Beirut, Lebanon, which killed 58 French paratroopers and 241 U.S. Marines; the bombing of a TWA Boeing 727, en route from Rome to Athens, which killed four; and the bomb attack in the La Belle disco, West Berlin, which was packed with American soldiers and killed two GIs and a Turkish woman.

As a direct result of these last two incidents, President Reagan approved a U.S. attack against Libya. By April 1986, the 4450th had taken delivery of 32 Nighthawks and taking into consideration the intense, sophisticated nature of the Libyan defense network, it was deemed that the aircraft's unique characteristics made it an ideal candidate to mount an attack on the country's leader, Colonel Mu'ammar al-Gadhafi. Following intense debate within the highest echelons of power, however, Secretary of Defense Casper Weinberger decided not to commit Senior Trend, thereby ensuring that its secrets were not compromised.

First Loss

The bat-like existence—sleeping during the day and flying only at night—was both highly demanding and chronically tiring on F-117 pilots. The root of the problem was the 4450th flying schedule which, in order to balance pilot proficiency against limited flight-time availability, split the hours of darkness into two shifts. The first wave off was known as the "early-go," the second the "late-go." Lieutenant Colonel John F. Miller, commander of the 4450th Test Squadron, penned a memo on Thursday, July 10, 1986, which turned out to be highly prophetic, he observed. "I believe that these extended hours are taking their toll on overall pilot performance. I have detected more and more instances of poor judgment that weren't evident two to three months ago."

At 0113 hours on Friday, July 11, 1986, in excellent weather and good visibility, Major Ross E. Mulhare departed Tonopah Test Range in aircraft 792, call sign Ariel 31, and flew northwest to the town of Tonopah. He then turned southwest, continuing his climb to 20,000 feet. After crossing the Sierra Nevada mountains, he turned south and flew along the east side of the broad San Joaquin Valley of central California. Flying in accordance with instrument flight rules (IFR) and in positive controlled airspace, Mulhare carried out radio calls to air traffic control centers at both Oakland and Los Angeles and received clearance to descend to 19,000 feet during the southbound leg. (To enable air traffic control facilities to track F-117s on radar when operating in accordance with instrument flight rules, corner reflectors are bolted on to each side of the aircraft fuselage.) Near Bakersfield he requested, and was granted, permission to fly "off-route" in accordance with his prebriefed mission. The time was 0144 hours. Just one minute later, 792 ploughed into a hillside at 2,280 feet above sea level, killing its pilot.

An accident investigation established that 792 was on a heading of 080 degrees at the time of impact. The aircraft was upright and in a steep dive, characterized as "no less than 20 degrees and probably in the neighborhood of 60 degrees." Impact was at "high velocity," and both engines were "operating at high power settings prior to impact." There was no indication of a precrash fire or that Mulhare had attempted to eject. Having received his bandit number (Bandit 198) on January 7, 1986, he was declared mission ready on March 18, 1986, and had accumulated 53.5 hours on the F-117A prior to his fatal accident.

In a report submitted to the accident investigation board, Robert McGregor, an aeronautical engineer at the U.S. Air Force Sacramento Air Logistics Center stated, "Without exception, in terms of physical damage to the aircraft, this is the worst crash that I have worked. Structural breakup was almost absolute." And "The right engine compressor drum . . .was crushed to half its normal length." The prime reason behind this horrific accident was almost certainly pilot fatigue and spatial disorientation.

On April 3, 1987, the 4450th received its fifth commander, Colonel Michael C. Short. Another officer to join the unit four months later was Major Jerry Leatherman who had graduated from the U.S. Air Force Academy in 1978 and gained his wings at Reese Air Force Base, Texas. His first operational assignment was flying A-10s with the 81st TFW, stationed at RAF

In true "fighter jock" style, the lead and his wingman taxi out to the holding point at TTR. *Lockheed Martin*

This is the outside world's first insight into the F-117's shape. Revealed at a Pentagon press conference by Assistant Secretary of Defense J. Daniel Howard on November 10, 1988, it clearly demonstrated how far off the mark all the aviation speculators were—especially the Testor Corporation's $9.95 plastic kit model of the "F-19 Stealth Fighter." *U.S. Air Force*

Bentwaters, England, where he arrived in May 1980. During his first tour, he was selected to attend and graduated through the Air Force Fighter Weapons School, at Nellis Air Force Base. Returning to England, he continued flying A-10s with the 81st until August 1985. Marked out as an exceptional pilot, Leatherman was next assigned to the 422nd Test and Evaluation Squadron, again flying A-10s at Nellis. Here he undertook weapons testing and helped develop and test tactics. By August 1987, he had accumulated a little more than 2,000 hours flying in the A-10 and was an instructor pilot. He often came into contact with friends that he had graduated with, Gary Frith, Mike Ritchy, and Mike Cook, on Friday nights at the Officers Club at Nellis. Here's Leatherman's story:

I was coming up to my third year at Nellis, and they usually gave you an assignment to another base. I had been talking to them to find out ways of staying at Nellis for a little while longer. Mike Cook said, "Our unit is looking for a weapons officer; if you're interested I'll tell the powers that be that you'd be interested in coming over and flying with us." I talked it over with my wife Nancy and told her that we would get to stay for at least another three years, but that what I knew about the job was that they were gone Monday through Friday and asked her if she was willing to put up with that.

About a week or so later I was sitting in my office up in director of tactics and test when I got a phone call from Col. Pickering who was the DO [director of operations] for the 4450th, and he asked me to meet him

at building 878, which was the A-7 squadron building at Nellis Air Force Base, next to base ops, at about 1 p.m.

I went over and you had to phone to get into the building. I said that I was over to see Col. Pickering. I got into the building and as soon as I entered there was an announcement over the PA system, "Unbriefed personnel in the building. Unbriefed personnel in the building." They escorted me over to one of the flight briefing rooms, where I sat with the door shut. After a while Col. Pickering showed up. He introduced himself and said that he had heard some good things about me from some of his guys and asked if I'd be interested in a job. He said he couldn't tell me what the job was until after I had accepted it, but basically he said, "I want you to be assigned to our unit, we fly mainly at night and fly Monday through Friday. If you accept the job you'll be checked out in the A-7 down at Tucson." I said I'd only been at Nellis for two years, and I didn't know if I could be released from my assignment very early. He just looked at me and said, "If you want to go, I have already spoken to Gen. Hall (who was the fighter weapons wing commander), and he has said that if you want to go you're released." I was somewhat surprised because this was at a time when they weren't letting anybody go early, and so I said, "What are we talking about here?" He replied, "We have a class date for you at the beginning of August." Which I thought was really fast. He said, "If you say the word,

high time A-7 drivers around that could ask questions. I went down for training with Jerry Howalt; we were the only two active-duty guys. The rest were being trained to go onto Guard units. We started in August and finished at the beginning of November. When we got back to Nellis P-Unit they gave us a little local area checkout, which consisted of five or six rides, flying around Nellis ranges and some low level; basically showing you how to fly around the local area. During that check-out procedure was when they set out a briefing for you. This was when you finally found out what you were going to be doing for a living, flying the F-117. There was always a backlog of guys going through the program, so you didn't get your F-117 checkout real quick. In my class, they had the first trained civilian contracted instructor to teach the academics and run the simulator program. One of the things that was unique in training was, before we got to fly the 117, they sent us down to Luke Air Force Base, and we got a VIP checkout in the F-15. We got to fly in the front seat and did just one ride with no flap landings because somebody had thought that to do a no-flap landing in an F-15 was pretty similar in speed and pitch as the 117. So we spent two days at Luke Air Force Base, getting academics and flying the simulator and then our one ride. I started academics for the F-117 in April of '88, so from November to April I was flying A-7s keeping current. Then in May '88 I took my first flight in an F-117. It was a normal training program; you had the simulator checkout and then the instrument check out and then the mission stuff. You were then assigned to your squadron, and you went through mission upgrade where you had to hit your targets. That was no different from any other fighter-type training that I had been through.

Before Leatherman joined his squadron, the 4450th lost a second F-117A. This occurred on October 14, 1987. Major Michael C. Stewart became airborne from Tonopah at 1953 hours, in Aircraft 815, call sign BURNR 54. The single-ship mission was conducted under visual flight rules (VFR) and remained within the boundaries of the Nellis range complex throughout. At 2033 hours, three-quarters of the way through its mission, the aircraft's radar return was seen to stray left of its planned track and disappear. In common with the loss of the 792, weather conditions at the time were clear with unlimited visibility.

The crash site was situated on gently sloping desert and the impact created a crater between 6 and 7 feet deep. The standby attitude indicator recovered from the wreckage showed the aircraft to have impacted the ground at an attitude of 28 degrees nosedown and in a 55-degree banked turn to the right. Yet again, there was no evidence of an in-flight fire, Stewart had made no attempt to eject, and the aircraft was intact prior to impact. Unlike the earlier accident, however, the 815's engines were operating at a low power setting. Stewart had notched up 2,166 hours of flight time, including 76.7 hours in the F-117; he became Bandit 231 on May 1, 1987, and was declared mission-ready 52 days later. As with the earlier accident, the report failed to clearly determine the cause, but yet again repeated references were made to pilot fatigue and disorientation.

Six days after the tragic loss of Major Stewart, the 4450th became the center of more unwanted attention, focused around the loss of yet another of its aircraft. On this occasion Major Bruce L. Teagarden (Bandit 222) safely ejected from an A-7D after the aircraft lost power. Unfortunately, the A-7 crashed into a Ramada

Dave Ferguson completed F-117/KC-10 compatibility tests. Refueling from these wide-bodied tankers is now a routine event for operational F-117 pilots. Seen here is a 37th TFW aircraft. *Lockheed Martin*

we'll start getting orders cut for you, and by the beginning of August you'll be down in Tucson flying A-7s." I said, "OK, count me in!"

On a Friday in the first week of August, I had my final flight in the A-10 with the 422nd; then on the Sunday, I was driving to Tucson to get checked out in the A-7. That was as far as I knew about the job, because they weren't briefing anybody until after the A-7 training.

At Tucson International Airport, I flew with the Guard guys in the A-7, as this was our cover. The A-7 was used, because in active duty nobody flew the A-7, therefore if you landed at another base, there wouldn't be

The first F-117 from lot 6, Aircraft 807, took to the air on September 13, 1984. Of note is the flush-mounted DLIR and the red rotating beacon, both off-set, to the right of the aircraft's underside. The beacon, together with a second unit located on the left upper fuselage, is bolted into position when required (during some training sorties only). *Lockheed Martin*

Depending upon all up weight, ambient air pressure, and temperature, the F-117 generally reaches V2 (take-off safety speed) at 90 knots. Note forward gear transition, which aids emergency extension. *U.S. Air Force*

Inn Hotel, near the Indianapolis airport, killing nine people in the process. Following a detailed accident investigation, however, Teagarden was cleared of all culpability surrounding the tragic incident. Although publicly acknowledged as being a member of the 4450th, the unit was not known to have any links with Tonopah, ensuring that Senior Trend remained in the black.

Another pilot to enter the Senior Trend program shortly after these incidents was Major Greg Feest. A graduate from the University of Wisconsin, Madison, Feest received his Air Force commission in May 1978. A year later, he completed undergraduate navigator training with a distinction and was assigned to the 366th TFW, Mountain Home Air Force Base, Idaho, to complete his training as an F-111 weapons systems officer (WSO). His first operational assignment from January 1980 until December 1982 was flying F-111Es with the 20th TFW, RAF Upper Heyford, England. While at Upper Heyford, he won the Wing "Top Gun" competition for 18 consecutive months and was given his call sign, "Beast." Such notable accomplishments as a WSO led to Feest being selected to attend undergraduate pilot training. Upon graduation in

December 1983, he completed conversion training on the F-15 and was then assigned to the 1st TFW at Langley Air Force Base, Virginia. By September 1987, he had become an instructor pilot (IP), a flight standardization examiner (Stan/Eval), and a flight commander.

Then one day he was approached by his squadron commander regarding an assignment to the 4450th Tactical Group. Feest was unaware of how this seemingly, out-of-the-blue opportunity came his way. The 1st Tactical Fighter Wing commander, Brigadier General Buster Glosson, had personally requested the F-117A assignment from General Robert D. Russ, commander of Tactical Air Command. Russ levied the following criteria: "I want your number one fighter pilot, both as an officer and pilot, a future wing commander." Glosson leaned over Russ's desk and wrote, "Captain Greg Feest, by a wide margin." Russ said, "I'll make it happen." Feest takes up the story:

I was told that I would be flying the A-7D and that most of the flying would be conducted at night. I was also told that if I accepted the assignment, I would live in Las Vegas, be stationed at Nellis Air Force Base,

Nevada, and would fly to work in a contract airline on Monday and not return until Friday. The F-117A program was still secret in 1987, so I was never told what I'd actually be flying. The requirements for the assignment were a stellar record of performance, references from pilots who were part of the Stealth Fighter Program, over 1,000 hours of flying fighter aircraft, and at least one tour as an instructor pilot. I currently had over 1,000 hours in the F-15 and was qualified as both an instructor pilot and flight examiner. I immediately told my squadron commander I was interested in the job, and two weeks later I received my orders. I was excited about the assignment since there were countless rumors about the 4450th Test Group and its mission. Many newspaper articles told of stories about a special aircraft flown in the Nevada Test Ranges, and many Air Force fighter pilots believed the 4450th was involved.

In March 1988, I arrived at the 4450th following A-7 transition training at Tucson, Arizona. For the first two weeks I received a local area checkout in the A-7 and flew several day and night missions. Upon arrival at the squadron during my third week at Nellis, my operations officer asked me into his office. After entering, he locked the door and proceeded to show me a classified videotape of the F-117A Stealth Fighter.

The tape lasted approximately 10 minutes and showed the aircraft on the ground and in flight. My immediate thought was how nonaerodynamic the aircraft looked, but the tape clearly showed it could actually fly. He told me this would be my primary aircraft and that the A-7 was a cover story, to help keep the program secret. This was my first introduction to the Stealth Fighter.

In May 1988, I entered F-117A training. After countless hours of academic instruction and simulator missions, the day finally came for me to fly my first sortie. Since there are only single-seat F-117As, the first sortie was solo. However, an instructor pilot chased the mission while flying an A-7. The feeling of lifting off the ground for the first time was awesome, and I can honestly say that I felt extremely proud to be in the Air Force on that day.

Feest became Bandit 261 on May 26, 1988, and this outstanding officer would play a key role in Senior Trend's operational achievements. Some three months after Feest successfully completed his first F-117A flight, Colonel Antony J. Tolin took over as commander of the 4450th on August 10. Two months later in the run up to a presidential election, the Reagan administration

Captain Matt Byrd's (Bandit 348) personal mount supports a new and impeccable paint job. Note all antennas have been retracted and the fuselage reflectors removed. *U.S. Air Force*

requested the Pentagon to schedule a public unveiling event for the F-117. Such a move would undoubtedly boost George Bush's campaign against Michael Dukakis. Embroiling such a prized national asset in a blatant piece of cheap electioneering infuriated some senior congressmen and the event was delayed until November 10, 1988, one week after the outcome of the election had been decided. On that day, at a Pentagon press conference, Assistant Secretary of Defense J. Daniel Howard held up a fuzzy photograph of the F-117 and all the rumors about the "F-19" and its shape, circulated by those who

hadn't a clue what they were talking about, were instantly shot to pieces. Underlining one of many favored quotes of Ben Rich, "Those who don't say, know. Those who say, don't know."

Mike Mahar graduated from the U.S. Air Force Academy in 1977, having earned a bachelor's degree in international affairs. His first posting was to Williams Air Force Base, Arizona, for undergraduate pilot training. In January 1979 he was assigned as a security assistance training program instructor pilot, and for the next two years he trained pilots from seven European,

Until elements of the Senior Trend Program were made public, A-7s provided a cover story for the 4450th's "raison d'etre." *U.S. Air Force*

KC-10s of the 22nd Air Refueling Wing based at March Air Force Base often provide the F-117A air-refueling support. *U.S. Air Force*

African, and Middle Eastern countries. He went on to serve as the 47th Flying Training Wing flight safety officer and was selected for assignment to the National Guard Bureau in Washington, D.C., as part of the Air Staff Training Program (ASTRA).

Following his ASTRA tour, which lasted 12 months, he was assigned to Strategic Air Command as an FB-111A flight commander and assistant operations officer. A member of the 528th Bombardment Squadron at Plattsburgh Air Force Base, New York, until January 1988, he then moved to the 530th Combat Crew Training Squadron, and it was from there that he was hand-picked by Air Force senior officers to fly the F-117A Stealth Fighter. Mahar remembers:

I was informed of my F-117 assignment in September 1988 by my FB-111 wing commander, who could not offer any details of the assignment other than the fact that it was very selective and involved relocating my family to Las Vegas, Nevada. He added that the assignment was done "at the highest level" and implied that it was an offer that I could not (or should not) refuse. At that time, I was unaware of the existence of the F-117, so I didn't apply for the job. I was "volunteered" by my supervisors. I was to be an exchange officer from the USAF strategic bomber community on loan to the tactical fighter community to learn low-observable tactics and training procedures. This arrangement was presumably in preparation for a future assignment to the B-2 stealth bomber program (although

after my F-117 tour of duty I was subsequently assigned to fly F-15E Strike Eagles, thus remaining in tactical fighters).

Nellis Air Force Base, in Las Vegas, Nevada, is acknowledged as "The Home of the Fighter Pilot." As a career strategic bomber pilot, I had difficulty understanding why I was being assigned there. In November 1988, the Department of Defense officially acknowledged the existence of the F-117 Stealth Fighter and released a grainy black-and-white photograph. This was the first time I realized what I would be doing during my F-117 assignment. I was very excited about having an opportunity to participate in this very selective program, but a little apprehensive about the lifestyle which included frequent family separation and extensive security. In fact, during this three-year assignment, I would spend Monday through Friday in Tonopah, Nevada, about 150 miles away from my wife and children in Las Vegas.

Prior to my first flight in the F-117, I received extensive academic and flight simulator training. The day prior to my first flight, I strapped into an F-117 and performed a supervised high-speed taxi down the runway to gain familiarity with the aircraft ground-handling characteristics and drag chute operation. I also received a brief AT-38 landing currency course at Holloman Air Force Base, New Mexico, to get some hands-on flying currency with an instructor prior to jumping into the Black Jet solo. Unlike the earlier pioneers in the Stealth program who flew exclusively under cover of

Captain John Massee (Bandit 372) studies target imagery and plans offsets that will enable him to confirm and accurately track his target during simulated attacks conducted over wide areas of the United States. *U.S. Air Force*

darkness, my first flight was during daylight hours, on 6 July 1989. I flew a one-hour familiarization mission with an instructor flying chase in an AT-38. The jet was remarkably easy to fly and my academic and simulator training had prepared me very well. The cockpit offered somewhat constrained but acceptable outside visibility. The Stealth was very maneuverable in roll and slightly sluggish in pitch. It was relatively slow to accelerate on take-off without afterburners, but accelerated nicely in flight and required attention to keep from getting too fast. After completing my first flight, I

became Bandit 304 and proudly earned a place for my scarf, embroidered with "Bandit 304," on the wall in the TOCACL (Tonopah Officers Club and Chinese Laundry)—which was our postflying gathering place and was actually a converted laundry facility.

Now that the general shape of the aircraft was no longer classified, the 4450th began daylight flights, which naturally led to sightings being reported. On April 12, 1989, 10 of the aircraft were observed flying separately at eight-minute intervals, maintaining an estimated altitude of between 5,000 and 6,000 feet and a west-to-east track. The sightings took place a few miles north of Edwards Air Force Base, and a further six F-117As with their lights on adhered to the same route, between 10:00 and 11:00 P.M., later that night. Further similar sightings took place in the same general area six days later.

Easing Senior Trend into the White World had other spin-offs. Gone was the need to shelter the 4450th's covert activity behind a valid aircraft type. Consequently, in September 1989 the Wing said farewell to the trusty "Sluff" and instead operated far more economical T-38A Talons, and later AT-38Bs, in the chase/pilot proficiency role. Yet another change took place on October 5, 1989: The 4450th TG, together with its component squadrons, was redesignated. The parent designation was changed to the 37 Tactical Fighter Wing (formerly an F-4G wing, based at George Air Force Base, California). The 4450th (Night-stalkers), together with the 4451st Test Squadron, became the 415th (Night-stalkers) and the 416th (Ghost Riders), respectively. The 4453rd (Grim Reapers) Test and Evaluation Squadron continued in its responsibility as the

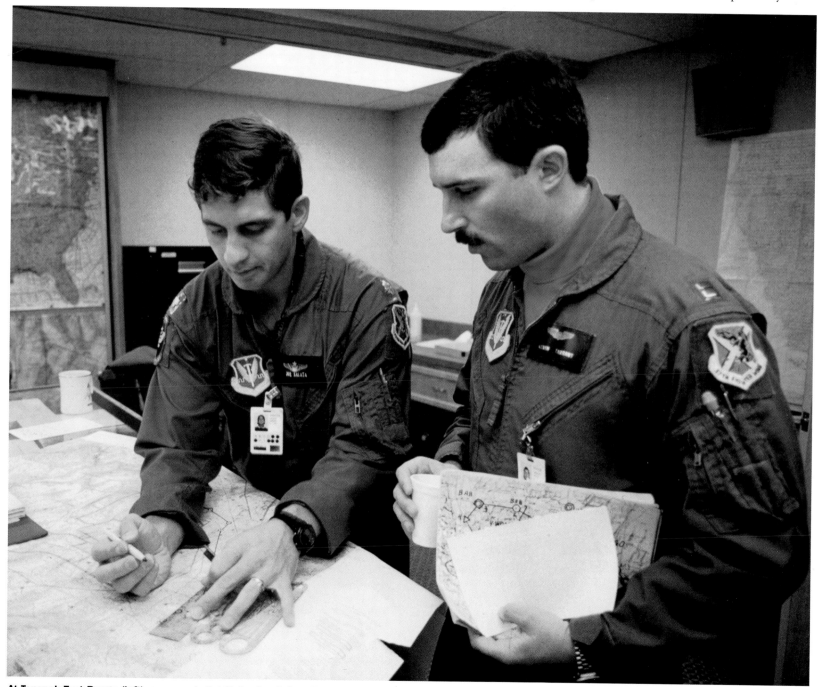

At Tonopah Test Range (left), command pilot Major Joe Salata (Bandit 295) plans a sortie with Captain Kevin Tarrant (Bandit 335). *U.S. Air Force*

Ghost Riders attend a scheduling/training meeting. Pictured from left: Major Mike Mahar (Bandit 304, operations officer); Captain Skeeter Kohntopp (Bandit 355, scheduler); Captain Terry Foley (Bandit 327, flight commander); Captain Mike Mahan (Bandit 323, scheduler); Major Rich Treadway (Bandit 336, flight commander); Captain Gregg Verser (Bandit 310, flight commander); Captain Steve Troyer (Bandit 334, flight commander); and Major Mike Daniels (Bandit 336, assistant operations officer). *U.S. Air Force*

Wings training squadron, becoming instead the 417th (Bandits) Tactical Fighter Training Squadron (TFTS). The new designations had a firm foothold in a proud history, being the first U.S. night-fighter squadrons of World War II.

Just Cause

Indicted by two Florida grand juries on charges of laundering drug money, Panama's military dictator, General Manuel Noriega, dismissed the country's president, and then ordered his "Dignity Battalion" to beat up opposition candidate Guillermo Endara. Endara won the presidential election, but Noriega prevented him from taking office. On October 5, 1989, an attempt to oust the loathsome dictator failed and the following day, the coup leaders were executed. United States/Panamanian relations continued to deteriorate to a point where, on December 15, 1989, Noriega declared a state of war between the two countries. The following evening Panamanian Defense Force (PDF) troops killed a marine lieutenant and arrested a navy lieutenant and his wife, who had witnessed the shooting. The officer was beaten and his wife threatened with sexual abuse.

The despot had to be removed, and in response President Bush issued orders to invade Panama. The objective was to strike at PDF forces, capture Noriega, and rescue political prisoners.

Since joining the Senior Trend program, Greg Feest's highly competitive nature and ability ensured he won the squadron Top Gun award for two consecutive years, while maintaining an incredible 100 percent hit rate. Recognized as the 37th TFW Top Gun for 1989, Feest was selected to lead the Wing's planning effort for Operation Just Cause, the code name for the U.S. invasion of Panama. As mission lead for the operation, he was the first to employ the F-117A in combat.

Panama didn't have a radar defense network; the reason to deploy the F-117 on this mission was based on its bombing accuracy. On the night of December 19, 1989, eight F-117s from the 415th TFS took off from Tonopah. Two aircraft were airborne spares and returned to Tonopah following the initial AR; two aircraft in the lead cell were targeted to attack an army base at Rio Hato, 65 miles southwest of Panama city. The four remaining aircraft were to take part in an operation that remains classified but involved special forces capturing Noriega. This element of the mission was later canceled when intelligence reports indicated that the target wasn't at any of the known sites. The 3,000-mile roundtrip required five ARs, which were supported by KC-10s from the 22nd Air Refueling Wing, out of March Air Force Base. This ever-dependable unit actually escorted the 117As from Tonopah, all the way down to the Panamanian coast and back! The objective of Major Greg Feest, flying Aircraft 816, and his wingman Major Dale Hanner (Bandit 239) was to drop two weapons in an open field adjacent to the barracks belonging to Battalion 2000, a unit known to be loyal to Noriega. The purpose was to stun the sleeping soldiers and disorient them before they had an opportunity to engage parachute landings by the 2nd and elements of the 3rd Ranger Battalion.

Three hours before the invasion was due to begin, however, the PDF was tipped off and had deployed to one of the Ranger's objectives—an airstrip. As the two F-117As approached their target area, the wind changed direction, a target change was called, causing confusion, the subsequent bombing results being not as effective as had been planned. The chairman of the House Armed Services Committee, Les Aspin, later stated that target acquisition problems had also added to the pilots' confusion because "The humid, varied, vegetation . . . lowered the contrast and gave the [IRAD] system problems."

Despite the inauspicious start, General Steiner, the XVIII Airborne Corps commander who had planned the invasion and requested the F-117As, maintained that, despite the PDF having already deployed, the explosions still produced considerable confusion. Several Rangers, however, were killed and more than a dozen wounded in the ensuing firefight before the island could be secured. As for Noriega, having initially taken refuge in the papal nunciature, he was eventually extradited to Florida.

Graham's story

The special relationship that exists between the United States and Great Britain has provided a basis for pilot exchanges in even the most sensitive programs. Graham Wardell attended officer training at Royal Air Force (RAF) Cranwell in 1976, having received a bachelor of science degree in aeronautics and astronautics from Southampton University. He completed his initial training in Hawks at RAF Valley, Anglesey, North Wales, and his weapons training in Hawker Hunters at RAF Brawdey. His first operational assignment was with 14 squadron, at RAF Bruggen, West Germany, flying Jaguars. In 1982 he was assigned to 41 Recce Squadron, again flying Jaguars but from RAF Coltishall, Norfolk. As a deputy flight commander with five years of operational flying, Graham's next posting was as an instructor pilot on Tornadoes at the Operational Conversion Unit (OCU), RAF Honington, Suffolk. In 1987, he was successful in his application to undertake a test pilot course and was particularly pleased when he was informed that this would be as an exchange officer with the U.S. Navy at Patuxent River (Pax River). Everything seemed to be shaping up rather well, until the day he received a strange telephone call and life changed quite a lot. . . .

In September of 1987 I received a call from a gentleman who introduced himself as a group captain from the Ministry of Defense. I initially thought it was one of the boys from work winding me up, and when he continued saying that he wanted to come and see me at the weekend and that I wasn't to mention this call to anybody, I became even more convinced that someone was definitely winding me up.

Sunday duly arrived and a man dressed in a suit and driving a unmarked car pitched up on my doorstep. He asked if I'd like to see his ID card, and up until this point I was still convinced I was on the receiving end of somebody's practical joke. But I couldn't see anything wrong with his ID, and he was in fact genuine.

The reason for the home visit was to get my wife Sue's reaction as all he could disclose about the job to us at this initial meeting was that it would entail a three-year tour of duty in the United States of America, it would be flying, and that it would involve having to spend an awful lot of time away from my wife. He left us saying that he would give us a few days to think it over.

Sue and I weighed it all up. We ruled out space shuttle training and decided that my options were that either I was going to spend a year at Pax River working my socks off or three years in the States doing something that involved flying. We were also expecting our first child at the time. He was due about the time I was to start at Pax River, so by taking this unknown job the baby would be a little older by the time we came to travel. Finally we decided to go for the mystery option, so I made the phone call and was told to travel to London.

I met the same man at the Ministry that had visited the house, this time he was accompanied by an American brigadier general who had

The lighting angle boldly etches out the contours of the 802's fuselage facets as it flies over Lake Tahoe. *Lockheed Martin*

come over to brief me. Also present was a group captain, David Cousins, who was my sponsor.

The American brigadier showed me a picture of the F-117, at which I promptly giggled and thought to myself "this clearly can't fly"; he continued to explain that it was a stealthy airplane and that he had a whole unit of them. He went on to say that I would be away from home from Monday to Friday and that nobody, not even my wife would be allowed to know where I was; however, there was a system in place that would enable me to be contacted in the event of an emergency. The American brigadier wanted me to fly the F-117 with the USAF as part of a team! He concluded with the statement that if I said yes then everything was ready to roll, but if I said no then I was never to breathe a word of this meeting again. I was still worried about the test pilot course that I had been accepted for and mentioned this to the group captain. He smiled and said

that the chief of the Airstaff had said that if I wanted to do the test pilot course when I came back, then he would permit it. It's a standing joke within the RAF that when high-ranking officers promise you things for postings, they never actually write it down; but this was written in my file at Insworth, so it was bulletproof. It seemed like the perfect dream, flying in the U.S.A. for three years, then picking up where I left off. Having agreed everything I went home to give Sue the news.

From November 1987 until February 1988 while waiting to start my new assignment, I went to Boscombe Down, flying with the ETPS (Empire Test Pilot School) to get an idea of flying different types of aircraft. During this period I flew Jaguars, Andovers, Gazelles, Hunters, the BAC-111, and Tornadoes; this helped in my preparation for the States. The news obviously got out that I wasn't going to Pax River, especially as my replacement on the course was brought back from Germany and was told

Illuminated by the hangar lights, the suck-in doors and FLIR turret are clearly visible. *Lockheed Martin*

not to unpack, as he wouldn't be staying after all but joining the course at Pax. I went back up to Honington and flew there for a few months undertaking my last flight in Tornado ZA404. During my dining out night at Honington, my station commander, Dick Bogg, gave the customary speech and announced to everybody that I wouldn't be attending the test pilot course at Pax after all. Instead I was going to America, but I wouldn't tell him what I was going to be doing, other than it involved flying. Suddenly there were about 100 pairs of eyes all looking at me, asking what was going on. So I used the cover story that I was going to fly the A-7, which was true to a degree. Luckily no more questions were asked.

The day before we were due to fly from Brize Norton to Washington, D.C., my wife's passport hadn't turned up even though the Air Force had promised that there wouldn't be a problem. The group captain had offered, "if you ever have any problems give me a call," so I telephoned him, explained the position, and said that I was not prepared to leave my wife and our four-month-old son behind. By 10 p.m. that evening a guy arrived hot foot in his RAF transport and said, "I think you need this Sir," as he handed over Sue's passport. I thanked him and gave him a cup of coffee (which was all he had time for) before he disappeared into the night again.

We had a couple of days in Washington. Air Commodore Peters was the air attaché and to a certain extent was "in on the plot" and was able to help out with awkward questions about exchange numbers—the system for tracking RAF personnel on exchanges. We then flew down to Las Vegas and were met at the airport by a previous American exchange officer, George Doran, and his wife. George had been on exchange at Honington flying Tornadoes and had disappeared off to fly the A-7! They looked after us for a few days, then we traveled down to Tucson, Arizona. There I joined the 162nd Tactical Fighter Group to undergo the A-7 conversion training with the Air National Guard. My first flight took place on June 20, 1988, in a two-seat A-7K, serial ATO287. The course lasted 30 hours and ran from June until August.

The Air National Guard [was] a little surprised to be training a Brit and [wasn't] quite ready for the British approach to life. You often find on exchanges that we all do things differently. I felt that as the U.S. Air Force is much larger than the United Kingdom's they tend to have a lot more rules and concentrate on the fact that you are part of a huge jigsaw. Whereas the British rely much more on the individual to think while he is airborne and react accordingly to circumstances.

The Air Guard knew that there was this "funny team" up in Nellis that flew A-7s. Various stories were put around about it, that they did secret stuff, etc. But the Americans are very good at not embarrassing people by pushing them into disclosing secrets. Having been kitted up with U.S. Air

Force flying suits, I was allowed to wear my RAF insignia, which showed my rank as squadron leader. The first time that I walked into the bar at Nellis the place went deathly quiet. You could almost hear people thinking, not only is there this "secret thing," but there's a Brit in on it and he was flying!

I joined the 4450th Tactical Fighter Group at Nellis in August and had my first flight on the 11th in A-7D serial 741760. Interestingly, I did my first air-to-air tanking at night in a two-seater just one week later, so it was a quick learning curve. I continued flying the A-7 throughout October, then moved onto the F-117.

My first 117 trip was in 809 on the 14 December, when I became Bandit 282. The flight lasted 1 hour and 30 minutes, during which time I was chased by an A-7 pilot. I had already completed all the ground school and simulator training. The simulator was a fixed based unit because operationally the aircraft was flown mainly at night so no aerobatics and hence no requirement for g simulation. I completed about 5 hours in the simulator, and as with most modern airplanes, by the time you have completed the ground school and the simulator training you're fairly well up to speed by the time you actually get into the airplane.

Takeoffs were interesting; there's no afterburner so there wasn't much thrust from the (relatively) small engines. In my opinion the takeoff was at least as good as the Jaguar, which surprised people who had seen the Jag on Ref Flag exercises and had wondered why it had traveled such a long way down the runway. Once they understood why, I think they were more respectful of Jaguar pilots. The takeoff speeds were higher, as it was generally warmer; Tonopah is 5,500 feet above sea level and at plus-90 degrees Fahrenheit I've seen some ground speeds on the INS that you wouldn't believe!

A typical working week would be to leave home on Monday around 11:00 a.m. At Nellis Air Force Base. If you were lucky, you'd get an A-7 to drive to work. This meant that you could leave a little later, and if you were also lucky enough to get one on a Friday to drive back then you'd be home early for the weekend too. Nobody knew where you were going; you just used to check in and fly off.

The first briefing, which would be a basic brief and target study, was at 3:00 p.m. The targets would be anything from a hangar at the end of a runway to someone's garage in the middle of L.A. As for material, in theory you could basically use whatever you wanted; long-range angle shots from roughly the attack direction, overhead shots, and satellite material. These would give you a lead in to the target; the idea being that you had to train your eye to pick up from the photo or image what would show up in the FLIR [forward-looking infrared], to guide you onto the target.

Everything was videotaped, and there was always a lot of analyzing of all video films from the previous night. All attacks were assessed but not actually with the crew member present. I was also the squadron weapons officer, so this was one of the jobs each night. You either hit or missed a target, and all results were logged. Crews were very keen on their hit rates, and if they had a miss now and then, it made a huge difference and caused a lot of bitter complaints. Many misses were down to not tracking the target. We were made to manually track as well as autotrack and were

Boeing's indefatigable KC-135s have been the backbone of Air Force AR support since before Pontius Pilate obtained his flying license. *Lockheed Martin*

The barns of Tonopah were "drive-through" and grouped in blocks of six. Note the odd numbers by each hangar door and the sparse "tumbleweed and tarantula" world that existed beyond the perimeter fence. *Lockheed Martin*

very hard-nosed about it. We had to be, as we set the standards. Annoyingly, I was continually second best on the squadron. My great rival was Greg Feest, an ex F-15 driver. As much as I tried, I just couldn't beat him; he seemed to have a natural flair for it.

There were lots of other duties that seemed to use the day up; we would take it in turns to be mission planner, and this was a fair workload. We would also do air refueling once or twice a week and then maybe have a big one about once a month; we also had to book the ranges to drop practice weapons.

When you went flying, you'd get your kit on and check out at the desk, much the same as you would anywhere else. You'd find out which aircraft you would be flying, and more importantly where it was parked as it was pretty dark outside! Then you'd get to the hangarette in a little buggy, meet your crew chief, and check the aircraft over. Check the book [the aircraft servicing log], leap in, start up, and trundle out into the night.

Everything for the mission was in a TDM [transportable data module], which if it failed was a major disaster as they were route specific and there were no spares. You could take off in any direction but were generally restricted to 20,000 feet or so because of mixing in with the airliners. I remember on one occasion an airliner coming in the opposite direction and on hearing him being told that he had an F-117 opposite at 1,000 feet below. I instantly turned my lights off (which you weren't supposed to do), only to hear the response from the airliner that he couldn't see me. I couldn't help but responding with "but that's the idea; you're not meant to." He still didn't see me when I put the lights back on! On another occasion when we had started flying during the daytime, an F-18 pilot requested permission to come and have a look. When he came alongside he said something along the lines of, "It sure makes you feel proud to see what America can build"; however, he looked somewhat surprised when he heard my response in my best British accent!

We would trundle up and down the airways, in and out of various big ranges. The Utah range was huge and practice bombing their targets ranged from easy to near impossible. For example, if they'd scratch a runway out in the sand it can be extremely difficult to see; but it was meant to be challenging! You were also able to drop real weapons quite often. Watching 2 tons of bomb dropping in the middle of the Nevada desert was great—something we can't do back in the United Kingdom. We blew up some SAC targets one night that we weren't supposed to. We had requested to drop real weapons and were given the go-ahead, but we were allocated the wrong targets. They had just built some huge infrared targets on the Nellis range for the B-52s, and we flattened them with a 2,000-pound bomb!

Sometimes you'd fly in an early wave with perhaps a second sortie later, or you'd fly just one long sortie. By the time you came back, cleared up, caught the bus back to Main Camp (which was 5 miles from the airfield), it could be about 3 in the morning. You'd have your breakfast and then go to bed. It seemed strange that it was a nighttime operation yet half of this was worked during a normal day, so you'd go to bed after having breakfast then get up for lunch. It was like living in Las Vegas and going to work in Korea Monday to Friday, which meant that you had two lots of jet lag every week.

The DO [director of operations] was Klaus Klause, and we had frequent "interviews" about my flying. Normally these would be along the lines of "what the hell was I doing!" There were areas that differed between the two air forces, such as visual flying in the circuit at night. In the Royal Air Force we practice them quite regularly, but in the USAF they tend not to. Instead they focus on instrument approaches in the dark. The first time I did a night visual circuit, it was seen as an incredible first.

Another discussion I had with the DO concerned what I considered to be at that time the F-117's biggest shortcoming: stopping the aircraft on the ground. It was a large aircraft, but its brakes were relatively small. If you suffered a brake chute failure, the procedure in the USAF is for the aircraft to land, bring it to a halt as soon as possible, and wait for the fire service to arrive. I had witnessed this on one occasion and the aircraft tires were literally glowing. When I was unfortunate enough to suffer a similar problem I followed the RAF procedure. Having landed I kept rolling along the taxiway to maintain some cooling airflow over the brakes and tires. I shut down with the aircraft into wind, just as the fire service arrived. I wasn't too popular with them as I wasn't where they had wanted me to be, and they were even more surprised to see me at the bottom of the airplane!

Initially I was in the 4450th Fighter Tactical Group. We had initials for squadrons and I was in I, reporting to Bill Lake. We then went through a whole tirade of redesignations, and eventually I ended up in August 1989 in the 415th Tactical Fighter Squadron of the 37th Tactical Fighter Wing still reporting to Bill Lake until his departure in November 1989, when he was replaced by Ralph Getchel.

When the 415th departed for Desert Shield, I was left on my own and I was absorbed into the 416th. During my last few months I spent a lot of time training the new flight refueling operators, which meant spending a lot of hours each night getting plugged by anybody and everybody. Initially I was unable to join the rest of my squadron as there were the obvious practical aspects on what was effectively an American operation. Behind the scenes in Washington I was asking to join my squadron in Saudi, but this was taking longer than I had expected. As I was trying at my end, the guys in the squadron were pushing at theirs, expressing in no uncertain terms to the DO Klaus Klause that they wanted me to join them, to which he agreed; but again getting the clearance was taking time. I was nearing the end of my exchange and was due to come back to the United Kingdom for January to start the ETPS course. By the time the clearance came for me to go and join the squadron, it was too late; I was committed to going back to the test pilot course.

Prior to the war starting, we back planned targets, duplicating the work of the pilots in theater. These were then banked. It was interesting to be able to identify on a news report during the war something I had planned prior to my return to the United Kingdom.

Having been a weapons instructor at Coltishall on the Jaguar and then becoming one on the Tornado at Honington, I was the obvious choice to become the squadron weapons officer. I later became the senior flight commander, which is quite unusual but very nice. I had been considered for my squadron, but for security reasons this was not permitted. However, as senior flight commander I did have an impact on the squadron, and luckily it was well received, the proof of this being that they had wanted me to join them when they were deployed to Saudi Arabia.

chapter five

THE STORM

Kuwait was created by the West at the beginning of the 20th century, an act never recognized or accepted by its neighbor, Iraq. When the state received its independence from Great Britain on June 19, 1961, Baghdad almost immediately claimed it as part of its own territory, basing such assertions on the fact that the region had once been part of the Ottoman Empire. Threatened by invasion, Britain's military intervention in July 1961 forestalled Iraq's short-term designs on Kuwait. Oil ensured that Kuwait became spectacularly rich and admitted into the United Nations and the Arab League; Iraq however, never renounced its claim on the small state.

A resurgence of Islamic fundamentalism was sparked off by the Ayatollah Khomeini on April 1, 1979, when he declared Iran to be an Islamic republic. At the time, most Western intelligence sources predicted that Islamic fundamentalism would become the most destabilizing influence throughout the Middle East. They were right.

The new Iranian Shiite state was messianic, intent on expanding its influence throughout the Islamic world and beyond. More than half of Iraq's population was Shiite, but the country was ruled by its Sunni minority. It wasn't long before Iran began to interfere significantly in Iraqi affairs. On September 22, 1980, a simmering border war between the two nations flared into full-scale hostilities. Despite initial successes by the Iraqi army, the war turned into a stalemate with both sides digging in and fighting a long bloody trench war. It was during this time that Iraq began to develop nuclear, biological, and chemical warfare capabilities. In 1984 and again in 1985 and 1986, Baghdad used its chemical warfare capability against Iranian forces and its own Kurdish population.

In January 1983, alarmed by events within the region, the United States created a new unified command, Central Command (CENTCOM). During the Iran/Iraq war, tens of thousands had been killed on both sides. To finance the war with Iran, Iraq had racked up a bill of $80 billion borrowed from its neighbors, Saudi Arabia and Kuwait. Despite Iraqi arguments that Iranian messianic fundamentalism represented a potential threat to both countries, Kuwait refused to write off Iraq's $65 billion debt. Other issues also strained Iraqi/Kuwaiti relations, especially alleged Kuwaiti oil drilling in the disputed Rumeila oil field. The straw that Iraq would use as the excuse that broke the camel's back, however, was Kuwaiti overproduction of oil which, they alleged, contributed to an oil glut on the spot market, driving prices down and frustrating Iraqi efforts to use its own oil revenues to clear its debts.

On July 17, 1980, Iraq's Saddam Hussein threatened to use force as retribution for Kuwait's oil overproduction, which he claimed had cost his country $14 billion in lost revenue. While stalling, prevaricating, and lying to the Arab League and the United States about his true intentions, Saddam Hussein prepared for an all-out military assault against Kuwait.

On August 1, 1990, final Iraqi preparations for war were complete; attending supposed negotiations with Kuwaiti counterparts in Jidda, Saudi Arabia, Iraqi officials conducted a stage-managed walk-out. That conference would prove to be the last of such smoke-screen meetings. The next day at about 2 A.M. Baghdad time, three Iraqi Republican Guard divisions invaded Kuwait. One division thrust down the coastal road to Kuwait City, a second

As noted on the front nose wheel strut, Aircraft 818 is pictured in its HAS at King Khalid Air Base. Operated by the 415th TFS, *The Overachiever*, completed 38 missions. *U.S. Air Force*

provided by the United States showing Iraqi troop positions along the Saudi border, however, the Saudis relented and conceded that an Iraqi invasion was probably imminent. The King invited Western troops into Saudi Arabia on August 6.

Within two days, F-15C Eagles from the 1st Tactical Fighter Wing (TFW), Langley Air Force Base, Virginia, KC-10 Extender tankers, E-3 AWACS, and C-5 Galaxy transporters carrying advanced elements of the 82nd Airborne Division had arrived to draw a line in the sand. Operation Desert Shield had begun.

Back at Tonopah, Colonel Tony Tolin's tenure on the 37th TFW was coming to an end. In August he would take up his new assignment at Langley. After an absence of five years, Colonel Al Whitley was to assume command of the F-117 wing for a second tour. Whitley recalls:

Colonel Al Whitley took the 37 TFW (Provisional) to war in the F-117. He is depicted here in his "personal" aircraft (serial 813, *The Toxic Avenger*), in its HAS at Khamis Mushait. *U.S. Air Force*

You can only imagine the emotions I experienced in August of 1990 when I was all set to leave the Tactical Air Command staff as the director of fighter training and operations, and the situation in Kuwait developed with no warning. I had known for a couple of weeks that I was scheduled to take over as commander on August 16, 1990, but the circumstances of the moment seemed likely to impact that. I continued on with my duties, which included many hours on the TAC battle staff as personnel, aircraft, equipment, and supplies were being pushed to the Middle East. I could see the magnitude of the effort firsthand and sincerely believed that my assignment might be put on hold; however, Hussein decided to take a break and things continued on schedule.

My family and I departed Langley on August 9, 1990, to visit family in South Carolina before proceeding to Nevada. In accordance with instructions, I called my former boss, General Mike Ryan [who was then the TAC director of operations and is now the Air Force chief of staff] everyday, until we arrived in Nevada on late Wednesday, prior to the change of command on Friday, August 16, 1990. Each time he assured me things were on track and to continue on my way. On the day prior to the change of command, I visited Tonopah with Tony Tolin for the first time in over five years. Much had changed, but Gen. Tolin brought me up to speed quickly.

The change of command was at 10 o'clock on Friday morning. Following the ceremony and reception, I saw my new boss, 12th Air Force

seized inland oil fields, and the third sealed off the Kuwait/Saudi border. The size and the power of the Iraqi onslaught overwhelmed the small state. Elements of the Kuwaiti Army and Air Force fought valiantly for up to three days before lack of fuel and ammunition compelled them to surrender.

In just four days Iraq had secured the annexation of Kuwait and was amassed, menacingly along the Kuwaiti-Saudi border. A successful invasion of Saudi Arabia would not only establish Iraq as the secular leader of the Arab world, but would result in the country's control of 45 percent of the world's oil.

Between August 2 and November 29, no less than 12 resolutions were passed by the United Nations condemning Iraqi aggression against Kuwait. The first, Resolution 660, demanded that Iraq withdraw from Kuwait, and it was passed unanimously. Four days later Resolution 661 was passed, which imposed an embargo on Iraq. The 12th resolution, number 678, approved the use of all necessary means to drive Iraq from Kuwait after January 15, 1991. The vote was 12 to 2 in favor.

Initially, King Fahdibn Abd al-Aziz Al Saud of Saudi Arabia was not convinced that Saddam Hussein had aggressive intentions toward his country. Following a series of border incursions, together with satellite imagery

Each Nighthawk pilot was given one of these sheets, known as "chits," with them on every flight into Iraq in case they were shot down. They describe in many languages that rewards will be offered to those who help the bearer of the chit make it back to friendly soil. Note the four tear-off "coupons" on the corners that enable a pilot to reward several people along the way to safety.

Commander Lieutenant General Peter T. Kempf, to his airplane at base operations and watched him take off. I went back to the temporary housing quarters to join my family and soon got a phone call to proceed to the command post for a priority message. As you might expect, it was notification of our deployment order. We were tasked to deploy our first squadron (415th TFS) on Sunday morning. Unfortunately, all my shot

Outside of Tonopah, the layover at Langley Air Force Base was the biggest state-side gathering of F-117As. *U.S. Air Force*

records were in the removal van, which was parked at Nellis and wasn't scheduled to deliver to our new quarters until the following Monday morning. Consequently, I had to get several shots and chemical warfare training accomplished and documented (lesson learned for me: be responsible for your shot record).

Later that evening, several of us (many had just returned for the weekend), departed for Tonopah. These folks knew what was going on in the world and had been mentally and physically preparing for this moment for many years. Of course I was quickly brought up to speed on the status of the aircraft, intelligence, logistics, and people; but all I really had to do was stand back and let these highly skilled young men and women exercise talents they had been practicing for a long time. I was certainly drinking from a fire hose, but it tasted awful good.

Major Jerry Leatherman and Captain Marcel Kerdavid were the wing's weapons officers and together formed the nucleus of a contingency planning group. Leatherman remembers:

I had just got back from my mother-in-law's funeral when Iraq invaded Kuwait. I had watched the news footage on TV in West Virginia, which is where my wife's folks are from. I said to my wife, 'We've got to get back to Vegas.' On arrival, I called up Tonopah, to find out if they needed me. They sent a C-12 down to pick me up because part of my job in the wing was to plan missions for the F-117. I went up and phoned through to the Checkmate planning staff in the Pentagon. They had drafted one of our ex-F-117 drivers, Mike Ritchy, in, who was calling me and asking me to run stuff through our flight planning computers. He'd ask, "If we place you here, how much gas would it take for you to get to Baghdad and back?" They needed to know in order to get a base for us, and secondly, when they got a base, they needed to know how much gas we would need to hit the targets and come back. I spent a lot of time on the secure phones passing back the information they requested. We did all this in an area up at the wing called the rubber room, so-called because the inside walls were lined so that they were soundproof. This wasn't new; it was where we did a lot of our covert planning stuff. It was set up to be self-contained. The big delay for the deployment was mainly from Checkmate figuring out how and where they wanted to base us. Once they had that figured, we were off.

A C-5 Galaxy departed Tonopah early Sunday morning; among those onboard were the mission planners, including Jerry Leatherman and Colonel Al Whitley who recalls, "Lieutenant Colonel Ralph Getchell, 415th TFS commander, accompanied me and did one heck of a job of bringing me up to speed on his unit's capabilities. It was on that deployment that he suggested the title of 'Team Stealth,' which we would use throughout Desert Shield and Desert Storm.

"We had a refueling stop at Westover Air Force Base, Massachusetts, and then proceeded to Rhein Mein Air Base, Germany. The crew informed me we had aircraft problems that would necessitate a night on the ground there. I immediately went to the wing commander, explained our situation, and got his support in getting our aircraft repaired and a fresh crew assigned. After only a few hours, we were on a nonstop flight to Khamis Mushait, Saudi Arabia. We arrived only a few minutes before a C-141, which was transporting additional personnel, equipment, and supplies for our unit."

At 0645 hours on Saturday morning, KC-135 tankers from the 9th Strategic Reconnaissance Wing, based at Beale Air Force Base, California, began lifting off the runway and heading for the first Air Refueling Control Point (ARCP). This would allow them to rendezvous with their single-seat black charges. Twelve tankers, including an airborne spare, were organized into three cells and provided tanker support for 22 F-117s. Cruising between 22,000 and 25,000 feet, a total of three ARs per aircraft completed the initial leg of the deployment to Langley Air Force Base. Strong head winds resulted in a higher fuel burn, which caused three tankers to divert into Plattsburgh Air Force Base. After just a few hours on the ground, the 135s were airborne again and continued their deployment to the Middle East, without the company of their friends from the 37th. Around midafternoon on Monday, August 20, the F-117s were airborne, this time for the 15-hour, nonstop haul to Saudi Arabia.

A Team Stealth photograph taken at King Khalid in late 1990. Front row, crouching, from left: Greg Feest, Rob Donaldson, Lee Gustin, Jerry Leatherman, Wes Wyrick, Ralph Getchell, Barry Horn, Blake Bourland, Bob Warren, Mark Lindstoem, Dan Backhus, and Marcel Kerdavid. Back row, standing: Clarence Whitescarver, Phil Mahon, Brian Foley, Joe Bouley, John Savage, Bill Behymer, Dave Francis, Kevin Tarrant, Paul Dolson, Lou McDonald, Bobby Bledsoe, George Kelman, Joe Salata, and Mike Riehl. *U.S. Air Force*

On this occasion, tanker support was provided by KC-10As of the 22nd Air Refueling Wing, from March Air Force Base. After successfully completing the initial AR shortly after takeoff, 4 of the 22 Black Jets designated airborne spares peeled away from the formation and headed back to the Eastern Seaboard. The main formation, led by Lieutenant Colonel Greg Feest, then continued east, for King Khalid Air Base where they arrived around noon local time on Tuesday, August 21. Back at Tonopah Major Mike Mahar recalls, "I was assigned to the 416th TFS (Ghost Riders) during Operation Desert Shield. When our sister squadron, the 415th TFS (Nightstalkers), deployed to Saudi Arabia, the mood in our unit was similar to watching your twin getting ready for a big party to which you'd not been invited. We expected that they would have a once-in-a-lifetime opportunity to be employed decisively in combat, and we'd be left to read about it in the newspapers."

Soon nicknamed Tonopah East, King Khalid Air Base was nestled in the Asir Mountains at an elevation of 6,776 feet (2,065 meters) above mean sea level, just outside the small city of Khamis Mushait. Located in the extreme southern tip of Saudi Arabia, the base was well beyond the range of Iraqi Scud-B missiles. Completed in 1980 and built under the direction of U.S. Army Engineers to U.S. military standards, it boasted two 12,000-foot runways and its hardened aircraft shelters (HASs) were each capable of holding eight aircraft. Bedrooms attached to the shelters provided accommodation for the pilots who slept in bunk beds, four to a room. In the event of a nuclear, biological, or chemical (NBC) attack, massive generators with their own fuel supply could be fired up to provide electricity and to overpressurize the shelters, preventing contamination seepage from outside. Divided into four sections, the aircraft inside were parked, nose-to-tail, two to a bay. The facilities offered at King Khalid were second to none; however, on the down side, the return distance from the base to Baghdad necessitated the need for three ARs per sortie, with a typical mission lasting five hours.

On August 23, the 415th TFS launched eight aircraft, which in company with four F-5s, three F-15s, and a Tornado from the Saudi host wing, conducted an orientation flight to familiarize pilots with their new surroundings. It would prove to be the first and last daytime sortie until after the hostilities ended. Three days later, the 415th assumed alert duty for the first time in its history. This consisted of between six and eight aircraft at any one time fueled, bombed up, and ready to go. The pilots had their flight plans and target photos ready, and if the Iraqis decided to roll into Saudi Arabia, a robust, defensive plan was in place.

The air armada ranged against Saddam Hussein continued to build. Work on exactly how this awesome force could be used to maximum effectiveness for minimum losses proceeded in parallel. Colonel John A. Warden III had been appointed director of a new strategy office to rethink how to use air power. Believing the doctrines of both Strategic Air Command (SAC) and Tactical Air Command (TAC) were "too limiting," Warden's "five rings" paper of 1988, depicted the modern battlefield much like a dart board. At its center, the bull's-eye, was the command control communications centers (c3), the decision-making capability of the enemy. By severing this, Warden believed it might be possible to end the enemy's ability to stay in power or run affairs of state, including its ability to wage war.

The next ring represented the enemy's military and economic production capability—factories, electrical grids, powerplants, refineries, and so on—all essential to sustaining a war. The third ring was his means of transportation,

On August 19, 1990, 22 F-117s from the 415th TFS arrived at Langley Air Force Base, Virginia, on a one-night stop-over, en route to King Khalid Air Base, Saudi Arabia. The next day, 18 of the aircraft resumed the journey. The remaining four, having completed their duty as airborne spares, returned to Tonopah. *U.S. Air Force*

movement, and distribution—bridges, highways, airfields, and ports—once destroyed all traffic would be paralyzed. The fourth ring was population and food sources, but carpet bombing this ring he believed, was both repugnant and unethical in today's world. The outer ring, and therefore least important of all the target categories, was the enemy's military forces, which, Warden reasoned, existed only to protect the inner rings—and in particular the bull's-eye. In essence, the paper sought to reaffirm and update arguments that a war could be won by aerial bombing raids, using nonnuclear weapons, against "centers of gravity," rendering a land campaign unnecessary.

Warden presented his outline plan for the execution of the air war in the gulf, to General Norman Schwarzkopf and other senior members of CENT-COM. He, together with three lieutenant colonels, were then instructed to brief Lieutenant General Chuck Horner, who was acting theater commander at the time, pending Schwarzkopf's arrival. The team of four arrived in Riyadh on August 19, 1990, but Horner had already seen a copy of the proposed "Instant Thunder" campaign and wasn't impressed. (Instant Thunder represented the complete opposite of the disastrous Rolling Thunder campaign that was pursued in Vietnam, where force was only deployed in increments.) Instead, Horner, commander of Joint Air Forces (CENTAF), selected a white-haired North Carolinian to develop the air campaign, one Brigadier General Buster Glosson. It had been noted that "unlike Warden, Glosson had a rapport with Horner and Schwarzkopf, was well connected, and while Warden had

Two F-117s taxi out to the holding point prior to launching another raid from King Khalid. *U.S. Air Force*

An F-117 leads a mixed formation of aircraft from the Royal Saudi Air Force over scrub desert. It is made up of a Tornado air defense variant: Northrop F-5, McDonald Douglas F-15, and Tornado ground attack aircraft. *U.S. Air Force*

built his reputation as a theorist within the Pentagon, Glosson was an operator through and through, a weapons school graduate, skillful politician, and good at getting things done." All that aside, Glosson and Warden had one thing in common: They were both Billy Mitchell and Trenchard disciples.

An F-4 jock in Vietnam, Glosson's background had a profound impact on the management of Senior Trend during the war planning process. As an executive for the commander of the Tactical Fighter Weapons Center at Nellis Air Force Base, his initial exposure to the F-117A program was, as he recalls, the difficulty in preparing accident-related news releases and answering news queries concerning a program that "did not exist." As commander of the 414th Fighter Weapons Squadron, his unit was located adjacent to the 4450th Tactical Group. Reflecting, he stated, "The 414th paid for many things that we never received." Finally, as chief of Tactical Forces Division

Headquarters, U.S. Air Force, Washington, D.C., one of Glosson's responsibilities was to ensure that every aspect of the F-117 program was fully funded in the Air Force annual budget, without the expenditure being detectable. His most memorable experience of the F-117, however, occurred in 1987. While as commander of the 1st Tactical Fighter Wing and flying an F-15C, he attempted to detect and engage an F-117 over the Nellis range. He describes the effort as his most humbling experience as a fighter pilot; however, this event was one of the driving forces behind his unflinching confidence in the F-117 later during the planning and execution of the Gulf War.

On August 21 Lieutenant Colonels Dave Deptula and Ben Harvey (both part of Warden's delegation) briefed Instant Thunder to Brig. Gen. Glosson and Colonel Larry Henry (the latter would command electronic warfare programs in the Gulf). Later that evening, the two lieutenant colonels learned that it

The failure of one weapon to penetrate the HAS in the foreground is more than made up for by the other three that did. Note the doors of all six hangars have been blown out by the blast of weapons exploding inside. *U.S. Air Force*

would be Glosson, not "their boss," who would oversee the planning of the air campaign. This would be a highly compartmentalized operation, with the Special Planning Group (later referred to as the Black Hole) operating initially from a third-floor conference room at Horner's headquarters in the Royal Saudi Air Force (RSAF) Headquarters building in Riyadh. The Spartan room contained a large table, one secure phone to Washington, and another for theater operations. In October, Glosson moved the Special Planning Group to a semihardened underground office in the RSAF headquarters.

The plan interested Glosson, although he believed it required additional planning and vectoring of strategy beyond the proposed six days, as a hedge against the campaign failing to deliver the victory envisaged by Warden. In addition, Schwarzkopf directed Glosson to initially develop a retaliatory plan, lasting three or four days, giving the allies the capability to respond, if Saddam did something stupid. The strategic plan would be step 2. Glosson reminded Deptula that the battle would be launched against a nation that had fought Iran for eight long bloody years and that the plan was not cognizant

of the need to deal with the Republican Guard. On the plus side of Instant Thunder, Glosson liked the idea of taking the war to Baghdad at the outset. Mindful that Deptula had previously worked for both Warden and Horner, and the need to successfully integrate the planners at the Pentagon and in Riyadh, Glosson cleverly appointed Dave Deptula as his principal planner and sent the others back to Washington. Eleven days later, the two had refined the air campaign, a plan that embodied the same general principles as Instant Thunder. On September 2, Glosson presented the air campaign plan. Horner accepted the plan's basic thrust and asked that the first 24 hours of the attack plan be incorporated into an Air Tasking order, a formal directive to units in the field that would expedite early implementation should Saddam Hussein move against Saudi Arabia.

Working from a completely different doctrine, however, Instant Thunder found no allies in the U.S. Navy, whose representative in the Black Hole referred to it as "Distant Blunder"—*distant* because the original draft had been prepared in Washington and *blunder* because of the intention to attack

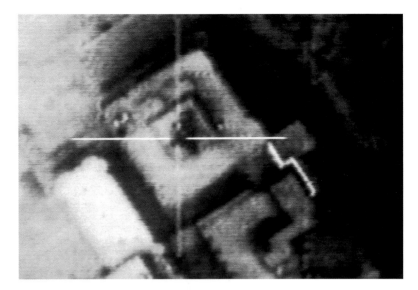

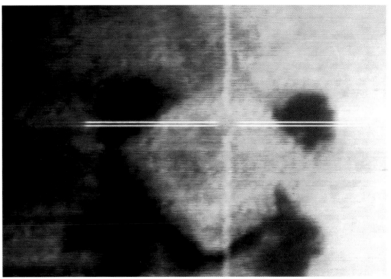

Bandit 307, Captain Mark Lindstoem, attacked the new Iraqi Air Force Head-quarters building. These views recorded from his IRADS, depict perfect tracking of the target, culminating in black smoke billowing out as the weapon blows out all four sides of the building. *U.S. Air Force*

Baghdad from the outset. The Air Force rolled over these objections, how-ever—numbers and rank providing the immovable mass. On September 5, Glosson presented the plan to Schwarzkopf, and it was enthusiastically endorsed and approved.

In theater there remained problems. These included a lack of fuels and coolant for the F-111s based at Taef and F-15E Strike Eagles, which still awaited their Low Altitude Navigation and Targeting Infrared for Night (LANTIRN) targeting pods. There was also a lack of reliable intelligence, relating to the location of scud launchers in the west of Iraq and a shortage of satellite imagery required by the 117 crews to locate their targets in Baghdad, which didn't arrive until mid-October—notwithstanding, Glosson assessed the plan as "doable" from mid-September.

General Schwarzkopf's theater campaign had four phases: Phase 1, the strategic air campaign, necessitated the destruction of Iraq's vital centers: the leadership; national communication centers including radio, television, and land lines; nuclear, biological, and chemical weapons research and production facilities; military focusing on the Republican Guards, Iraqi Air Force, and Scuds; and infrastructure such as the transportation system, including rail-roads, bridges, and oil distribution. To implement this phase, a detailed under-standing of the Iraqi defense network was obviously a prerequisite, and it was to this end that the U.S. Navy made an outstanding contribution. A Navy intelligence cell had been set up in a federal office complex in Suitland, Mary-land, to improve that service's tactical intelligence on Soviet and Third World threats, after two aircraft were lost and a third suffered severe damage during a 1983 raid in Lebanon. Entitled SPEAR, for Strike Projection Evaluation and

Anti-Air Research, the unit had just prior to Iraq's invasion of Kuwait begun to focus its attention on Iraq. Having expanded the team to include experts of Iraqi equipment from the other two services, they shared their information with the Air Force's Checkmate planning office in the bowels of the Pentagon. Like layers of paint, SPEAR was able to strip back the various layers that con-stituted the Iraqi air defense network and identify its core. This was a system known as Kari (Iraq spelled backwards in French). It was driven by a main-frame computer designed by the French aerospace company Thomson-CSF and completed in 1988. Like pulling teeth, the team slowly managed to extract details of the system's capabilities from Thomson. Meanwhile, Air Force air-craft acted as ferrets flying to Iraqi border areas to stimulate their air defenses. This enabled satellites, Rivet Joint RC-135s, Compass Call EC-130s, and U-2Rs to record communications intelligence (COMINT) together with the signal characteristics of radar emissions or electronic intelligence (ELINT). This information then enabled intelligence officers to map Kari's structure and establish Iraq's electronic air order of battle (EAOB)

The sophistication of Kari was briefed to Checkmate and the Joint Chiefs of Staff; its destruction would chronically disable the Iraqis' tight central control system. The various layers of Kari consisted of more than 400 observation posts from which basic heading and altitude data could be simply set to a command post. This data was supplemented by 73 radar reporting stations, which in turn fed into 17 Intercept Operations Centers (IOCs). These command posts were mobile units, often located in hardened concrete shelters, and could process such inputs using computer technology that permitted air defense officers to transmit targeting data via the touch of a light pen, to an aircraft's track on his radar screen. Four Sector Operations Centers (SOCs) then controlled the IOCs. From these three-story, reinforced concrete centers, the defense of enormous areas of Iraq could be planned. One SOC was located at airfield H-3 in Western Iraq; another to defend the south was situated at Tallil air base; the north was covered by the SOC at Kirbuk; the fourth, at the Taji military base,

protected the country's interior; and Baghdad itself (work on a fifth SOC at Ali al Salem air base, had begun, but the unit did not become operational). Kari then provided this basic targeting information to missile batteries, thereby minimizing the time needed to operate radars in target acquisition mode. This, in turn, provided the batteries with a degree of defense against an attacker's antiradiation missiles. These acquired their targets by locking onto the missile batteries' radar emissions.

To delay detection from these long-range systems and possible engagement by high- and medium-altitude SAMs, an interdictor might instead elect to fly a low-level flight profile. The Iraqis tried to seal off this option by complementing the Kari system with Soviet SA-16, SA-13, SA-9, and SA-7 heat-seeking missiles, SA-8 and SA-6 low-altitude radar-guided SAMs, and literally thousands of 57-, 37-, and 23-millimeter AAA batteries. To knock down their target, the AAA units didn't independently target an aircraft, but instead

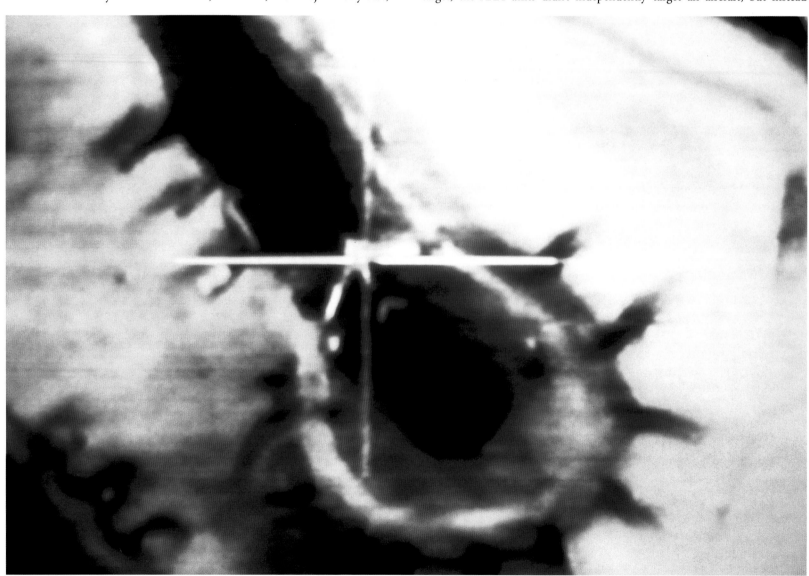

Several aircraft of the 416th were rescheduled to hit Iraq Tu-16 Badger bombers, spotted in open retrievements at Al Taquaddum. Of the eight bombers targeted, three were destroyed by the 416th and three more were taken out later that day by nonstealthy aircraft. *U.S. Air Force*

employed the Soviet technique of setting up a "wall of steel" in their sector, allowing the aircraft to fly into it.

By providing detailed information of the Iraqi air defense system, SPEAR enabled Gen. Glosson's planning group to further refine its initial Kari planning. But post-World War II statistics showed that 85 percent of all aircraft losses occurred within 12 miles of the target area and were attributed to AAA or shoulder-fired SAMs. With a strong likelihood of similar losses over Iraq, Glosson ordered that low-level missions flown during the first two nights would give way to strikes conducted at medium and high altitude—beyond AAA range, from day three onward. The exception to this was F-117 sorties.

Carving out this "medium-altitude sanctuary" was a loadable pursuit, but its creation necessitated the dismembering and destruction of the Kari system. The military nomenclature for such an exercise is SEAD, suppression of enemy air defenses, and the basic principles of its successful prosecution were highlighted in a classified memo compiled by Glosson, Henry, and Deptula then sent up the line by Horner to Schwarzkopf and the Joint Chiefs of Staff. The attack had five objectives:

· Destroy/disrupt C2 nodes
· Disrupt EW/GCI coverage and communication
· Force air defense assets into autonomous modes
· Use expendable drones for deception
· Employ maximum available high-speed
   antiradiation missile (HARM) shooters

Like dismembering an Octopus, its head—the SOCs and IOCs that ran the defense network—would be taken out by the F-117s at the outset, as would key early-warning radars and communication links. The flaying tentacles would then be dealt with by other, nonstealthy assets. If successful, the

This is all that remains of an Iraqi command bunker, located at one of the many airfields visited by the F-117s. *U.S. Air Force*

plan would have two benefits; without the Kari system, SAM batteries would be forced to use their radars longer, making them more vulnerable to attack from antiradiation missiles. Cut off from their ground control intercept controllers, Iraqi fighter pilots would become easy prey for allied air defense assets.

If a war did break out in the Gulf, it would be the F-117's first true operational test. General Buster Glosson takes up the story:

I was totally confident as I planned the air war that the F-117 would live up to its expectations. There were a lot of doubting Thomases around, but I had spent enough time in the F-15 trying to successfully intercept the F-117 that I was a believer! The air campaign was built with the F-117 as its backbone; you must believe it's going to work or it's foolish to make it the backbone of your entire effort. In fact, during early September, I decreed that stealth would work and did not permit discussion to the contrary.

The initial 24 hours of the Gulf War [were] meticulously planned. I directed the planners to ask themselves three questions about every target they considered, what system had the highest probability of destroying it, what system had the highest probability of its pilot coming back alive, and what system had the highest probability of no civilian casualties. As you may expect, 99 percent of the time, the answer to these questions was F-117. We did not have enough F-117s to attack every target. So I directed the F-117 to be used against the most critical, the most highly defended and difficult-to-hit targets. That gave us the greatest probability of accomplishing our strategic objectives and creating the utmost confusion and disruption. I used all the other systems, be they cruise missiles, fighters, or bombers, as fillers.

On September 22 two C-141 Starlifters delivered the 37th's avionics maintenance vans from Tonopah to King Khalid Air Base. These units were just part of the specialist equipment that had been developed to support the

The damage wrought by an exploding GBU-27, having penetrated 3 feet of reinforced concrete, is total. *U.S. Air Force*

Despite Iraqi HASs being constructed to the highest standards, they were no match for the GBU-27s. *U.S. Air Force*

Black World program. The unit also boasted its own satellite link to national intelligence assets, which provided them with threat information needed for the F-117's mission planning system. This didn't go down at all well with CENTAF intelligence officers, as they intended to control the flow of all intelligence resources and information to the units deployed to the region. Rather than working with the 37th to sort out complementary capabilities, or discover what the unit needed to supplement that capability, elements within CENTAF worked with the appropriate government agencies to shut them down. When CENTAF refused to reinstate its collection capability, the 37th started using the address of a duplicate system located at Tonopah. Unfortunately for them, CENTAF eventually learned what had been going on and tension over the issue persisted until better communications between the two led to a more cooperative atmosphere. Although such instances were an exception to the rule, it demonstrated a lack of understanding or appreciation of the wing's unique requirements borne from the need to develop such stand-alone systems in isolation, in the Black World. On October 8, Gen.

A destroyed and abandoned Iraqi ZSU-23-4 mobile anti-aircraft gun at an airfield. The weapon is fully automatic and gas-operated with a breech block of the vertical sliding wedge type. *U.S. Air Force*

Major Joe Bouley (Bandit 331) is strapped into the jet by crew chief, Staff Sergeant David Owings. *U.S. Air Force*

Glosson described the problem as CENTAF Intelligence arrogance and stupidity. He directed Col. Whitley to get the best planning information available, whatever the source.

October 3 saw the execution of the first of three exercises, code named "Sneaky Sultan." Devised by Col. Whitley, the aim was to test the 37th response capability. Upon receiving the exercise message, pilots on alert duty grabbed their flight plans and photography packs, while maintenance had the aircraft ready and waiting for them. They would actually taxi out, before the order was given to stop everything, the aircraft never getting airborne as they were loaded with live munitions. Fifteen days later, on October 18, Colonel Klaus Klause, the 37th's deputy commander for operations, assumed command of the deployment while Al Whitley returned to Tonopah to requalify in the F-117. It had been five years since his last flight in the aircraft, and many changes were made over the intervening period. Three days after Whitley's

departure, Sneaky Sultan 2 was initiated, and on November 12 Team Stealth participated in a major six-day exercise, codenamed "Imminent Thunder." During this exercise, they flew 32 sorties.

By the end of November, the 415th's sister squadron, the 416th "Ghost Riders," were committed to Desert Shield. On Sunday, December 2, they, like the 415th, positioned to Langley Air Force Base. At 1903 hours the following evening, their squadron commander, Lieutenant Colonel Gregory Gonyea, became airborne. Leading a six-plane element, he headed for the first ARCP. They were followed 30 minutes later by another six-ship element; there then followed two four-plane elements, each interspaced by 30 minutes. Having successfully completed the three-month conversion course in just six weeks, Colonel Al Whitley returned to Saudi Arabia, flying in the third cell. All 20 aircraft arrived safely at King Khalid the next day, December 4, despite one aircraft developing severe engine problems on the final leg of the deployment.

The planners were eager to check on the effectiveness of stealth technology, as Major Jerry Leatherman recalls:

Towards the latter months of Desert Shield, myself and Marcel Kerdavid were one night given a mission that only Col. Whitley, Marcel, and I knew about. We rendezvoused with a KC-135 that came out of Riyadh and got gas, we then flew towards the border, basically mimicking the tanker tracks that we were going to use during Desert Storm. At the same time, the guys at Riyadh had EC-135s, a RC-135 Rivet Joint, and other intel-gathering platforms airborne at the same time as we were doing this. As we got within 30 miles of the border, Marcel and I dropped off the tanker and stealthed up. One of us flew at about 10,000 feet; the other flew at between 15,000 and 20,000 feet, and we flew this mirror image right along the border. We then turned, rejoined the tanker, got gas, and headed back to Khamis. During this exercise, Riyadh noted that the Iraqis seemed unable to detect us; however, they could certainly detect the tankers, and when they flew toward them it scared the crap out of them for a few minutes, and they went onto a high-alert status. Over the next few months we kept repeating this exercise, flying the same profile, but with different guys from the squadron. This was a bait/decoy thing for the Iraqis, so for weeks they would see tankers going up to the border and doing the same thing, except they never knew that the 117s were dropping off and flying along their border. It gave confidence to the guys in Riyadh that we could get in there and back out without being seen; it also gave the pilots a warm feeling that "Hey, this stuff will work."

We were staying up and flying almost every night. I used to stay up until just before sun rise, to try and keep my body clock adjusted. I knew that if the war started, we'd be flying nothing but nights. We were always a little more on edge every time the moon cycle came to zero moon illumination. We imagined that would be the best time to start the war, and it turned out that we were right. One day in January, at about 10 a.m. local time, one of the command post men came into my room and woke me. He said I was needed in the command post right away, so I put on some shorts and flip-flops and went over, somewhat half asleep, as I'd only been asleep for three or four hours. Col. Whitley and Col. Klause were already there and they handed me a message, which as I remember was headed something like "Top Secret." It went on to read, "Execute Wolfpack 'H' hour is 0100, Zulu." Execute Wolfpack was the code word for Desert Storm to go. [Wolfpack was derived from the North Carolina State Athletic Team Mascot, underlining Buster Glosson's roots.] "H" hour was to be the start of the war, which was 3:00 a.m. Baghdad time. That gave us all our Time Over Targets (TOTs), as these were based on "H" hour. I remember looking at the note and then the two colonels and saying, "Well, 'just like Slim Pickings in Doctor Strangeways,' I guess we got the go code." One of the colonels then asked if we were ready, to which I replied, "Yeh." I then went over to wake up Joe Bouley and his team. The deal I made with these guys was, since I was the chief of the mission planning cell, I would plan it out, on condition I got to fly in the very first mission. I wasn't going to spend all my time planning and not get to fly. During the course of the mission cell planning, we split into various teams which concentrated on planning missions for the subsequent night. You couldn't fly the mission you had planned because the planning cycle took

Major Jerry Leatherman (Bandit 259) takes a final look out of the hangar doors before strapping in and getting down to business. *U.S. Air Force*

anywhere from between 24 and 36 hours. After being awake for that length of time, it would have been impossible to fly the mission.

Joe Bouley was going to be flying the second night, so it was pre-planned that his team was responsible for when we got the go code to finalize the first night's plan. I was told not to tell the other pilots, so I woke Joe up, and he dragged his guys over to the mission planning area to start running the final details on the plan, coordinate with the tankers for the rendezvous, etc. After I had got all that going, and with our brief time set for 9:00 p.m. that evening, I looked at my watch and decided it

This warning was prepared by the 18th Psychological Operations Task Force based in Riyadh. One of several leaflets featuring the F-117, it was dispersed over selected Iraqi air bases and reads, "This location is subject to bombardment! Escape now and save yourselves." *U.S. Air Force*

was time for some sleep, as I figured that at 3:00 in the morning, I would need to be pretty much awake! I actually managed to get a few hours sleep in. I then got up and checked with mission planning; there were a few glitches, but nothing insurmountable. Once we got things sorted out with the tankers, nothing really changed for us. What we had on paper was pretty much what we were going to go with. The funniest thing about the briefing was it took less time than one of our peacetime briefings. I think part of the reason for that was, that number one, we were ready to go, everybody had been assigned their targets for months on end, we had been briefing guys on a fairly routine basis of what our plans were, how many guys were going in at any time, and the sequence. At the end of it Col. Klause, being a Vietnam veteran and one of the few guys to have flown combat, got up and told us what it would be like to be shot at. He said that we would get a big dry taste in our throat, and the thing was, that after it was all over, we would look back and think, "Well, that wasn't so bad." He told us to rely on our training and make sure that we did what we needed to do.

When the briefing was over, we had more than a normal amount of time prior to stepping out to the jets. A bunch of us went over and checked our personal equipment, like our harness and the "g" suit, as we were going to have to carry our search-and-rescue maps, blood chits, and weapons. We were being a little more thorough; we got some bottles of water to take and checked the batteries in our Walkmans so that we had something to listen to on the long flight back. Even after that, there was

time left, so some of us went out in front of the hangar for an idle chitchat and a cigarette. When it was time, we got into the vans. Maintenance had got all the weapons loaded, coordinated specifications needed for the targets; it was just like any other night. The planes were sitting there, with the INS all spun up. While I was traveling in the van with Joe Salata, he looked at me and said, "Boy, I hope this stealth shit works." I looked at my watch, smiled, and said, "Well, I guess in about three or four hours, we're going to know aren't we?" Spare planes were in the hangars as backup, and a spare airplane had been positioned out at the arming area. So if you had a problem, you could change planes and complete your mission. I remember Marcel Kerdavid had to go to a spare plane because his port engine wouldn't start for whatever reason. But it wasn't a problem. We'd allowed plenty of time for changing planes, so it wasn't a big rush. Everything went pretty much as planned and I remember thinking, Murphy's law is going to come into play at any moment. Something bad has got to happen; something has got to throw a monkey wrench into this plan, but it didn't.

Colonel Greg Feest recalls the night that validated stealth technology in the ultimate arena, which would forever thereafter revolutionize air warfare:

I had mixed emotions stepping to fly the evening of January 16, 1991. As an Air Force fighter pilot, I had spent my entire career preparing to fly combat operations. This is what I had trained for and I was ready to go. However, in the back of my mind I wondered, as did the other F-117A pilots, would this stealth technology really work? After all, we were flying into the heart of the Iraqi air defense system and this mission would be the ultimate operational test of stealth technology. Hopefully, the Lockheed engineers were correct and the "Black Jet" would perform to expectations. After the mission, I discovered that even the wing commander was not completely confident in stealth technology. After the first wave of aircraft launched, he called all senior leadership into a meeting and expressed his view that "We might lose some aircraft tonight." He wanted everyone to be ready for that possibility. After all, the F-117A is low-observable, not invisible.

Arriving at the hangar, I proceeded to preflight my jet as well as the two 2,000-pound GBU-27 laser-guided bombs strapped in the weapons bay. My crew chief and I did not talk much this night. He and the weapons troops had written numerous messages to Saddam Hussein on the bombs. Hopefully, I'll be able to deliver them, I thought to myself. Having started engines in the blacked-out shelter, my crew chief told me to, "Kick some ass!" and he disconnected his communication lead from the aircraft. These would be the last words I would hear until airborne.

The entire first wave of F-117As launched without radio communications; we didn't want the Iraqis to get a "heads-up" as to our plan. My call sign was Thunder 36 and wingman Captain Dave "Dogman" Francis was Thunder 37. We took off and flew to the tanker without saying a word to each other. My radio was on but remained silent. Since the F-117A is a single-seat fighter, there was no copilot to talk to and the next several hours would be extremely quiet. Having rendezvoused with the KC-135

Depicted in one of the "canyons" at King Khalid, a segmented ladder, unique to F-117 operations, has been placed on the aircraft for cockpit access. *U.S. Air Force*

tankers, we air refueled and headed north, towards Iraq, while flying on each wing of the tanker. The night was extremely dark and I was thankful, since I did not want the moon to silhouette my jet as I flew into Iraq.

At approximately 2:30 a.m., I topped off with fuel, "stealthed-up" my aircraft, and departed the tanker. In 20 minutes I would drop the first bomb of Operation Desert Storm. [The fact that Feest dropped the first bomb of Desert Storm was by no means a coincidence. This action, unbeknown to him, was the result of a personal directive from General Buster Glosson.] Crossing the Iraqi border, I was nervous as I armed my weapons. My target was an IOC located in an underground bunker, southwest of Baghdad, near Nukhayb. This IOC was a key link between border radar sites and the air defense headquarters in Baghdad. Destroying it would allow other non-stealthy aircraft to enter Iraq undetected.

Approaching the target I was apprehensive. Two thoughts crossed my mind. First, would I be able to identify the target? Second, did the Air Force really want me to drop this bomb? These thoughts only lasted several seconds. I had practiced for three years, and I could find and destroy any target within one second of my scheduled time-over-target. Having trained for so long, nothing was going to stop me from dropping my bombs. All I had to do was play, what I called, a highly sophisticated video game, and in 30 minutes I would be back in Saudi Arabia.

As I approached the target area, my adrenaline was up and instincts took over. My bomb was armed and my systems checked good. I found the target on my infrared display and concentrated on tracking the target by slewing the crosshairs over the aim point. The target had been easier to find than I envisioned. I was able to take time to glance outside the cockpit. Everything was dark except for a few lights in the town. It appeared that no one knew I was in the sky. Looking back at my display, my laser

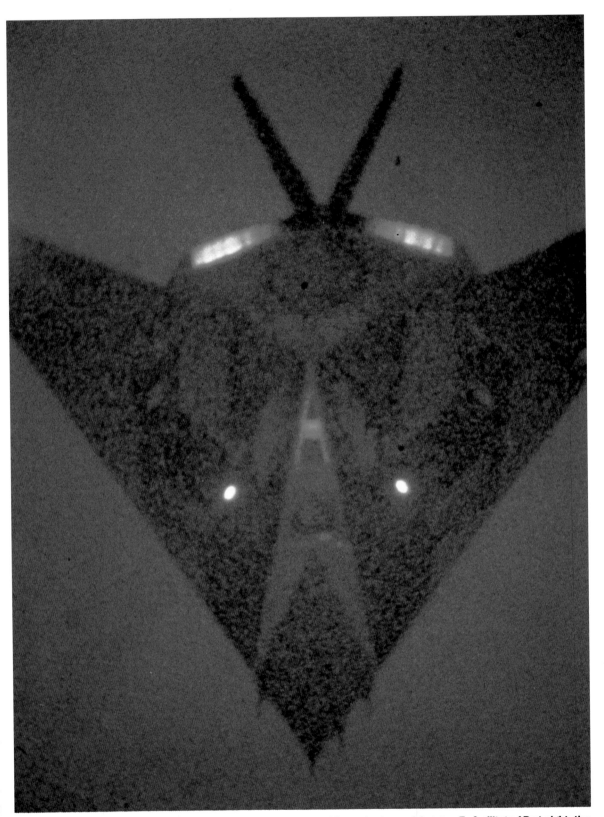

A "Boomer's-eye view" of an F-117, stabilized in the precontact position, prior to receiving gas. To facilitate AR at night, the apex of the canopy frame houses a rear-facing light to provide illumination of the inflight refueling receptacle. *U.S. Air Force*

began to fire as I tracked the target. I waited for the display to tell me I was "in range," and I depressed the "pickle" button. Several seconds later the weapons bay doors snapped open, and I felt the 2,000-pound bomb depart the aircraft. The bay door slammed closed as I watched the IR display while continuing to keep the crosshairs on the target. The bomb appeared at the bottom of the display just before it hit. At exactly 2:51 a.m., I saw the bomb go through the crosshairs and penetrate the bunker. The explosion came out of the hole the bomb had made and blew out the doors of the bunker. I knew I had knocked out the target. The video game was over.

Having destroyed the target, I turned my aircraft 210 degrees left to head for my second target. While in the turn, I decided to try and see my wingman's bomb hit, since his was due one minute after mine. As I looked back I saw something completely unfamiliar. It looked like fireworks, big bursts of red and orange, flying at me and lighting up the sky. After being stunned for several seconds, I realized it was tracers from AAA. During all my peacetime training missions flying exercises like Red Flag, I had never anticipated what actual AAA would look like. After all it cannot be simulated. I snapped my head forward and pushed the throttles up as far as they would go. I wanted out of the target area as fast as I could.

As I headed towards my second target, an Iraqi SOC at the H-3 airfield in western Iraq, I looked out in front of my aircraft. I now saw what everybody at home saw on television. Tracers, flashes, and flak were all over the place. The whole country had come alive with more AAA than I could ever imagine. I watched several SAMs launch into the sky and fly through my altitude both in front and behind me, but none of them appeared to be guided. Stealth technology really seemed to work! Even if the AAA and SAMs were not guided, the intense "barrage fire" in my target area was scary. All it would take was a lucky hit.

I decided to ignore what was happening outside my jet. I lowered my seat and concentrated on my displays. After all, what I couldn't see couldn't hurt me! I dropped my second bomb and turned as fast as I could back towards Saudi Arabia. I don't think I ever maneuvered the F-117A as aggressively as I did coming off my second target. For a second time in less than 30 minutes, I wanted out of the target area as fast as possible.

On December 4, 1990, F-117 representation at King Khalid was increased, as 20 aircraft from the 416th Ghost Riders arrived. *U.S. Air Force*

Having made it safely out of the area, my thoughts turned to my wingman. Dogman was again one minute behind me. I knew he had to fly through the same air defenses I had just flown through. I didn't think he would make it. For both of us to survive untouched would require too much good luck.

Major Jerry Leatherman recalls:

Everybody took off on time; we joined up with the tankers near Taef. We had two tanker tracks that we flew up on; the first wave of us was a flight of 10 planes and our targets were due to be hit at H hour, which was 3:00 in the morning. My target was the 14-story Al Karak skyscraper, what we called the "AT&T building," because it was the main telephone switching center in Baghdad. My call sign was Hail 02. I was to be the second guy to hit that, one minute behind Paul Dolson, Hail 01. We dropped off the tankers and flew our routes. Everybody had a different route, as we were attacking from all different points of the compass. The idea being that the first four or five guys would be hitting the targets right

on H hour. I was to hit my target one minute past, to allow for any debris kicked up from Paul's bomb to settle down enough so that I could find the target. I was to drop two GBU 10s right into the AT&T building, while Paul would fly on to attack the IOC at Al Taqaddum with his remaining GBU-27. My flight profile was to come in from the northeast of Baghdad; we only had a five-minute window for all of us to hit the targets. Our TOT was to be no later than five minutes after 3:00 in the morning, so 0305 hours was the drop-dead point. Later on, the planning staff gave us an hour block of time because the Iraqis were shooting as we arrived. It was random, sporadic, triple-A fire flying all over the city. I think that some of it was due to some of the radars along the border screaming out something just before they got hit; so Baghdad itself was lit up like a Christmas tree. I remember turning in toward Baghdad and seeing the bright lights of the city out on the left side of my plane. When I looked at the sensor display, the cursor was laying right on the Baghdad AT&T building. When I looked at this I thought That's not right; it's too perfect. I checked one of the off-sets that we had: their memorial to those killed during their war

with Iran. I flicked over to that and again my cursor was right on it, so I clicked back and looked at my photograph. I probably checked over my switches about 30 times in this two-minute run. When I had the target, I looked outside for a while, and the first thing I remember thinking was, Man these people are pissed. It was like swarms of bees flying around. You could see all the tracer ammunition from the AAA, and every now and then, you could see the explosions as the rounds fused. I decided that it wasn't the thing to do, to be looking outside, so I concentrated on looking at the target. I kept saying to myself, OK, just let me get to release, let me get to release. I spent most of the time living my life in small bites of time. So when the bombs came off I said, OK let me guide it to impact, let me guide it to impact. Then, when the bombs impacted, I said, Just let me get the hell out of here, let me get the hell out of here. Paul had punched a hole through the roof of the Al-Karak with a GBU-27; that was my aim point for two standard GBU-10s. Once I was clear of Baghdad, one of the first things I remember thinking was that there was no way of all of us surviving that.

Coming back towards the tanker, I was tail-end Charlie because of my egress route. I ended up going out to the north of Baghdad, then having to swing to the west before heading back down to the tankers. I knew that there were supposed to be six guys in my cell, but I only counted five. I thought we'd lost one, and I was trying to figure out who it was, when it suddenly dawned on me that I was the sixth guy! The tanker called over and found out that the other cell had all four of their guys, so everybody came back without a nick on them. The only depressing thing about the whole situation was the prospect of a two-and-a-half-hour flight back to Khamis. I put my headset on, and putting my Walkman in my ears, I listened to some Def Leppard, "Pour Some Sugar On Me!" Approaching Khamis, we learned that all the F-111s that had flown out of Taef had had to divert into our base due to fog. This added an extra 30 minutes to an hour, to the length of our sortie, as we had to wait for them to recover first.

Having hit both targets, Feest remembers the flight back to King Khalid:
Just prior to crossing the border into Saudi Arabia, I performed my de-stealth procedures. My task now was to find the postmission tanker, so I could top off with fuel and make it back to home base. After confirming the tanker was on-station and waiting for my two-ship, I headed for the rejoin point. At a predesignated time, I called Dogman on the radio to see if he was ready to rejoin. I prayed I would hear a response. I didn't hear an answer, so I waited several seconds and tried again. This time I heard him answer. He said he had my aircraft in sight and was ready to rejoin. Now the question was, how many other stealth fighters would make it home? During our mission briefing, all pilots were given line-up cards. These listed all the pilots flying in the first wave along with their call signs. I had this list on my kneeboard and checked off each name as I heard the pilots check-in with the tankers. After approximately 30 minutes, I looked down at the list and saw I had checked off all the names. All pilots had made it out of Iraq, but had any aircraft been hit?

It was a two-hour flight back to Khamis Mushait after departing our postmission tanker. It seemed like it took forever. Thankfully, the sun was rising so we would be able to land in daylight. The six-and-one-half-hour mission had been quite tiring. Upon landing, I was met by my wife, Captain

Assistant Chief of Weapons and Tactics for the 37th, Major Jerry Leatherman headed up the unit's Combat Mission Planning Cell at King Khalid. In recognition of his outstanding achievements in planning and coordinating the use of F-117s in Desert Storm, he was awarded the 1991 Chennault Award. *U.S. Air Force*

As demonstrated during Desert Storm, successful integration of the F-117A, IRADS, and the GBU-27 produced the most survivable, accurate, and cost-effective weapons system in military aviation history. Shortly after the war, however, some elements began rewriting history, cynically manipulating statistics in an attempt to turn the F-117 and the achievements of Team Stealth into antiheroes. *U.S. Air Force*

Bridget McGovern. During Operation Desert Storm, she served as the resource manager and was responsible for all of our logistical requirements. She relayed to me that none of the F-117As had sustained any battle damage. She had listened intently in the command post while each pilot called in with his aircraft status before landing. We were both relieved. I immediately told her, for the first time in my life, I was happy I would be mission planning the next day instead of flying during the second night.

Feest was also met by the 37th's chief of maintenance, who asked him which aircraft he had flown during Just Cause. When checking his log book later, he discovered that it was the same aircraft that he had just taken into combat over Iraq—Aircraft 816.

On arrival back at King Khalid, Leatherman remembers, "One of the first things I did after I shut down, was open the bomb bay door. I then retrieved the two Kevlar lanyards, used to fuse the bombs as they dropped; they remained on the pylon, and so I gave one of them to the crew chief and I kept

the other as a souvenir. The plane had worked great and I had no write-ups. I ran into some of the other guys as we rode back in, and we were all slapping each other on the back and talking about how well everything had worked. We went back into the mission debrief area where we had our videotape machines set up. There were a lot of F-111 guys there; I knew a couple of them, because they had worked on planning with me at Riyadh. One had been flying a jamming pattern in an EF-111 near Baghdad, so he'd seen the AAA coming up. He'd seen all of our videotapes of everybody nailing the targets that they were going for in downtown Baghdad. He came over to me and shook my hand and said, 'You know what, I saw that stuff. Anytime you guys need anything, you call and you've got it. Man I cannot believe what you guys just did and to have everybody shack the targets, its just amazing.'"

Once the first wave of F-117s were clear of the capital, the next strike occurred between 0306 and 0311 hours and was conducted by six or so Tomahawk Land-Attack Missiles (TLAMs) aimed at various government ministries and smaller telephone exchanges. With EF-111 Ravens continuing to provide blanket ECM coverage, BQM-74 target drones, together with 137 tactical air-launched decoys (TALDs), were launched to provide realistic targets to draw Iraqi SAMs. While these were being engaged, high-speed antiradiation missiles (HARMs), fired by Air Force F-4G Wild Weasels and Navy F/A-18 Hornets, engaged the missile batteries. Shortly after 0330 hours, more than 200 HARMs were simultaneously homing in on their targets. Within just five minutes of this massive, coordinated launch, most of Baghdad's tactical radars had been obliterated.

The second wave of 12 F-117s began reaching Baghdad at 0400 hours, just as hundreds of coalition aircraft struck Iraqi airfields to the south. Al Whitley had been directed by General Buster Glosson to fly on the first night's operations, like all other 14th Air Division wing commanders. During that second Nighthawk raid, the capital's SOC was visited a second time, as was the air force headquarters and IOCs at Al Taqaddum and Ar-Rutba. Also attacked was the IOC at Rasheed Air Base and the presidential bunker in Baghdad. A third raid consisting of eight Nighthawks hit SOCs, a chemical/biological facility and ammunition stores.

Lights under the wings and fuselage of the KC-135s help receivers position themselves in readiness to receive the boom. *U.S. Air Force*

Home for the 37th TFW (Provisional) throughout Desert Shield, Desert Storm, and beyond. *U.S. Air Force*

Having been concerned about missing all the action back in August, Major Mike Mahar flew the final Team Stealth strike on day one. Mahar recalls:

My mission called for me to deliver a 2,000-pound GBU-27 on a munitions storage bunker just outside Baghdad. My TOT was 0501 hours, which was less than desirable, because this was more than two hours after the first shots were fired and gave the enemy plenty of time to prepare a welcome. Additionally, dawn would be rapidly approaching, and I certainly didn't want to overstay my visit in Iraq and be highlighted by daylight. I rendezvoused with a KC-135 tanker shortly after takeoff and then flew to the Iraqi border, nearly two hours away. As I took my final on load of

fuel and departed the tanker, I knew I'd crossed the point of no return. I was now alone and isolated, on a preplanned route, through enemy territory to my target. I went over my check list again and again to ensure that I hadn't made a fatal mistake, which could be as trivial as forgetting to turn off my exterior lights. It was a very dark, peaceful night, as I flew high above the Iraqi desert. I soon began to relax and review the photos of my target.

Approximately 30 minutes after crossing the Iraqi border I noticed the first indication of trouble. I was approaching Baghdad from the south, still several hundred miles away. Below me, was a long ribbon of light, pointing the way to my target. I realized that this was a line of vehicle head-

lights, moving south from Baghdad—a mass evacuation. I realized that I could no longer count on the element of surprise. As I approached within 100 miles of Baghdad, I could clearly see the lights of the city. I saw numerous explosions that reminded me of cluster bomblets. My first reaction was that we had clearly seized the upper hand and must be keeping the enemies' heads down. Then, I realized I wasn't watching air-ground cluster bomblets, but rather ground-air AAA and missiles. Up until this time, I had never actually seen actual anti-aircraft fire. The sky over Baghdad was lit up with a breathtaking display of multicolored fireworks. The 23-millimeter projectiles looked like long curving ropes of red fire. The 57-millimeter AAA reminded me of flash bulbs exploding in a darkened sports arena. Surface-air missiles were corkscrewing menacingly through the air from all directions. I never imagined a spectacle quite so dramatic. The density of the barrage fire looked impenetrable. I thought I would probably

never see another sunrise. As my aircraft entered the dome of anti-aircraft fire over the city, it began to shake from the turbulence. I could actually smell the distinct odor of exploded munitions. I looked off to the side of the airplane to see a flash of light as an enemy missile exploded in front of me. The explosion was so large that the flash was blinding. As my vision began to come back, I noticed the standby altimeter on my instrument panel winding down, I was in a dramatic descent and within just a few seconds I'd be impacting the ground. As rapidly as the altimeter wound down, it began winding up again. What had actually happened was an anomaly within the instrument, the aircraft hadn't been hit at all and was flying straight and level just as it had been programmed to do, but the effect was jolting.

The activity outside the cockpit was so bright, I didn't need a light to view my target photos. I electronically lowered my seat to eliminate the distraction of the enemy's fire and concentrated on delivering my weapon

Aircraft 839 first flew on June 14, 1989. Operated by the 415th TFS during Desert Storm, the aircraft, christened _Midnight Reaper,_ completed 39 sorties. _U.S. Air Force_

via the small television screen in front of me. As rapidly as I entered this cauldron of enemy fire, I exited into a calm and peaceful desert night. During the previous 30, 40 minutes, I had experienced an amazing extreme of emotion: from the terror of facing almost certain death to elation at having somehow survived, which in turn led me to feel guilty, for surely, most of my colleagues must have perished. I was absolutely amazed when we later broke radio silence to report in prior to crossing back into friendly territory. Somehow we had all survived.

For me the most memorable event of this first mission was watching the sun rise over the Saudi Arabian desert, during my return to home base. Earlier that night, I hadn't expected to see daybreak again and the gift of witnessing another sunrise became a very emotional event. When I arrived back at our home base after this first night of combat, I really didn't expect to see too much activity. The base was very much geared to night operations and mornings were reserved for sleep. Even though I was the last aircraft to return that morning, hundreds of "Team Stealth" men and women lined the taxiways and saluted as I taxied by. It was clear that everyone was proud of the part they played in this highly successful air battle. Although physically and emotionally exhausted, I lifted myself out of the cockpit after shutting down the engines and waded through the crowd that greeted the jet. Someone slapped me hard on the back and said, "Great job, but you'd better get some rest because you're on the schedule to fly again tomorrow." This was the first time it had occurred to me that we might have to return to Baghdad. It was convenient never to think too far ahead when you were "on the tip of the spear." In fact, for 42 nights we continued to launch sorties attacking critical targets in Iraq. Although the element of uncertainty decreased over time and my confidence in the F-117's capabilities grew, flying into combat never became routine.

The burden of command lay heavily during the early hours of January 17, as Buster Glosson recalls:

H Hour, of the first attack on Baghdad, was at 3:00 in the morning. At about 2:00 in the morning, Gen. Horner and I walked separately into the ops center and sat down. In front of us was a large screen, which electronically depicted every airplane, color coded. It was amazing how little conversation we had; it was a very sobering time. The thought process of Gen. Horner and myself was probably the same; we both knew that we had done the best we could do, and that some of those people, in all likelihood, would lose their lives. The loss of human life is so revolting dwelling on it would be debilitating, so you force yourself to think of the task at hand. You must stay ahead of the unknown. Everything will not go as you planned. You hope you have created such confusion by so massive and disruptive an attack, that Iraq wouldn't be able to do anything. But we had no assurance that chemical or biological weapons wouldn't come flying back the other way.

During the first three hours I was pleased with how the war was unfolding, but I was concerned that it was unfolding too perfectly. Just as I was about to permit myself to succumb to the euphoria of things going perfect, one of the F-117s due to low fuel, diverted to another base for landing. The first call I got was, "F-117 such and such is missing." It was only for a brief

Under a sky similar to that found back at Tonopah, Aircraft 821, *Sneak Attack* (foreground), was the personal mount for Major Wes Wyrick (Bandit 330). It completed 32 combat missions. *U.S. Air Force*

Parked in a riveted taxiway and with a unique four-section ladder in place for access to the cockpit, an F-117 receives some TLC from avionics technicians. *U.S. Air Force*

just three days was an incredible achievement and a tribute to not just those who conducted the air strikes, but also to the planners who had devoted hundreds of hours to "getting it right." In order to attack more highly defended Baghdad targets each night, eight more Nighthawks left Tonopah for Langley Air Force Base at 0800 hours (Pacific time) on January 17 on the first stage of their journey to King Khalid. As the war continued, F-117s of the 37th TFW (Provisional) continued to score spectacular results.

Day three of the air campaign, January 19, was to see the start of a series of attacks on targets in the Baghdad area made by nonstealthy aircraft in daylight. A formation consisting of 32 F-16s would strike the Daura petroleum refinery together with Baghdad's nuclear research center. Sixteen F-15Cs provided a combat air patrol, four EF-111s supplied jamming support, eight F-4G Wild Weasels provided defense suppression, and 15 tankers provided AR support.

period of time, 10 minutes or so, and then another call came in from the base where he had landed to say that the F-117 had refueled and was heading back to Khamis Mushait. During a war there is always something that keeps you alert and focused. The time to celebrate is after it's all over; you cannot afford the luxury of losing concentration or focus. If you do, the result will be unnecessary loss of life. You absolutely must be obsessed with minimum loss of life; if you're not, you have no business being in command.

As the battle continued to unfold, it was almost eerie, how precise everything was happening. We were concerned we weren't getting all the information, but as it turned out, God smiled on us. A lot of people worked very hard, and most important, those pilots were absolutely tremendous; they never flinched. When things got a little tough they did exactly what they'd been trained to do, what the technology permitted them to do, and that's why we were so successful, eye-watering successful, in the first 24 hours. The world saw it on TV, or at least, to a large extent. As the first three hours unfolded, Horner and I felt both pride and humility; but it's not something that you dwell on. You can't afford to be a bystander when people's lives are on the line.

The sheer number of Iraqi AAA weapons ensured that low-altitude flight remained a no-go area for allied aircraft for some time to come; however, the success of the coalition in neutralizing the multibillion-dollar Iraqi integrated air-defense system to create a safe (in relative terms) medium altitude haven in

Codenamed Package Q, a combination of enemy smoke screens, bad weather, and heavy AAA conspired to ensure that no damage was inflicted on the reactors, and two of the F-16s were shot down. The idea of taking the war to Baghdad 24 hours a day had to be shelved, at least for the immediate future; the skies over the capital remained the preserve of the F-117s.

The first wave of day seven of the 37th's air war consisted of 14 Nighthawks from the 415th TFS targeted to hit the Balad Southeast air base. Twenty-one of the GBU-10s dropped on the airfield's HASs hit their targets; however, the bombs' fuses were set on instantaneous (instead of delay). They penetrated the outer layer of concrete only to be deflected by a "sandwich" of dirt and hard core that lay packed beneath, thereby failing to penetrate the inner concrete shell, leaving the aircraft parked inside unscathed. An embarrassing mistake, but to err is human.

The next night, intelligence received information that eight Tu-16 Badgers at Al Taquaddum Air Base were being loaded with chemical weapons for a dawn strike. Several F-117s of the 416th were retargeted at the last minute to attack the bombers. Three of the Tu-16s were taken out by GBU-10s dropped by the 416th; three more were destroyed by nonstealthy assets later that day.

The first wave out of King Khalid on the night of January 27 had some unfinished business to attend. Six Nighthawks from the 415th attacked the HASs at Balad Southeast for a second time; on this occasion, however, their weapons bays touted GBU-27s with delayed fusing. During the five intervening days since the last attack, the Iraqis had mistakenly concluded that the construction of their HASs at Balad could withstand bomb attacks and had therefore packed more aircraft in for "safe storage." The GBU-27s penetrated the shelters, causing devastation among the tightly packed aircraft inside. With four Nighthawks from the 416th enjoying similar HAS-bursting success at Rasheed and the same airfields receiving a further visit from the 37th's second wave of the night, Iraqi fighters were being systematically wiped out on the ground.

The success of the Black Jet wasn't just restricted to attacking strategic targets in Baghdad and other highly defended targets, as General Buster Glosson recalls, "I used them to destroy the pipelines that fed the fire trenches Sad-

dam intended to fill with oil and ignite as the ground attack started. The F-117 took this option away from him. I also used the F-117 to attack targets others had been unable to destroy. A particular case in point was one of the bridges across the Euphrates, near Basra. Eight airplanes dropped more than 36 bombs, and the bridge was still up. I sent one F-117; he dropped two bombs and disconnected the bridge from both banks."

The third and final wave of F-117s on the schedule for February 13 consisted of ten aircraft, four from the 415th TFS and six from the 416th TFS. The target list included various headquarters buildings, miscellaneous bridges, a missile site at Al Adbaliyah, and a C3 bunker that had been on the Black

Aircraft 816 (foreground) first flew on October 30, 1985. During the Gulf War, it was christened *Lone Wolf*. **It was operated by the 415th TFS and completed 39 combat missions.** *U.S. Air Force*

Hole's target list for some time. Originally constructed as 1 of 25 similar shelters for the civilian population of Baghdad, the Al Firdos bunker together with two others, had been upgraded and further reinforced by western contractors to serve as a hideout for the Iraqi leadership. At the beginning of Desert Storm, U.S. intelligence noted that the Iraqis had camouflaged the bunker's roof and, together with other activity in the vicinity, concluded that the Iraqi Intelligence Service, located several blocks away, was using the facility. Two Nighthawks each dropped GBU-27s on the structure, scoring direct hits. According to Iraq's Foreign Ministry, as many as 400 people were killed in the attack, many of them women and children. Satellite reconnaissance had failed to establish that the families of intelligence officials in addition to others from the Ameriyya suburb used the facility each night; and although a classified intelligence report later revealed that a senior Iraqi security official and a third of his staff had been killed in the bunker, such peripheral assertions couldn't possibly justify the raid and neither were they intended to do so. If U.S. intelligence had been in receipt of all the facts, the attack clearly would not have been approved.

The Al Firdos incident would have a profound impact on the conduct of the rest of Desert Storm. General Colin Powell immediately placed a moratorium on all Baghdad targets; none could be attacked unless it had his specific approval. Glosson would later remark, "There's no question it had an impact. It took the pressure off the leadership in Baghdad at a crucial time, and that was not to anybody's advantage and was the wrong decision. The Iraqis had structured or attempted to set up a communications capability to the field army, using mobile assets. These backup systems had not been used before. To not take those switching nodes and fiber-optic connectors out permitted the leadership in Baghdad to maintain more direct command and control of the field army and scud units, than would have been possible, if Baghdad had not been effectively put off limits."

Aircraft 826, first flew on March 2, 1987. During Desert Storm, *Nachtfalke* was operated by the 415th TFS and completed 29 missions. Note both the stars and stripes and the Saudi flags hanging from the HAS roof. *U.S. Air Force*

On January 17, three Tornado GR1s from XV Squadron, RAF, operating from Bahrain got airborne for a coordinated attack on the Ar Rumaylah airfield complex. Having successfully completed a prestrike AR from Victor tankers, the aircraft proceeded at low level to the target area. One of the Tornado's involved, ZD 791 (call sign, Norwich 03) was flown by Flight Lieutenant John Peters and his navigator, John Nichol. The formation split up, but remained within visual contact. Flying over the desert floor at 50 feet and 540 knots, with one minute to go, Nichol performed three target offset checks to update the aircraft's navigation system. Thirty seconds to go and the target bars were perfectly aligned. Exactly on schedule, Peters initiated a 4-g pull-up. During the loft-delivery maneuver, eight 1,000-pound bombs should have arched away from the attacking Tornado and slammed into the airfield's runways and taxiways. However, a malfunction failed to release the weapons at the predesignated point. With the aircraft's energy depleted, Peters completed the pull-up and rolled the lumbering aircraft off its back. He then jettisoned the bombs and slammed the aircraft into a 4-g turn, holding 60 degrees of bank to take them onto their escape heading. It was then that a shoulder-fired SA-16 infrared missile found its target, ZD 791's right exhaust outlet. The aircraft bucked as the missile impacted and turned into a burning meteorite. Successfully firing their ejector seats, they were catapulted into another nightmare after being subsequently captured by the Iraqis.

On February 19, General Buster Glosson received information from previously reliable, regional intelligence sources, that troubled him deeply. The reports expressed concern about the well being of our POWs. These sources had established that all our POWs, including a CBS news team, were being held at the Baath Party's intelligence service headquarters facilities in Baghdad.

Ordnance specialists attach the forward canards to a GBU-10, which is to be hauled by John Hesterman's (Bandit 339) mount, Aircraft 791, *Lazy Ace*. This aircraft first flew on November 22, 1982, and completed 33 missions during Desert Storm. *U.S. Air Force*

With the suck-in door open and the crew chiefs intercom lead disconnected from its front nose wheel bay jack-plug, this F-117A is about to taxi. *U.S. Air Force*

Its staff was renowned for brutal interrogation methods that routinely included torture. The next day, another report indicated that treatment of the prisoners had further deteriorated. A day later, Glosson directed that an attack should be planned against the intelligence facility. Glosson remembers:

On the 22nd February, I was informed that our POWs were all in one building located furthest from the complex's car parking lot. I was also advised that people mysteriously disappeared from that facility. Therefore, based on the proceeding, I directed that the 23rd February air tasking order be changed as follows:

1. *Four (4) F-117As will attack target L-42 (Baath Party regional HQ intelligence complex).*
2. *Weapons: 4 GBU-27s (2,000-pound and instantaneous fuse).*
3. *Aim point: Multistory building closest to car parking lot.*
4. *Attack must occur before 2100 local on 23 February.*

The next day I reviewed specifics on the intel HQ mission on a secure phone to the 37th TFW commander, Col. Whitley. I discussed with him the specific aim point and indicated that no other aim point was acceptable; furthermore, if the pilots had any doubt, they were not to drop their weapons. I did not at any time discuss POW location with Col. Whitley. It was during the course of this telephone conversation, that I learned Lieutenant Colonel Greg Feest was to be one of the pilots flying this mission. Colonel Tony Tolin and Lieutenant Colonel Rick Lewis were the only people knowledgeable of all aspects of this POW mission. On the night of 23 February '91, I made the following diary entry: " . . . God, I pray you will guide these bombs!!"

John Nichol now eloquently describes what happened next:

There came a low moaning, a rush through the air, almost human at first, then swelling to a metallic shriek, until the sound of something screaming filled the universe. There was a blinding flash. I normally counted the interval between flash and bang. There was no interval. The whole building shook to its foundations, tottering. The blast wave from the bomb lifted me bodily off the floor. It took me so long to come back down, that for one moment of terrifying eternity I thought the whole floor had been blown away from under me, that I was falling down through the building.

The noise came again, the same low whining to begin with, then the rushing noise cutting in on top, louder this time even than before, more like an express train, a heavy locomotive, thundering in with its whistle shrieking. It hit. The pressure-wave from 2,000 pounds of high-explosive ripped through the prison, the massive building quivering in its path. Every bone in my body rattled. The smell of burning filled the air, along with a hissing sound, as though a gas main had ruptured. I noticed that the floor was covered in dust.

That's two, I thought. How many more? I scrambled out of the sleeping bag and into my clothes. I wanted to be ready to run from it if the building came down around my ears. I had carefully saved some water, in a spare bowl I had conned out of the guards, intending the next day to have my first wash in four weeks. Now, I put this next to me, in case a fire broke out. Then I tore a big square of cloth from my blanket, folded it carefully into the larger bowl, and put the whole thing on my head, like a tin helmet, for protection. It was the only thing I could think of doing. I had nothing else to hide under.

Outside, I could here people banging on their cell doors. Someone was screaming, "Let me out, let me out. I'm on fire, the walls are coming in. . . ."

The next bomb came thundering towards the prison. Three. I remembered books about the Second World War, the kind of book in which someone says: "It's the one you don't hear that kills you." It didn't help. It sounded as though a jet was about to crash on us; the noise of the bomb was deafening, its mass disturbing a gigantic volume of air as it rushed towards the end of its trajectory, its kinetic energy enormous. Now the boot was on the other foot: Instead of sitting up there ourselves, watching the radar, clinically ticking off the initial point of the bombing run, clearing down the offsets, pickling the bombs onto the target, we were the target. It was a bloody odd feeling.

This time, part of the ceiling came in. Chunks of plaster fell round my head and shoulders. Bits of chocolate-brown boredom came whizzing round my ears, as the tiles pinged off the walls. I could hear rubble falling and everybody was yelling now, at the tops of their voices, to be let out. The bombing was more and more accurate. I was petrified, waiting for number four to hit the bull's-eye—me.

I didn't have to wait long. An American shouted the obvious and inevitable: "Incoming . . . !," the grinding roar of the bomb trucking in, swallowing the end of the word. The first three explosions had loosened the building's joints; the fourth blew it apart at the seams.

A moment or two of shocked quiet, then the yelling started again. The Americans were trying to calm everything down, to formulate a plan of action. "OK," said one of them, "OK, it's all right; it's all right! Let's see if we can sort everything out. . . ."

Greg Feest flew Aircraft 796 during the POW attack, the after action report indicated three direct hits and one near miss. The aircraft video review indicated four hits. Regional sources informed Gen. Glosson that at 2345 hours, all POWs were alive and moved to another facility.

On February 24 at 0300 hours (local), the coalition ground assault began. In true blitzkrieg fashion, it was all over in just three days. On February 27 Kuwait City was liberated and a cease-fire declared.

In June 1991 Gen. Glosson met some of those POWs and remembers, "During discussions they mentioned being bombed. I was stunned, to say the least. Clearly, their exact location was the intel complex building closest to the car parking lot, not the building farthest from the car parking lot. The POW mission was the toughest decision I was confronted with during the Gulf War. I knew the risk was high, but to me the alternative was unacceptable."

At the end of the Gulf War, Glosson noted, "Reflecting on the Gulf War, and specifically the F-117 and what it was able to accomplish, only one word seems appropriate: *awesome*. People have said, correctly, that its success was eye-watering. But the real issue is why? The technology, the air crew training, the willingness of leadership to believe in stealth, and the understanding of what was to be accomplished—all of those things fit together. The single most important accomplishment of the F-117 during the Gulf War, however, was that it saved thousands and thousands of lives. Very close behind is the fact that it revolutionized the way we're going to fight wars in the future and the way people think about wars. Additionally, in the future belligerent nation states will pause to reflect, before they get carried away with mischief."

F-117A 415th Fighter Squadron weapons bay artwork used during Operation Desert Storm.

Aircraft 789, *Black Magic*, completed 31 combat missions. *Jim Goodall collection*

Aircraft 790, *Deadly Jester*, completed 30 combat missions. *Jim Goodall collection*

Aircraft 791, *Lazy Ace*, completed 33 combat missions. *Jim Goodall collection*

Aircraft 793, *Wiley E. Coyote's Tritonial Express*, completed 33 combat missions. *Jim Goodall col-*

Aircraft 794, *Delta Dawn*, completed 35 combat missions. *Jim Goodall collection*

Aircraft 796, *Fatal Attraction*, completed 29 combat missions. *Jim Goodall collection*

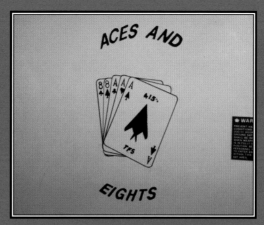

Aircraft 798, *Aces and Eights*, completed 34 combat missions. *Jim Goodall collection*

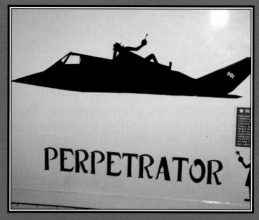

Aircraft 801, *Perpetrator*, completed 38 combat missions. *Jim Goodall collection*

Aircraft 806, *Something Wicked*, completed 39 combat missions. *Jim Goodall collection*

Aircraft 807, *The Chickenhawk*, completed 14 combat missions. *Jim Goodall collection*

Aircraft 808, *Thor*, completed 37 combat missions. *Jim Goodall collection*

Aircraft 811, *Double Down*, completed 33 combat missions. *Jim Goodall collection*

Aircraft 812, *No Name*, completed 42 combat missions. *Jim Goodall collection*

Aircraft 816, *Lone Wolf*, completed 30 combat missions. *Jim Goodall collection*

Aircraft 818, *The Overachiever*, completed 38 combat missions. *Jim Goodall collection*

Aircraft 821, *Sneak Attack*, completed 32 combat missions. *Jim Goodall collection*

Aircraft 825, *Mad Max*, completed 33 combat missions. *Jim Goodall collection*

Aircraft 826, *Nachtfalke*, completed 29 combat missions. *Jim Goodall collection*

Aircraft 839, *Midnight Reaper*, completed 39 combat missions. *Jim Goodall collection*

Aircraft 843, *Affectionately Christine*, completed 33 combat missions. *Jim Goodall collection*

F-117A 416th Fighter Squadron weapons bay artwork used during Operation Desert Storm.

Aircraft 786, *War Pig*, completed 24 combat missions. *Jim Goodall collection*

Aircraft 797, *Spell Bound*, completed 8 combat missions. *Jim Goodall collection*

Aircraft 799, *Midnight Rider*, completed 21 combat missions. *Jim Goodall collection*

Aircraft 802, *Black Magic (Witch)*, completed 19 combat missions. *Jim Goodall collection*

Aircraft 803, *Unexpected Guest*, completed 33 combat missions. *Jim Goodall collection*

Aircraft 810, *Dark Angel*, completed 26 combat missions. *Jim Goodall collection*

Aircraft 813, *The Toxic Avenger*, completed 35 combat missions. *Jim Goodall collection*

Aircraft 814, *Final Verdict*, completed 34 combat missions. *Jim Goodall collection*

Aircraft 817, *Shaba*, completed 18 combat missions. *Jim Goodall collection*

Aircraft 819, *Raven Beauty*, completed 30 combat missions. *Jim Goodall collection*

Aircraft 829, *Avenging Angel*, completed 23 combat missions. *Jim Goodall collection*

Aircraft 830, *Black Assassin*, completed 31 combat missions. *Jim Goodall collection*

Aircraft 832, *Once Bitten*, completed 30 combat missions. *Jim Goodall collection*

Aircraft 833, *Black Devil*, completed 30 combat missions.

Aircraft 834, *Necromancer*, completed 34 combat missions. *Jim Goodall collection*

Aircraft 835, *The Dragon*, completed 26 combat missions. *Jim Goodall collection*

Aircraft 836, *Christine* (Red F-117A), completed 39 combat missions. *Jim Goodall collection*

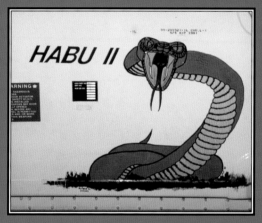

Aircraft 837, *Habu II*, completed 31 combat missions. *Jim Goodall collection*

Aircraft 838, *Magic Hammer*, completed 36 combat missions. *Jim Goodall collection*

Aircraft 840, *Black Widow*, completed 32 combat missions. *Jim Goodall collection*

Aircraft 841, *Mystic Warrior*, completed 18 combat missions. *Jim Goodall collection*

Aircraft 842, *It's Hammertime*, completed 33 combat missions. *Jim Goodall collection*

chapter six

HOLLOMAN
AND PALMDALE

Leading the first element of eight F-117As to return home from King Khalid, Colonel Al Whitley and two KC-10s containing 130 support personnel touched down at Nellis Air Force Base in front of a crowd of 25,000 on Monday, April 1, 1991. During the following months, all but a handful of the 37th's F-117As returned home. Those remaining in Saudi Arabia, plus some 100 tactical reconnaissance and support aircraft, made up the backbone of Operation Southern Watch. To staff the F-117A deployment, a three-month rotation cycle was established for some 200 pilots, maintenance staff, and other key personnel. Back at Tonopah, arrangements were being finalized to relocate the 37th Wing to Holloman Air Force Base, New Mexico. The first aircraft to be delivered was the 791, which arrived from Tonopah on January 7, 1992, for maintenance familiarization. The move officially got underway, however, on May 8, when Aircraft 814, flown by Lieutenant Colonel "Moose" Merritt of the 416th TFS touched down. On July 8, 1992, the 37th FW at Tonopah Test Range took part in an inactivation ceremony. "Later that day, we had a reception at Nellis Air Force Base Officers Club, recognizing the 37th FW's accomplishments and thanking the Nellis community for all their support over the years," says Colonel Al Whitley. "On July 10, I proceeded to Clemson, South Carolina, to join my family and to start my final assignment at the Clemson University Senior ROTC unit as a professor of aerospace studies."

For 14 years, Holloman had been an F-15 Eagle base. Boosting a long proud heritage, its wing—the 49th—had roots established in the Pacific theater of operations of World War II. Senior Air Force staff officers decided that the F-117A wing should adopt the lineage of the 49th FW. Consequently, commensurate with the inactivation of Tonopah, the 37th FW was deactivated and its assets transferred across to the 49th FW. Similarly, command of

the F-117A wing was also transferred from Al Whitley to Brigadier General Lloyd "Fig" Newton. Unusually, however, the squadron designations of the F-117A units remained initially unchanged. The move at last reunited families, enabling them to join their loved ones in living quarters on or close to the base. It also eradicated the need for Key Airlines to shuttle more than 2,500 personnel on 75 weekly flights to and from their place of work, an action that would, in itself, save millions of dollars a year.

On Tuesday, August 4, 1992, the first Holloman-based F-117A was lost in an accident. Captain John B. Mills of the 416th FS was forced to eject from Aircraft 801 (not 810 or 802, as reported elsewhere), after it entered an uncommanded roll and caught fire. The crash occurred just 8 miles northwest of Holloman, and Mills, a former A-10 pilot, landed safely, just half a mile from the blazing wreckage. The pilot then hitched a ride back to the base with a highway patrolman, having sustained just a cut chin and a few bruises in the incident. A crash investigation identified the cause as an improperly reinstalled bleed air duct, which led to a hydraulic line malfunction to flight controls and a fire.

The move to Holloman also signaled a steady integration of the F-117A into theater operational planning, enabling it to become a true "force multiplier," something that was impossible to achieve during its years in the black. Accordingly, the 416th participated in Exercise Team Spirit, a short deployment to South Korea. In June 1993, eight F-117As from the 415th deployed briefly to Gilze-Rijen, in the Netherlands, for Exercise Central Enterprise.

Aircraft 800, the personal mount of the 8th FS commander, first flew on November 10, 1983. *Lockheed Martin*

was postponed until 2115 (Baghdad time) the next day. Six F-117As participated in the measured strike, each equipped with just one bomb. The GBU-27 designated to hit the Al-Amara IOC found its target; however, bad weather again intervened, highlighting the shortcomings of a nonradar-directed, target acquisition and designation system. The aircraft tasked against the rebuilt Tallil SOC failed to locate its target. Of the remaining four aircraft targeted to hit SA-3 radar sites, one knocked out the unit at Ashshuaybah, two failed in their attempts to hit the Nasiriya site, and the pilot of the fourth aircraft misjudged his turn point losing his laser-guided bomb into a large single-story farmhouse, a mile from his designated target, the radar site at Basra. This action was followed up four days later by a cruise missile attack against the Za' Faraniyah complex, a site known to be responsible for the manufacture of machinery for Iraq's nuclear program.

By mid-1993, an argument concerning the squadrons designations that had continued since the F-117As arrived at Holloman was finally resolved. The synergy of Senior Trend's operational environment and that of the squadron's night-fighter roots during World War II failed to carry the argument for its designation to remain unchanged. Consequently, on July 30, 1993, the 415th and 416th Fighter Squadrons were redesignated the 9th and 8th Fighter Squadrons, respectively. Then in December 1993, the training unit, the 417th, also succumbed and became the 7th FS.

Following the disbanding of the Soviet Union and the Warsaw Pact, budgetary considerations and other issues focused the Air Force's attention on other priorities. The number of war-ready F-117As declined from 37 out of a fleet of 45 in 1992 to a mere 28 aircraft in 1994. Acknowledging the problem, the Air Force allocated an additional $12 million to help alleviate chronic maintenance shortfalls to Senior Trend in 1993, assigning a further $174 million to the program in 1994.

As the threat of Iraqi aggression against Saudi Arabia faded, so too did Saudi willingness to provide the United States with offensive bases. Therefore, the Senior Trend deployment to King Khalid Air Base came to an end. Saddam Hussein remained in firm control of Iraq, however, and the games of brinkmanship continued. In August and early September 1996, he ordered a vicious attack against Kurdish factions in northern Iraq. The United States responded by firing 44 cruise missiles against four air defense sites in southern Iraq. In addition, President Bill Clinton announced an expansion of the southern no fly-zone, to further help protect Shiites in the region. On September 11, 1996, Iraq fired an SA-6 at two Air Force F-16s patrolling in the northern no-fly zone. In response, Secretary of Defense William Perry announced that four B-52s, equipped with cruise missiles, would be deployed to Diego Garcia, a tiny island in the Indian Ocean, and a number of F-117As would also be dispatched to the region. As the Saudis refused to allow the Black Jets to be based in their country, agreement was gained to station the aircraft in Kuwait. Consequently, on September 11, eight F-117As of the 9th

In addition to being the first pilot to drop a weapon in anger from Senior Trend, and first to drop a bomb at the start of Desert Storm, Greg Feest was also the first Air Force pilot to reach 1,000 hours of flight time in the F-117; a milestone achieved on February 11, 1995. *Colonel Greg Feest*

During the intervening two years, post-Desert Storm, Iraq's Saddam Hussein continued to test the resolve of the West to respond to various provocations. These included cat-and-mouse games with United Nations weapons inspectors, numerous cross-border incursions into Kuwait, and a practice of locking onto Coalition aircraft that were patrolling the no-fly zones established in the north and south of Iraq, to protect the Kurds and Shiites.

On Tuesday, January 12, 1993, the Bush administration lost its patience with the loathsome dictator and ordered the 49th's F-117A Saudi detachment to strike against air defense targets. Due to bad weather, however, the attack

Fighter Squadron together with its commander, Lieutenant Colonel Greg Feest, deployed to Al Jaber Air Base, Kuwait, in Operation Desert Strike. The flight from Holloman was direct and lasted 16 hours, establishing in the process yet another milestone in Senior Trend's formidable career—the longest nonstop flight to date.

During the night of Friday, April 5, 1995, Aircraft 824 came close to being written off when it was forced to conduct an emergency recovery back into Holloman. The aircraft caught fire and was badly damaged, but the pilot escaped unhurt. Considerable work was necessary by Lockheed Martin to restore the aircraft to an airworthy state, which was finally achieved on July 15, 1995, when Tom Morgenfeld successfully completed its functional check flight.

The 49th lost its second F-117A from Holloman (the fifth to date) on May 10, 1995, at 2225 hours. Aircraft 822 was being flown by Captain Ken Levens of the 9th Fighter Squadron on a night-training flight when contact was lost. The aircraft crashed on Red Mesa at the Zuri Indian Reservation. The pilot hadn't attempted to eject prior to the crash, and 822 gouged out a 20-foot deep crater upon impact. Having received his bandit number (Bandit 461) on December 16, 1994, Capt. Levens had accumulated just 70 hours on the aircraft prior to the incident. An accident investigation team established that there were no signs of mechanical or electrical failure prior to impact and that pilot disorientation seemed yet again to be the most likely cause of the tragedy.

Major Lee Gustin (Bandit 297) and his daughter are re-united at Nellis following a triumphant return. *U.S. Air Force*

The sixth F-117A to be lost in an accident occurred publicly and in spectacular fashion. On September 14, 1997, Major Bryan Knight, an instructor with the 7th FS flying Aircraft 793, was coming to the end of his expertly choreographed display routine during an air show at Chesapeake Bay, near Baltimore, Maryland. Flying at 380 knots and at a height of between 600 and 700 feet, he entered a 15-degree climb when the left outboard elevon made at least four rapid oscillations, causing a 2.5-foot section of the inboard elevon to become detached. The aircraft then rolled rapidly left (90 degrees within 0.8 seconds) and then pitched sharply up into a high angle of attack. The landing gear was seen in the down position, and the aircraft was completely out of control. Knight managed to eject safely before the disintegrated aircraft hit the ground. About a dozen spectators escaped with only minor injuries in what could so easily have been a disaster. The subsequent accident investigation determined that the incident had occurred because four Hi-Lok fasteners used to secure the elevon hydraulic actuator to a spanwise, "Brooklyn Bridge" I-beam, had not been reinstalled following maintenance conducted at Holloman in January 1996. Over the intervening 20 months, this subjected the assembly to additional air loads and vibrations, causing three L-brackets and

Colonel Al Whitley stands next to his aircraft, the 813 *The Toxic Avenger*, on return to Nellis. Displaying the 37th Wing patch on his left shoulder, he also wears a Tactical Air Command patch over his right breast pocket. Following extensive reorganization of the Air Force, TAC, SAC, and MAC became part of a unified command structure known as Air Combat Command. *Lockheed Martin*

both T-brackets that secured the assembly to break. This, in turn, lead to the inevitable. A postaccident inspection conducted on the rest of the F-117A fleet discovered some loose fasteners, but no missing ones. The accident prompted the Air Force and Lockheed Martin into discussions to redesign the actuator, enabling its removal, while leaving the "Brooklyn Bridge" modification in place.

Flight Test the Improvements

The move from Area 51 to Palmdale was authorized on March 25, 1991, and completed on March 27, one year later. Activity from the new base continued at a brisk pace with Aircraft 831, flown by Lieutenant Colonel Chris Seat completing Detachment 5's first flight from Palmdale the day before. The first Senior Trend test sortie for Palmdale was a weapons evaluations flight, flown in Aircraft 784 by Jim Thomas on April 23, 1992.

On July 29, 1989, a proposal was made to improve IRADS. Following the results of a design competition nearly two years later, Texas Instruments (now called Raytheon), provided a system with increased target detection range and a longer laser life. These components were mounted in a new, F 3 turret, the first of which was delivered to Palmdale on May 1, 1992. The system underwent flight testing in Aircraft 784 and 831 between August 14, 1992, and February 12, 1993, after which a comprehensive report was compiled and submitted on July 26 that same year. Having successfully demonstrated its enhanced capabilities, a decision was made to proceed with a fleet modification program. The first units for this became available on August 30, 1994, with the first production turret modification completed on October 1.

Once an F-117A was stealthed up during an operational sortie—retracting antennas and the like—it was fully committed to execute the mission as briefed. Further communication was impossible until the aircraft arrived back at a prearranged contact point and once again had extended its antenna. Aware of the shortcomings of this procedure, a low-observability communications study was authorized on October 23, 1991, to identify methods of overcoming such problems. The study was completed in February 1992, and on August 31 that same year, Jim Thomas flew Aircraft 783 on its first low-observability antenna evaluation sortie. The test program lasted for two months, during which time the "stealthy antenna," located on the aircraft's underside, was thoroughly evaluated. Following submission of a final report on November 13, 1992, the go-ahead for full-scale development of the system was received on May 12, 1993. Work started four months later, on September 16, to upgrade the fleet.

On October 10, 1994, the Ring Laser Gyro Navigation Improvement Program (RNIP) commenced. Initially designed to evaluate the proposed replacement of SPN-GEANS by the Honeywell H-423 Ring Laser Gyro, the program was subsequently broadened (based on earlier successes achieved by the low-observability communication antenna program) to include the addition of a Global Positioning System (GPS). A "dry bay" was created by forming a recess in the fuselage fuel tank on the upper surface of Aircraft 784. Into this was located a stealthy antenna, capable of receiving the relevant satellite-generated data. The first RNIP flight occurred on December 12, 1994, and the accuracy advantages were immediately apparent. This improvement package is also being incorporated on the entire F-117 fleet.

Full house. The entire 9th Fighter Squadron, including their 18 Black Jets, form behind "The Boss," Lieutenant Colonel Greg "Beast" Feest, for a photo-call in 1996, at Holloman Air Force Base. *Colonel Greg Feest*

"The Iron Knights" take some time out for a photo call during Operation Desert Strike. The crew was on temporary duty (TDY) at Al Jaber, Kuwait, for 90 days, after which they returned home in a KC-10, leaving their mounts to be tended and exercised for 90 more days by crews from the 8th Fighter Squadron. Despite the fire power of a Carrier battle group remaining within striking distance of Saddam Hussein, it is interesting to note how the dictator backed down in 1996 when deployment of the Black Jets was broadcast. *Photo courtesy Colonel Greg Feest*

Attending a preflight brief at Al Jaber are, from left: Lieutenant Colonel Greg "Beast" Feest, Captain Todd "Meat" Flesch, and Captain Damian "Opus" McCarthy. Having first been attacked by the Iraqis and then the allies during Desert Storm, the conditions at the Kuwaiti base were in marked contrast to those enjoyed by both crews and aircraft at King Khalid. *Colonel Greg Feest*

The advantages of a low-observable antenna, located in the F-117's upper fuselage capable of receiving satellite-generated data, was further developed when, in December 1997, the IRRCA (or Integrated Real-time Information in the Cockpit/Real-time Information Out of the Cockpit) for the combat aircraft flight test project got underway. By June 30, 1998, the first phase of the program, "real-time information into the cockpit" had been successfully demonstrated. Phase 2, "real-time information out of the cockpit" was expected to begin in early 1999.

At the heart of IRRCA is the integration of a real-time symmetric multi-processor facilitating 1.2 billion instructions per second. As the F-117A receives threat updates from satellite broadcasts, a moving map displays new threats and the processor automatically evaluates the situation. Should analysis of the threat determine that the aircraft is in jeopardy, the processor replans the route and displays the option on a new color liquid crystal diode multi-function display. Decision criteria used in the proposed reroute includes threat exposure, flying time, and landing fuel. The pilot can then accept or reject the proposed option. In addition to mission information, text and images also update the pilot on key events and weather. Evaluations carried out by the 410th Test Squadron at Palmdale indicate that the F-117A is capable of reacting to mission updates or target changes and pop-up threats, while still remaining in a stealth configuration.

On June 24, 1992, Colonel Al Whitley completed his last F-117 flight, a sortie from Wright Patterson Air Force Base, Ohio, to Tonopah Test Range. Clearing the last step, he was doused with a fire extinguisher—the traditional ceremony for a last flight (he accumulated a total of 573.9 hours in the Black Jet). *U.S. Air Force*

Next Page: Having completed 308 hours of invaluable test flying, the first FSD F-117 was retired. Following restoration by the 37th FW Logistics Group, the 57th Fighter Wing, and others, the aircraft now stands as a gate guard at Nellis Air Force Base, Nevada. *U.S. Air Force*

During the dedication ceremony of Aircraft 780, Colonel Al Whitley presented the aircraft's control stick to former test pilot Hal Farley, in recognition of his first historic flight in the aircraft. *U.S. Air Force*

On July 8, 1992, the 37th FW was deactivated at Tonopah Test Range. During a ceremony after the last aircraft had departed the base for Holloman; the 37th's standard was furled and presented by Colonel Whitley to Lieutenant General Tom Baker, the commander of the 12th Air Force. *U.S. Air Force*

In early July 1998, Jim "J. B." Brown, lead IRRCA test pilot, flew a simulated combat mission in the dedicated testbed, Aircraft 784. During the course of the sortie, a geostationary satellite transmitted a series of encrypted messages to the aircraft via its low-observable communications antenna. These messages included threat updates, mission updates, text information, and alternative target imagery.

Mission changes provided information for the real-time symmetric multiprocessor to replan the mission to an alternative target. This was followed by a text message and photos of the alternative target, which enabled Brown to verify the processor's planning results and study target details prior to acquisition and attack.

Other Evaluations

Over the years other parties have evaluated the F-117A's capabilities. The first of these being the U.S. Navy.

Lieutenant Commander Kenny Linn was just finishing his tour at Pax River when, one day in October 1984, he was contacted by the Office of the Secretary of the Navy and was requested to attend a meeting in Washington, D.C., at OP-O5. At that meeting, Kenny and one of his colleagues, Lieutenant Commander Ken Grubbs, learned that they were to conduct an aircraft evaluation on behalf of the Navy, with little more information being volunteered. They were later introduced to some Air Force personnel who briefed them into the F-117A program. The two were introduced to the aircraft in late November, and Linn remembers being surprised not only by its faceted shape but also by its large size. He also recalls, "We spent several weeks reading the 'Dash-1

manual' and whatever other documents that were available. We conducted our own emergency drills in a cockpit mock-up and also while sitting in an actual aircraft. The cockpit layout was very similar to that of the F-18, which both Ken and I were very familiar with, so transition onto the F-117A was fairly straightforward."

In total, the two Navy pilots flew the aircraft on eight occasions; during each flight they were chased by an instructor pilot in a T-38. Details of their flight log were:

Pilot	Date	A/c Serial	Time	Duration
Linn	23.10.84	783	08:38	1.3 hours
Grubbs	23.10.84	782	13:36	1.4 hours
Linn	24.10.84	782	13:18	1.6 hours
Linn	25.10.84	783	08:20	1.6 hours
Grubbs	25.10.84	783	13:05	1.3 hours
Linn	25.10.84	782	13:18	1.3 hours
Grubbs	29.10.84	782	12:33	1.5 hours
Grubbs	31.10.84	782	13:15	1.4 hours
			Total	11.4 hours

During IRRCA, evaluations the central IR sensor display, seen here, was removed and replaced with a color multifunctional display (CMFD) taken from an MH-53 helicopter. *Lockheed Martin*

143

Lead IRRCA test pilot Jim "J. B." Brown's first operational assignment, was flying F-4s with the 480th TFS, 52nd TFW at Spangdahlem Air Base, Germany. Next, he completed a tour flying F-5Es with the 527th Aggressor Squadron at Royal Air Force Alconbury, England, before being selected to attend the U.S. Air Force test pilots school. After graduating, he conducted flight tests on F-15As though Es. Between 1989 and 1992, he completed a Black World assignment before leaving the Air Force and flew Boeing 737s with United Airlines for two years before joining Lockheed. *Paul Crickmore*

In conclusion of the trials, Linn recalls, "We conducted a thorough performance review and evaluated the F-117A for suitability in the carrier environment. Unremarkably, it was not suitable at that time for CV use, although it had quite nice handling characteristics in the pattern, landing speeds were too high, and the sink rate limitations were too low. The F-117A had not been built as a CV aircraft and was not going to turn into one overnight!"

Evaluations of the F-117A were not just restricted to citizens of the United States.

The Reagan/Thatcher administrations built on an already sound relationship that existed between the United States of America and the United Kingdom. Their uncompromising stand against Communism and terrorism ensured even closer levels of cooperation. When the rest of Europe distanced itself from possible military intervention against Libya in April 1986, the U.K. government granted the necessary clearance for U.S. Air Force F-111's bombers, based in Britain, to strike at Gadhafi.

Having moved from Area 51 to Air Force Plant 42, Site 7, Palmdale, Detachment 5 of the 337th Test Squadron was redesignated the 410th Flight Test Squadron on May 1, 1993. *Paul Crickmore*

Black Magic: three aircraft representing the pinnacle of technological excellence, the U-2, SR-71, and F-117A; all products of the Skunk Works. *Lockheed Martin*

Aircraft 793 participated in a number of flight demonstrations at various air bases during the summer of 1997. It is seen here, at Langley Air Force Base, one week before being lost at Chesapeake. *Bill Crimmins*

This overt demonstration of goodwill was reciprocated by the U.S. government, when it gave two Royal Air Force pilots the opportunity to evaluate one of the United State's most closely guarded secrets—an event that up until now has remained undocumented.

While at home one evening in mid-April 1986, Squadron Leader Dave Southwood (Royal Air Force) received a telephone call from his squadron commander, Wing Commander Colin Cruickshanks. Southwood had finished an Empire Test Pilot School course in December 1985 and had gone straight onto A Squadron (the fixed-wing squadron, based at RAF Boscombe Down, Wiltshire). His decision to remain on flying status was much against the advice of many of his colleagues, who believed that the only way to move up the promotional ladder was to move out of the cockpit. Southwood vividly remembers the phone call that evening, together with the subsequent six weeks that landed him with an opportunity of a lifetime:

Colin asked me if I was available in a few weeks time, to go to the United States for a month. I replied "Yes," so the following day, both of us traveled as civilians to the Ministry of Defence (MOD) in London. There

we were briefed by the chief of air staff (CAS), Air Chief Marshal Sir David Craig. The CAS didn't have any pictures of the plane, but he had seen it on a recent visit to the States, where the opportunity for two British test pilots to fly the F-117 had been arranged. He had flown the simulator and told us that it was the most bizarre shape and that it was highly faceted.

Colin and I flew out to the U.S. in early May, again in plainclothes. This wasn't unusual, as Boscombe was then, and is now, effectively, an MOD civilian organization, although the air crew are military, which means that travel procedures are not the same as on a normal RAF station, so we flew out with British Airways. We were unable to tell anyone where we were going let alone what we were going to be doing. The station commandant at Boscombe gave Colin a hard time, as he was unable to tell him where he was going. The British Embassy in the United States was unaware of our trip, and our wives were just given a phone number in London to call if they had any emergencies. We were also issued a card which had the phone number on it of someone in the Pentagon. This was to use if we received any clearance problems.

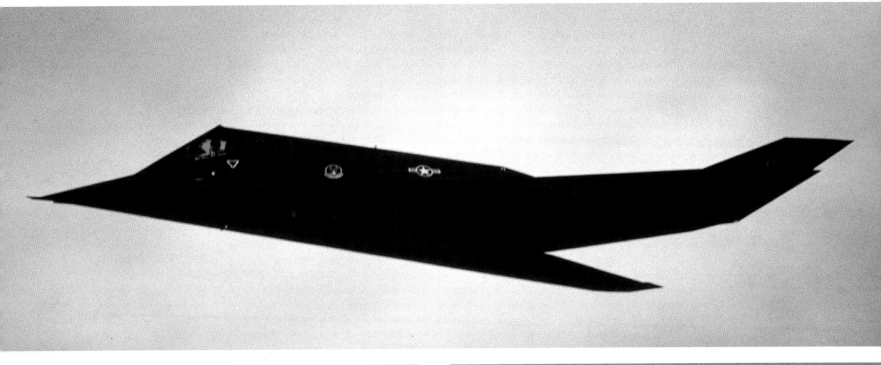

This sequence of three shots shows Major Bryan "B. K." Knight of the 7th FS demonstrating Aircraft 793 at the Chesapeake air show on September 14, 1997. Having made several passes and virtually completing his final flyby, everything then went very wrong. *Stan Piet*

Resplendent with three "Angel Fish" on the tail, this AT-38B belonging to the 7th FS is seen on the ramp at Palmdale in July 1997. *Paul Crickmore*

The three component squadrons together with the wing commander's personal aircraft are pictured at Holloman Air Force Base. From left: Aircraft 809, 9th FS; Aircraft 800, 8th FS; Aircraft 816, 7th FS; and finally Aircraft 803, 49th FW. *U.S. Air Force*

Lot 7, Aircraft 816, first flew on October 30, 1985. It is captured here, overflying the 7th FS's hangar area at Holloman Air Force Base. *Lockheed Martin*

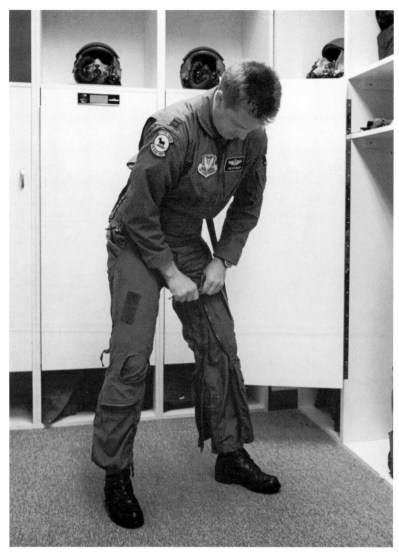

Senior pilot, Captain Jon Bachman (Bandit 390) of the 8th FS is seen zipping up his g suit prior to stepping for a training sortie. *U.S. Air Force*

We were met at McCarron airport, Nellis, by Major Robert Williams (Bandit 162). Bob was the boss of the 4452nd test squadron and was to be Colin's instructor pilot (IP). My IP for all the flying I did, was Major Byron "Buck" Nelson (Bandit 161). Bob took us for a few beers and got the essentials out of the way, and from there on in he was basically our escort and first point of contact throughout.

We stayed in Vegas during the weekend and went out and flew the airplane during the week. Colonel Michael Harris (Bandit 167) was the wing commander at Tonopah, and once we were on site with the training unit, it was much like any other airplane. They took us through ground

An F-117A of the 9th FS (Iron Knights) taxies out of to the holding point at Holloman. Note the open suck-in doors, located on top of the intake duct, for supplementary airflow to the two General Electric F404s during low-speed engine settings. *Lockheed Martin*

Aircraft 826 first flew on March 2, 1987. Today it is operated by the 9th FS. *Lockheed Martin*

The personal mount of the 49th's commander displays the insignia of each of three component squadrons. From left: the 7th FS, "Bunyaps/Screamin' Demons," got their nickname from a mythical fanged creature in Aborigine folk lore. Today the 7th FS is the F-117 RTU, Replacement Training Unit. The 8th FS, "The Black Sheep," like its two sister squadrons, saw combat in New Guinea, the Philippines, and Korea. Retaining its links with the Pacific, the 8th FS would deploy to Korea in the event of a theater crisis. The 9th FS, "Iron Knights," today retains the Atlantic contingency for the F-117 force and in the event of a theater crisis would deploy to Europe. *U.S. Air Force*

A post-Desert Storm gathering in the Ghost Riders Operations Lounge at Tonopah. From left: Lieutenant Julie "Jules" Harmon (squadron executive officer); Major Tom "TDY" Young (pilot); an unknown (flight operations specialist); Captain Gus "Skeeter" Kohntopp (scheduler); Captain Steve "Troy Boy" Troyer (flight commander); Major Doug "Cooch" Couture (pilot); Tom "Tinker" Bell (pilot); Lieutenant Colonel Jim "Whale" Phillips (pilot); and Captain Terry "Flo" Foley (flight commander). *U.S. Air Force*

Aircraft 794. All were day flights and totaled 6.25 hours flying time and were logged against existing bandit numbers of pilots who were away on leave at the time. The flying that we performed on the F-117A gave us the opportunity to explore its envelope in terms of its aerodynamic performance, flying qualities, and the operation of the systems. Much the same way as if it had been any other fighter or attack airplane. Similar previews and assessments happen fairly frequently at Boscombe Down. It was just the classified nature of the airplane that made it an unusual program.

The autopilot had some very impressive capabilities, being coupled to a mission planning system and the IRADs system. I suppose the most sophisticated avionics architecture that I had flown to that stage was in the Jaguar and the Hornet. But the F-117 was considerably further down the developmental road than both of those two airplanes. As an airplane to fly, most of the missions were flown on the autopilot, but even attacks without the autopilot switched in were perfectly feasible. The flying qualities were fairly straightforward; it did have a poor field of view, but when you consider that it was designed as a night medium- to high-level airplane, that wasn't a problem. It didn't have any flaps, so the approach speed

school lectures on the systems for the airplane and after that we completed approximately 10 hours on the simulator, which was spread over three days.

While flying we were chased by our IP in an A-7, which is pretty much as you'd expect on a single-seat airplane. On first seeing the airplane, I thought back to my initial conversation with the CAS and his description of it being a somewhat bizarre shape. I had to agree with him. I also realized that it had to be equipped with a highly augmented, fly-by-wire, flight control system in order to fly. But other than that, I think having a test pilot background, it was an aircraft I felt fully prepared to go and fly.

In all I was able to conduct five flights, the first being on May 27, 1986, in Aircraft 796. This was followed by another on May 28 in 791, two on May 29 in Aircraft 788 and 797, and my last flight on May 20 in

Lowered by the trapeze, a pilot undertakes preflight checks of a practice GBU-10. The trapeze dates back to the aircraft's initial design specification, which stipulated that it should be capable of hauling two of each weapon type in the inventory. Equipped with this device, it is therefore possible to haul target-acquiring weapons, for example the Maverick, AIM-7s, 9s, 120s, and even mini-gun pods. *U.S. Air Force*

Aircraft 799, operated by the 8th FS, touches at between 145 and 150 knots at Holloman Air Force Base. *U.S. Air Force*

was high, as was the threshold speed—about 170 knots, which meant that there was a fairly strong influence of ground effect on the airplane, which tended to make it float. It was therefore one of those aircraft that you had to minimize your rate of descent, but fly it positively onto the ground. If you were flying into an airfield with a significant elevation above sea level, your true air speed would be even higher. With the early standard brakes, if you lost your brake chute, and it was necessary to use just your brakes alone, it was extremely easy to trigger a brake fire. One thing I remember as being unusual about the F-117 was that when you put the gear down, a yaw bias fed in, which you had to re-trim out if you were being very precise and wanted to keep the slip ball in the middle. It was one of those things that I thought the flight control system should be able to take out, but it really made no difference to the way the airplane handled whether you trimmed it out or not.

I also did an air refueling (AR) off the boom of a KC-135. That was the first time that I'd tankered off a boom. Up until that point, I had done a lot of probe and drogue refueling. The piloting technique is different. It's a formation flying task. You were formatting off a tanker, and the responsibility was with the boom operator, who had to position a bit of his boom into your airplane.

A lot 7 aircraft, the 816 first flew on October 30, 1985. Today it is operated by the 7th FS at Holloman Air Force Base and is seen here flying over the north end of the Salton Sea, near the town of Imperial, California. *Lockheed Martin*

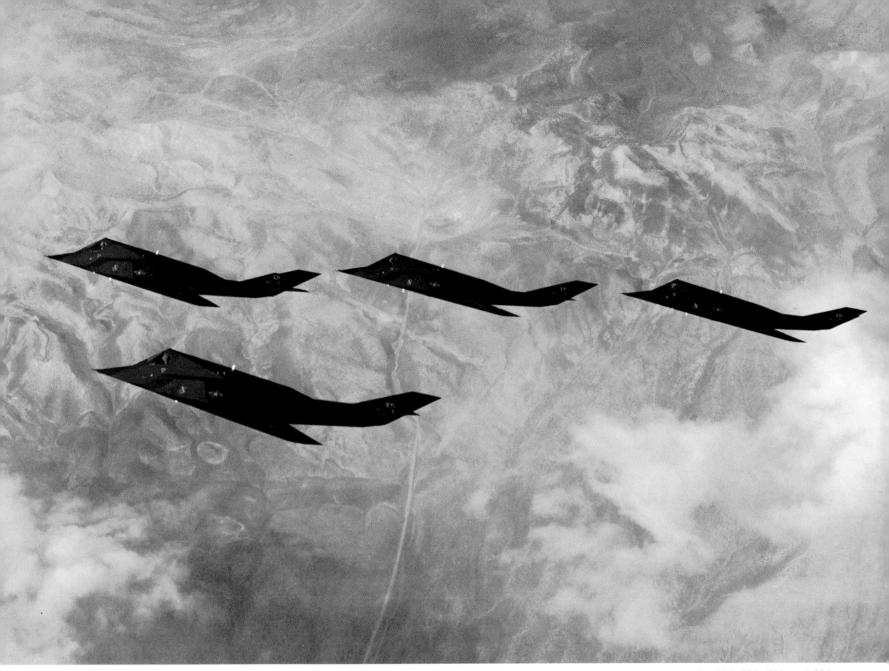

Aircraft 780 had already been retired when this Combined Test Force formation took to the air in March 1991. It was the last time that the 781, 782, 783, and 831 would operate together. Over the intervening months, the 781 had all test equipment removed, and on July 17, it was flown to Wright-Patterson Air Force Base, where it is now on permanent display at the Air Force Museum. *Lockheed Martin*

During our month on the program, we were also given the opportunity of flying an F-15. This was part of the F-117 pilot training, as it was suggested that a no-flap approach in the F-15 was similar to a landing in the F-117. Colin and I went to Luke Air Force Base for our flight, where the staff didn't know how to handle us, as the security didn't tie in with anything else. On this occasion we had to present our card with the contact at the Pentagon. That certainly worked, and they put us up to stay in the VIP Bachelors Officers Quarters (BOQs). I remember that in my room there was a visitor's book. Upon opening it, I found that two entries before I had arrived was an entry from a "General Charles E. Yeager." I elected not to add my name, as I didn't think I was in the same league of VIPs. We had one flight each in the F-15, which in my opinion is one of the easiest aircraft in the world that I have ever flown. It was the simplest. I flew a "B" model and Colin flew a "D." We took off as a pair, in a five-second stream takeoff. Max afterburner, we got airborne, canceled AB, and then went straight into close formation. It says a lot for an airplane that is capable of that sort of thing and was great fun to fly. Luke will always remain in my memory, though for something else. This was the place that Bob introduced me to Mexican fried ice cream, for which I will always be grateful!

Before we left the States at the end of our month, we debriefed with the people that had set the whole assessment up from the American side. Then we flew back to the United Kingdom and verbally debriefed the CAS. As our visit had been so classified, we were unable to add entries to our logbooks other than the flight times and dates. The rest of the book was scored with a pencil line and "classified" written through it. We had been unable to write up any detailed notes on performance, etc.; instead we could only write down a few cryptic numbers that had to be meaningless if they were read by anybody else. We also submitted our expense claims with no receipts or details of what they were for.

Colin and I then shut ourselves away in a secure office at Boscombe Down and worked on our report, which was to satisfy the objectives of the assessment that we had been set. The report was highly classified with an extremely limited distribution. Our notes were then locked in a safe,

On June 18, 1996, the Combined Test Force celebrated 15 years of F-117 operations. From left: Major Bill Gray, Tom Morgenfeld, Jim "J. B." Brown, and the 410th Flight Test Squadron commander, Lieutenant Colonel C. R. Davis. *Lockheed Martin*

Dramatically lit for a BBC documentary, Aircraft 782 continues its career with the 410th FTS at Palmdale. Pilots at the unit use the call sign "Dagger," followed by a two-figure number discreet to an individual. At the end of 1998, these were Lieutenant Colonel Greg Jaspers (410th Commander), 01; Major Bill Gray, 02; Tom Morgenfeld, 03; 04 was unallocated; and Jim Brown was 05. *Paul Crickmore*

for which only Colin and I had a key and combination. It wasn't until two years later that we were given permission for our notes to be destroyed completely, including our floppy disks.

The frustration Colin and I had after this assessment was keeping quiet, especially when we were working on the development of new planes with design engineers. In one particular case, we knew that an engineer was going up a "blind alley," but we were unable to offer any assistance by drawing upon our knowledge of the F-117. On another occasion that Colin was involved in, he was looking over the cockpit of the European Aircraft Project and noticed a switch marked "stealth." He

asked what the switch was for and was told that it retracted various antenna; he suggested that it was renamed, as the title seemed at best, a little overstated!

Stealth is Everything

In November 1981, the U.S. Air Force Aeronautical Systems Division issued a request for information on concepts for an advanced tactical fighter. Codenamed *Senior Sky* by the Air Force, the resulting document identified a clear need for an air superiority fighter, designed specifically to replace the McDonnell Douglas F-15 Eagle.

Test pilot, Sqdn Ldr Dave Southwood (pictured above in an ETPS Jaguar), together with his boss, Wing Cmdr Colin Cruickshanks, were the first two Royal Air Force pilots given an opportunity to evaluate the F-117. A fact that has remained shrouded in secrecy until now. *Crown © DERA, Boscombe Dpwn*

An earlier document produced by General Dynamics identified the application of stealth technology as the preeminent characteristic in achieving air superiority. At this stage Lockheed, Boeing, General Dynamics, Northrop, McDonnell Douglas, Rockwell International, and Grumman all bid on the concept exploration stage, which ran from September 1984 to May 1985. Grumman and Rockwell later dropped out of the competition. It was planned that four winning companies would each be awarded $100 million and participate in a demonstration/validation phase. When Advanced Tactical Fighter (ATF) engineering studies began in the Skunk Works, it is perhaps not surprising that these were based on a faceted design, owing to the success achieved by Senior Trend. Integrating these proven concepts into a platform that also required speed and maneuverability became a major challenge, however, eventually forcing the Skunk Works to reappraise and then abandon faceting, in favor of curved contours.

The Air Force totally restructured the program and a requirement to prototype two aircraft and avionics was added; the contractors were also encouraged to "team." As a result, in June 1986, Lockheed, Boeing, and General Dynamics signed a teaming Memorandum of Agreement, which also enabled

For a period of time, Aircraft 804 was assigned to Detachment 1 of the 57th Fighter Wing (formally 57th Fighter Weapons Wing) at Nellis. This small detachment carries out operational tests. *U.S. Air Force*

Unlike the European Fighter Aircraft, the Lockheed F-22 employs numerous low-visibility features, a deep-V fuselage cross-section intake ducts that shield the engine faces, internal weapons load, serrated edges to various doors, an overall clean exterior producing a minimal number of corner reflectors, to name a few. *Lockheed Martin*

The Skunk Work's Sea Shadow demonstrated a reduced RCS over a conventional ship of several orders of magnitude. The Small Water Area Twin Hull (SWATH) vessel displaced 160 tons, was 160 feet long, 70 feet wide, and had a crew of four: commander, helmsman, navigator, and engineer. The Navy wasn't interested. *Lockheed Martin*

each company to compete independently, with the winning company becoming the team leader. Northrop and McDonnell Douglas followed suit a few weeks later, and on October 31, 1986, the Air Force awarded two $691 million contracts to Lockheed and Northrop, designating each design submission the YF-22A and YF-23A, respectively.

On August 3, 1991, following the conclusion of an extensive demonstration/validation program, the Air Force signed contracts totaling $9.55 billion with the Lockheed consortia for the manufacture and flight test of nine single-seat YF-22s, two two-seat versions, and two fatigue and static test Engineering, Manufacturing, and Developing (EMD) aircraft.

Design studies for an advanced fighter utilizing stealth technology had been proceeded in 1978 by moves to produce a stealth bomber. As mentioned previously, the outstanding results achieved by Northrop during the XST program prompted DARPA to urge the design team to remain together. The sub-

sequent technology demonstration program, codenamed Tacit Blue, cost $136 million and lasted seven years, during which time 135 flights were logged. The 30,000-pound aircraft features a tapered wing and a V tail mounted on an oversized fuselage. Powered by two high-bypass-ratio turbo fan engines, which were fed air via a single-flush inlet located on top of the fuselage, the 55.8-foot-long craft, with a 48.2-foot wingspan, employed a quad-redundant, digital fly-by-wire flight control system and provided invaluable engineering data required for the subsequent B-2 program.

It is incredible to imagine that prior to 1974, the sole connotation of the word stealth was "an act or characteristic of moving with extreme care and quietness." Today it is also recognized as a collection of technologies that have a profound impact on the effectiveness of all military aircraft, ships, vehicles, and munitions. It is also a wonderful epitaph to a very fine gentleman, Ben Rich, "Father of Stealth."

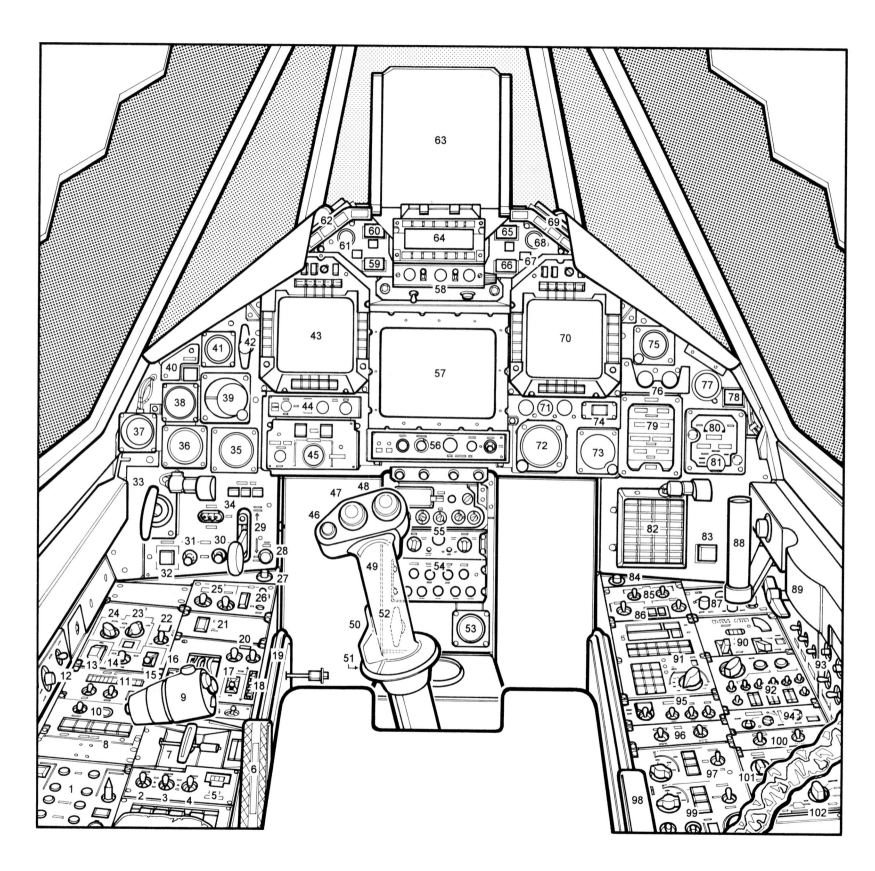

Lockheed F-117A
OCIP/Cockpit Layout

1   Left and right armaments panel (front to back: arm/safe/enable/unlock/lock)
2   Systems power On/Off
3   BCN power On/Off
4   Recorder switch
5   Recorder: minutes-to-go indicator
6   Ejection seat controls lock
7   Canopy/seat safe selector
8   Control surface centering rudders/elevons panel
9   Throttle (inc. R/H RADS viewpoint selector, zoom control, and black hot/white hot select; L/H cockpit dimmer "pinkie" switch: forward face contrast/brightness buttons, IRADS POV cursor and contrast lock "lock on")
10 Trim panel
11 Flight controls panel
12 Cockpit illumination control
13 Fuel dump button
14 Fuel feed switch
15 Fuel cross-feed switch
16 Left AMAD uncouple/norm control
17 Right AMAD uncouple/norm control
18 Throttle friction wheel
19 Ejection seat handle
20 Left and right engine start switches
21 Laser ground test button
22 Inner pressurization of tanks switch
23 Apex light
24 Air-to-air receptacle rotate control
25 Emergency power unit switch
26 Auxiliary power unit switch
27 Engine data event marker
28 Landing gear indicator
29 Gear up/down selector
30 Anti-skid braking on/off

31 Brake normal/reset
32 Brake emergency button
33 Emergency gear extension
34 Gear position indicators
35 Standby HSI (inc. ILS)
36 Standby altimeter
37 Clock
38 Standby ASI
39 Standby artificial horizon
40 Tailhook actuator
41 Rate of climb/descent indicator
42 Drag chute handle
43 L/H MDI, usually used for HSD
44 ILS and VOR controls
45 Master arm/bay doors/jettison indicator
46 Commit weapon release button
47 Trimmer and autothrottle disconnect
48 Attack mode selector (left, MDI/IRADS; right, MDI; up, HUD)
49 Control column
50 Nosewheel steering/autopilot and air refuel disengage
51 Nosewheel steering authority and autopilot reference
52 Rudder pedal adjuster
53 Cabin pressure gauge
54 Intercom
55 Radio
56 IRADS controls
57 IRADS display
58 HUD controls
59 Autopilot and autothrottle disconnect
60 L/H engine fire warning
61 AOA indicator
62 RCS warning
63 HUD
64 Attack profile and autopilot modes (LCD display with sort keys)
65 R/H engine fire warning
66 APU fire warning

67 Dual FCS
68 BETA indicator
69 PCS warning
70 R/H MDI, usually used for HSD
71 Trim position indicator (elev./rudder/aileron)
72 Radar altimeter
73 Standby artificial horizon
74 Turn and slip indicator
75 g meter
76 Hydraulics (flight utility) indicators
77 Lox indicator
78 Canopy unsafe indicator
79 Left and right engine indicators (top to bottom, core RPM/EGT/FF [fuel flow]/fan RPM/oil pressure)
80 Fuel quantity gauge
81 Fuel feed manual selector
82 Annunciator warning panel
83 Annunciator reset
84 INS fast erect button
85 Generator On/Off
86 Battery/external power panel
87 Compass
88 Canopy locking handle
89 Supplementary canopy depressurization lock
90 Oxygen regulator and flow indicator
91 INS panel
92 IFF panel
93 Heaters and deicers panel
94 IFF channel selectors
95 Computer panel
96 RLS panel
97 FLIR panel
98 Emergency manual seat separation handle
99 DLIR panel
100 Antenna retract switches
101 Laser control panel
102 Environmental control system selector

Lockheed Martin F-117A cutaway drawing key

1 Starboard ruddervator
2 Trapezoidal ruddervator section
3 UHF antenna
4 All-composite ruddervator structure
5 Hinge fitting
6 Honeycomb leading and trailing edge panels
7 Ruddervator torque shaft
8 Fixed stub fin
9 Port platypus exhaust duct
10 Parachute doors, open
11 Brake parachute housing
12 Auxiliary power unit (APU)
13 Rear equipment bay
14 Ventral emergency arrester hook stowage
15 Ruddervator hydraulic actuator
16 Rudder hinge control link
17 Starboard platypus exhaust duct
18 Exhaust lip heat shielding tiles
19 Slotted exhaust aperture
20 Tapered and flattened exhaust duct with internal support posts
21 Nickel alloy honeycomb, duct reinforce ment panel
22 Exhaust bay venting air grille
23 Close-pitched fuselage frame structure
24 Bolted wing root attachment fittings
25 Inboard elevon hydraulic actuator
26 Wing rear spar
27 Elevon rib structure
28 Honeycomb composite trailing edge panels
29 Starboard inboard elevon
30 Outboard elevon hydraulic actuator
31 Starboard outboard elevon
32 Faceted wingtip fairing
33 Starboard navigation light
34 Outer wing panel dry bay
35 Fuel tank end rib
36 Main spar

37 Wing panel integral fuel tank
38 Fuel system piping
39 Fuel capacitance unit
40 Composite leading edge panel
41 MXU-648 baggage pod, pilot's personal equipment
42 BDU-37 practice bombs

43 SUU-20 practice bomb carrier and rocket launcher (rocket capability not used)
44 GBU-10 900-kilogram (2,000 pound) laser-guided bomb
45 GBU-27 900-kilogram (2,000 pound) infrared guided bomb with BLU-109 penetrator warhead
46 Starboard main wheel, forward retracting
47 Wing auxiliary front spar
48 Landing light
49 Torque scissor links

50 Main wheel leg door
51 Main wheel leg strut
52 Wing root/tank end rib
53 Retraction breaker strut
54 Hydraulic retraction jack
55 Detachable radar reflector
56 Main wheel bay
57 Engine fuel control equipment
58 Main engine mounting
59 Full Authority Digital Engine Control (FADEC)
60 General Electric F-404 GE-F1D2 nonaugmented turbofan engine

61 Engine bleed-air heat exchanger exhaust
62 Engine bay firewall
63 Fuselage central keel
64 Port weapons bay trapeze mechanism
65 Dorsal integral fuel tank
66 Port engine bleed-air heat exchanger exhaust
67 Engine bay venting air grilles
68 Port inboard elevon, down position

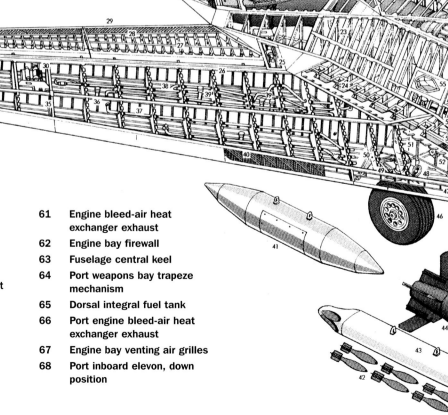

Mike Badrocke/98

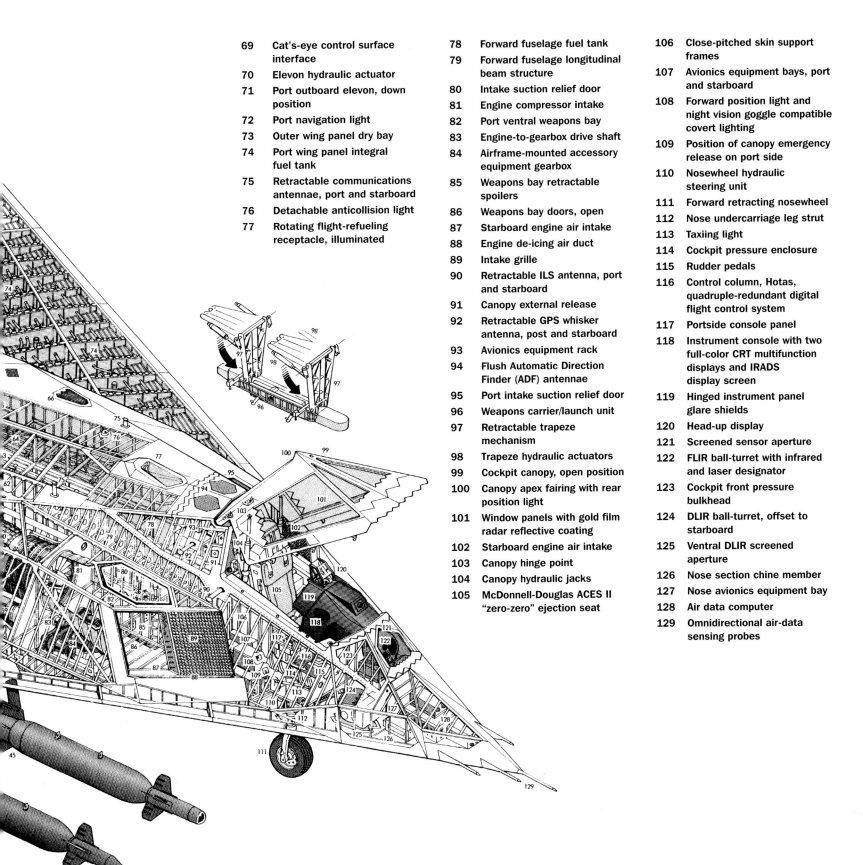

69 Cat's-eye control surface interface
70 Elevon hydraulic actuator
71 Port outboard elevon, down position
72 Port navigation light
73 Outer wing panel dry bay
74 Port wing panel integral fuel tank
75 Retractable communications antennae, port and starboard
76 Detachable anticollision light
77 Rotating flight-refueling receptacle, illuminated

78 Forward fuselage fuel tank
79 Forward fuselage longitudinal beam structure
80 Intake suction relief door
81 Engine compressor intake
82 Port ventral weapons bay
83 Engine-to-gearbox drive shaft
84 Airframe-mounted accessory equipment gearbox
85 Weapons bay retractable spoilers
86 Weapons bay doors, open
87 Starboard engine air intake
88 Engine de-icing air duct
89 Intake grille
90 Retractable ILS antenna, port and starboard
91 Canopy external release
92 Retractable GPS whisker antenna, post and starboard
93 Avionics equipment rack
94 Flush Automatic Direction Finder (ADF) antennae
95 Port intake suction relief door
96 Weapons carrier/launch unit
97 Retractable trapeze mechanism
98 Trapeze hydraulic actuators
99 Cockpit canopy, open position
100 Canopy apex fairing with rear position light
101 Window panels with gold film radar reflective coating
102 Starboard engine air intake
103 Canopy hinge point
104 Canopy hydraulic jacks
105 McDonnell-Douglas ACES II "zero-zero" ejection seat

106 Close-pitched skin support frames
107 Avionics equipment bays, port and starboard
108 Forward position light and night vision goggle compatible covert lighting
109 Position of canopy emergency release on port side
110 Nosewheel hydraulic steering unit
111 Forward retracting nosewheel
112 Nose undercarriage leg strut
113 Taxiing light
114 Cockpit pressure enclosure
115 Rudder pedals
116 Control column, Hotas, quadruple-redundant digital flight control system
117 Portside console panel
118 Instrument console with two full-color CRT multifunction displays and IRADS display screen
119 Hinged instrument panel glare shields
120 Head-up display
121 Screened sensor aperture
122 FLIR ball-turret with infrared and laser designator
123 Cockpit front pressure bulkhead
124 DLIR ball-turret, offset to starboard
125 Ventral DLIR screened aperture
126 Nose section chine member
127 Nose avionics equipment bay
128 Air data computer
129 Omnidirectional air-data sensing probes

APPENDIX 1

Desert Operations Chronology

The following chronology of the F-117 Stealth Fighter's operations and achievements during Desert Shield and Desert Storm was researched, compiled, and written by Senior Master Sergeant Harold P. Myers (retired), 37th Fighter Wing historian during his visit to Saudi Arabia. It was revised by Senior Master Sergeant Vincent C. Breslin and reviewed by Colonel Alton C. Whitley. The unclassified document was prepared and circulated to members of the Team Stealth community. It has subsequently been updated by the authors utilizing other available sources.

Desert Shield

August 1990

August 17

At 1000 hours, Colonel Alton C. Whitley Jr. assumed command over the 37th Tactical Fighter Wing (TFW) from Colonel Anthony J. Tolin. At 1400 hours, the wing received its deployment orders to Saudi Arabia.

August 18

The 37th TFW began processing people and cargo for deployment to Saudi Arabia for Operation Desert Shield.

August 19

Twenty-one F-117A Stealth Fighters from the 415th Tactical Fighter Squadron (TFS) were deployed to Langley Air Force Base, Virginia, completing their first leg to Saudi Arabia.

August 20

The first C-5 touched down at King Khalid Air Base in Saudi Arabia, with Col. Whitley and Lieutenant Colonel Ralph W. Getchell III, 415th TFS commander, onboard. They were officially greeted by Brigadier General Abdulaziz Bin Khalid Al Sudairi, base commander, and Colonel Faisal Eurwailli, flying wing commander.

August 21

Eighteen 37th TFW F-117As arrived from Langley Air Force Base, Virginia, at King Khalid Air Base, Saudi Arabia.

August 23

The 415th TFS launched eight orientation sorties with the Saudis. The host wing used four F-5s, three F-15s, and one Tornado to chase 37 TFW aircraft. General Buster Glosson (director of the air campaign planning for General Norman Schwarzkopf) directed CENTAF staff to use the F-117 as the backbone for all air campaign planning.

August 26

The F-117A assumed alert duty for the first time in its history.

September 1990

September 4

Major Guy C. Fowl, the deployed deputy commander for maintenance, initiated Shade Tree Aircraft Repair (STAR) procedures to repair broken line replaceable units (or avionics boxes). This was another F-117A first.

September 12

General Michael J. Dugan, the Air Force chief of staff, visited the wing at King Khalid.

September 22

Two C-141s brought the 37th TFW's avionics maintenance vans from Tonapah Test Range, Nevada, to King Khalid Air Base, Saudi Arabia.

September 23

Colonel Whitley issued special order #1 to assign all previously attached personnel to the wing for the duration of Operation Desert Shield.

September 25

General Norman Schwarzkopf, U.S. central command commander, visited the 37th TFW (Team Stealth).

October 1990

October 1

The 1880th Communications Squadron became a TAC unit and joined the 37th TFW as the 37th Communications Squadron.

October 3

Col. Whitley initiated Sneaky Sultan I, a limited operational readiness exercise, to challenge the 37th TFW's response capability.

October 3

His Royal Highness, Prince Sultan Abdul Aziz ibn Saud, Saudi defense minister, conferred with Col. Whitley and viewed an F-117A static display.

October 18

Col. Whitley returned to the Tonapah Test Range to requalify in the F-117A. The deputy commander for operations, Colonel Klaus J. Klause, assumed command over the deployed forces.

November 1990

November 12

Col. Klause initiated Sneaky Sultan II, an exercise to test the wing's ability to recall and generate aircraft on short notice to support D-Day planned operations.

November 15–18

The 37th TFS flew 32 sorties for Imminent Thunder, a six-day joint and combined exercise that enhanced warfare skills. Headquarters Central Air Forces tasked coalition air forces to attack a simulated "mirror image" of Kuwait and southeast Iraq.

December 1990

December 3

At 1903 hours, the 416th TFS Commander, Lieutenant Colonel Gregory T. Gonyea, took off from Langley Air Force Base, Virginia, leading an element of six F-117As to King Khalid Air Base. Another six aircraft left 30 minutes later, followed by two successive groups of four on 30-minute intervals. Colonel Whitley flew with the third group on his return journey to Saudi. The entire group of 20 F-117As arrived in Saudi on the following day.

December 5

Central Air Forces underwent an internal restructure resulting in the creation of the 14th and 15th Air Divisions. The command assigned the 37th TFW to the 14th Air Division, commanded by General Buster Glosson.

December 11

Team Stealth received a "how goes it" visit from Lieutenant General Charles A. Horner, the commander of Central Air Forces.

December 14

Representative Dave McCurdy (D-Oklahoma) and Brigadier General Buster Glosson, 14th Air Division (Provisional) commander, visited the 37th TFW. Glosson met with all air crews and senior maintenance personnel and stated, "The success of the air campaign is on your shoulders. . . . The pride of a nation and the lives of their sons and daughters are in your hands. . . . Failure is not an option."

December 20

To standardize and stabilize organizational structure, Central Air Forces redesignated all wings as provisional units. Thus, the 37th TFW deployed became the 37th TFW (Provisional). The command also established provisional combat support groups under each wing.

December 23

Headquarters, Central Air Forces, initiated Threat Condition Charlie to heighten the command's security posture during the Christmas holiday period.

December 23

Col. Whitley initiated Sneaky Sultan III to evaluate the wing's ability to accomplish tasks outlined in the D-Day tasking order.

January 1991

January 5

General Merrill A. McPeak, Air Force chief of staff, arrived in an F-15 to visit the 37th TFW (Provisional).

January 13

Brig Gen. Glosson canceled his scheduled January 14 wing visit and informed Colonel Whitley that the air campaign probably would start on January 17. The 37th TFW (Provisional) started a gradual load out to prepare for hostilities with Iraq.

January 15

The Joint Chiefs of Staff declared Defense Condition 2.

January 16

The 37th TFW (Provisional) received orders to execute its D-Day tasking against targets in Iraq; however, the first wave of F-117As did not take off until after midnight.

Desert Storm

January 17, 1991

Day 1, Wave One

At 0022 hours, the 415th TFS launched 10 F-117As against a combined integrated operations center/ground control intercept site at Nukhayb; two air defense control sector headquarters and the Iraqi Air Force headquarters in Baghdad; a joint integrated operations center/radar facility at Al Taqaddum; a telephone center at Ar Ramadi and two in Baghdad; an integrated operations center at Al Taji; a North Taji military related facility; and the presidential grounds at Abu Ghurayb. The 415th paved the way into Iraq for other Air Force units scoring 13 hits in 17 attempts.

Day 1, Wave Two

The 37th TFW (Provisional) sent 12 F-117As (three 415th and nine 416th jets) to repeat strikes on the Iraqi Air Force headquarters, air defense sector headquarters, and telephone exchanges in Baghdad; the Al Taqaddum integrated operations center/ground control intercept facility; military-related facilities at North Taji; and the presidential grounds at Abu Ghurayb. New targets included the Salmon Pak troposcatter station, television transmitter station, international radio transmitter, and the presidential bunker in Baghdad; Rasheed Airfield; a joint integrated operations center/ground control intercept site at Ar Rutbah; a troposcatter station at Habbaniyah; and the communications satellite terminal at Ad Dujayl. This wave scored 10 hits on 16 attempts.

Day 1, Wave Three

A third wave of eight F-117As proceeded to Salmon Pak, Nukhayb, Ad Diwamiyah, An Nasiriyah, Ash Shuaybah, Qabatiyan, and Karbala to strike sector operations centers, more headquarters buildings, ammunition stores, and a chemical/biological facility. This wave scored only 5 hits in 16 attempts, bad weather obscuring many of the target sites. The "Voice of America" reported anti-aircraft fire and bombs exploding in Baghdad at 0300 following the first weapons drop on the Iraqi capital by 37th TFW (Provisional) aircraft. At 0800 (Pacific time), eight more F-117As left Tonopah Test Range for staging out of Langley Air Force Base, Virginia.

Day 2, Wave One

Late in the afternoon, the 415th TFS launched 12 F-117As against Iraqi targets in Baghdad, Khan Al Mahiwil, Abu Ghurayb, Salmon Pak, North Taji, Al Taji, Al Kut, Al Amara, Ar Rutbah, and Al Taqaddum. Due to an air abort, only 11 aircraft completed successful runs against radio transmitters, command and control bunkers, the intelligence service headquarters, Baghdad's nuclear reactor, the Iraqi airborne warning and control system (AWACS), integrated operations centers, sector headquarters, and the national computer center. This wave achieved 10 hits in 18 attempts.

January 18
Day 2, Wave Two

The 416th TFS sent 12 jets to attack enemy-integrated operations centers, headquarters buildings, communications sites, a nuclear reactor, and ammunition bunkers. Target areas included Baghdad Salmon Pak, Nukhayb, Al Jahrah, Fallujah, Al Kut, and Qabatiyan. Stealth pilots achieved 13 direct hits out of 19 attempts.

January 18
Day 3, Wave One

The 415th TFS attacked communications sites, integrated operations centers, a nuclear reactor, sector headquarters, the Ministry of Culture and Information, Hawk missile sites and training centers, and the Ministry of Defense. Target areas included Umm Al Aish, Al Jahrah, Ali Al Salem, Baghdad, and Nukhayb. Above the targets the pilots found bad weather. As a result, they achieved only four hits on eight attempts.

January 19
Day 3, Wave Two

The 416th sent 10 F-117As against various targets, including chemical and biological bunkers, Scud missile sites; signals intelligence facilities; a highway bridge; and command, control, and communications facilities. Target locations included Baghdad, North Taji, Al Diwaniyah, Abu Ghurayb, Al Taji, Al Kut, and Al Amarah. The bad weather was so poor that the pilots only managed 2 hits on 18 attempts, leading to 9 no-drops. As a result, most pilots attempted to drop both bombs on alternate targets. Most missed.

Day 4, Wave One

The 415th TFS pilots attacked bridges, command and control bunkers, integrated operations centers and ground control intercept sites, sector headquarters, sector operations centers, radio transmitter stations, ammunition storage dumps, and two telephone exchanges. Target positions included Ash Shamiyah, Abu Ghurayb, Al Kut, Al Amarah, Ar Rutbah, Al Zubayr, Ali Al Salem, Ad Dujayl, Al Fallujah, and Karbala. Once again weather conditions limited pilot success as they scored seven hits with seven misses.

January 20
Day 4, Wave Two

Nine F-117As of the 416th TFS attacked a target list comparable to the previous three nights. This time the weather cleared up enough to permit a much

higher degree of success: 10 hits in 13 attempts. This wave concentrated on targets at Baghdad, Salmon Pak, Karbala, North Taji, Abu Ghurayb, and Al Taji. Types of target included Scud sector operation centers, chemical and biological warfare research facilities, ammunition storage dumps, a signals intelligence station, military-related facilities, bridges, command and control bunkers, and an integrated operations center. An air transportable hospital arrived at King Khalid on nine C-141s to provide rear echelon treatment for war casualties.

January 21
Day 5, Wave One

The 415th TFS initiated the fifth night of combat operations one minute after midnight. Due to two air aborts, only 10 jets flew their missions against the Taji biological warfare facility, the Salmon Pak troposcatter station, Tallil Airfield, a Tall King radar station, the Latifiya satellite ground station, the Baghdad television transmitter/radio relay terminal, and the headquarters for the Ministry of Defense and Iraqi Air Force in Baghdad. Stealth fighter pilots achieved 10 hits on 14 attempts.

Day 5, Wave Two

This wave's tasking obligated the 416th TFS to fly 14 combat sorties. One jet was aborted. The other 13 accomplished their missions with weather-impaired results against the presidential bunker, Ministry of Information headquarters, ammunition dumps, surface-to-air missile sites, Scud missile bunkers, a combined integrated operations center/ground control intercept site, a troposcatter station, and a Scud and Frog missile site. Attack areas included Salmon Pak, Ad Diwaniyah, Habbaniyah, An Nasiriyah, Abu Ghurayb, and Khan Al Kahawil. A combination of poor weather, unreliable aircraft systems, and target acquisition errors attributed to 14 missed targets of 21 attempted.

Day 6, Wave One

The night's first wave against Iraq pitted 14 F-117As from the 415th TFS against a radio relay terminal, Iraqi Air Force headquarters, the main signals intelligence station, the international radio communications transmitter-receiver, two telephone exchanges, and the nuclear research center in Baghdad; the Ad Dujayl communications satellite terminal; an acquisition and warning site at Bir Akirshah; the troposcatter station at Salmon Pak; a telephone exchange at Al Fallujah; Ubaydah Bin Al Jarrah Airfield; and a command control bunker at Abu Ghurayb. Two air aborts reduced the wave to an even dozen stealth fighters. Of 23 targets attacked, the squadron pilots registered 20 bomb hits and 3 misses.

January 22
Day 6, Wave Two

The 416th TFS sent a wave of 14 F-117As to bomb Iraqi targets at Baghdad, Al Taji, Al Taqaddum, and North Taji. Nighthawk attacks on surface-to-air missile sites, Internal Security, Ministry of Defense, Intelligence Service, Air Force headquarters, the presidential retreat, military-related facilities, telephone exchanges, a biological warfare facility, and a nuclear research center featured 26 hits and only 2 misses for the 37th TFW (Provisional)'s best performance so far.

Day 7, Wave One

With the setting sun in the background, the 415th TFS launched 14 F-117As toward the Balad Southeast Airfield. Stealth pilots scored 21 hits on the airfield and 1 hit on an alternate target. Only four bombs missed their targets.

January 23
Day 7, Wave Two

The 416th TFS had 14 combat sorties slated for this wave. Insufficient time for mission planning and photographic support, however, caused the unit to drop 4 sorties. The remaining 10 aircraft took off on time at midnight to bomb missile handling facilities, the main signals intelligence station, and transportation facilities in Baghdad; a VIP residence at Abu Al Jahish; highway bridges over the Euphrates River at An Nasiriyah and As Samawah; and a highway bridge at Al Kut. The 416th TFS pilots hit 16 of 18 attempts.

January 23
Day 8, Wave One

The 415th TFS launched 13 of 14 scheduled jets against road bridges in Iraq; however, bad weather limited the pilots to 3 bomb drops at Al Basrah, Um Al Aish, and Al Khirr, rendering only 2 hits, 1 miss, and 23 no-drops.

January 24
Day 8, Wave Two

The 416th TFS's combat schedule also called for 14 sorties against bridges, communication centers, and an airfield. All 14 F-117As launched on schedule, scoring 11 hits and 5 misses at As Samawah, Al Basrah, Al Qurnah, An Nasiriyah, Ar Rumaylah, Umm All Aish, Tallil, and Jalibah.

Day 9, Wave One

To increase the pressure on Iraq, Headquarters Central Air Forces tasked the 37th TFW (Provisional) to resume flying three waves of F-117As against military targets. For the first wave, the 416th TFS sent 14 aircraft against airfields at Qayyarah West, Al Assad, and Kirkuk. For the first time, KC-135 tankers supported the F-117A, flying 60 miles into Iraqi air space for postattack refueling. One aircraft aborted after takeoff due to a lack of tanker support; however, the other 13 jets scored 20 hits with 5 misses.

Day 9, Wave Two

The 416th TFS launched the day's second wave against highway bridges at Al Qurnah, An Nasiriyah, As Samawah, Al Kut, Al Fifl, Hachama, Samawa, Muftul, Ar Rumaylah, Al Madinah, and Saqash. The squadron dropped 20 bombs, scoring 14 direct hits and 6 misses.

January 25
Day 9, Wave Three

The wing's third wave combined resources from both squadrons. Seven 415th TFS and three 416th TFS jets concentrated on enemy airfields, but bad weather made all 20 targets impossible to hit (19 drops and 1 miss).

Day 10, Wave One

The 37th TFW (Provisional) combined unit operations again as the 415 TFS and 416th TFS each sent three F-117As after several bridges at Al Madinah, Ar Rumaylah, Al Qurnah, Muftul, Al Fifl, Al Basrah, An Nasiriyah, and As Samarah and an airfield at Tallil. On these targets, the pilots scored five hits, three misses, and five no-drops due to bad weather. Six more F-117As flew from Langley Air Force Base, Virginia, to King Khalid Air Base. These aircraft were assigned to the 416th TFS for maintenance and management.

Day 10, Wave Two

The wing launched this wave in two groups: four 415th TFS jets took off at 2200 hours; four more 415th TFS jets launched at 2300 hours. All eight jets attacked Iraq's H-2 and H-3 airfields. The wings poststrike assessment indicated eight hits, four misses, three systems malfunctions, and three no-drops due to bad weather.

January 26
Day 10, Wave Three

For this wave, the 416th TFS sent eight aircraft to bomb Iraq's H-2 and H-3 airfields. Their relative success reflected eight hits, three misses, and five no-drops for weather.

Day 11, Wave One

The 37th TFW (Provisional) launched 10 aircraft. F-117As attacked Iraqi airfields at Mosul, Kirkuk, and a joint integrated operations center/ground control intercept site at Al Mawsil. This raid proved largely ineffective as three F-117As air aborted and attacks by the other seven produced only eight hits and six misses.

Day 11, Wave Two

The wing dispatched 13 Stealth Fighters (8 415th TFS and 5 416th TFS) to strike Iraqi airfields at Qayyarah West, Al Asad, Kirkuk, Al Muhammed, and Tikrit. Also at Kirkuk, the F-117As bombed the integrated operations center/ground control intercept site, and the air defense control sector facility. The Qayyarah West Airfield went unscathed due to bad target weather, but the alternate target at Al Assad bore the brunt of seven direct hits. Kirkuk Airfield also quaked under the force of eight bomb strikes. Al Muhammed took three direct hits while the Kirkuk ground control site and sector headquarters were rocked by one each.

January 27
Day 11, Wave Three

The 37th TFW (Provisional) dedicated a third wave to the destruction of Iraq's H-2 airfield and various Scud missile sites. Six 416th TFS and four 415th TFS F-117As took part in the attacks, scoring 9 hits on 18 tries while suffering one air abort, four bomb failures, and five misses.

Day 12, Wave One

The 37th TFW (Provisional) sent three waves of F-117As to strike airfields, shelters, ammunition dumps, and other miscellaneous targets in Iraq. In the first wave, the 415th TFS and 416th TFS dispatched six and four jets, respectively, to attack airfields at Balad and Rasheed, communications facilities at Baghdad and Ad Dujayl, a troposcatter station at Salmon Pak, the Iraqi Intelligence Service headquarters in Baghdad, and a biological warfare facility at Abu Ghurayb. Stealth pilots scored 13 hits in 18 attempts.

Day 12, Wave Two

The second wave, with six F-117As from the 415th TFS and eight from the 416th TFS, achieved great success bombing Balad and Rasheed Airfields, a chemical/biological warfare research, production, and storage facility at Salmon Pak, highway bridges at An Nasiriyah and Al Madinah, and the Baghdad Nuclear Research Center. Twenty-four of 26 bombs found their targets.

January 28
Day 12, Wave Three

Ten F-117As raided Iraqi airfields, ammunition stores, and a missile site. Six 415th TFS jets concentrated on the ammunition storage facilities at Ad Diwaniyah, Ash Shuaybah, and An Nasiriyah, as well as H-3 airfields, shelters, and a surface-to-air missile site at Ar Rutbah. Four pilots of the 416th TFS spent their bombs exclusively on targets at Iraq's H-2 and H-3 airfields. The 10 jets bombed their assigned targets with much success, scoring on 16 out of 20 attempts.

Day 13, Wave One

The 415th TFS and 416th TFS contributed four and six aircraft, respectively, to this night's first wave. These aircraft, except for two jets that air aborted, hit various scud missile and communications facilities at Baghdad, An Nasiriyah, Ad Diwaniyah, and Ar Rutbah; hardened shelters at Rasheed Airfield; and the presidential grounds at Abu Ghurayb. Stealth pilots enjoyed a high margin of success, hitting 15 targets and missing only 1.

Day 13, Wave Two

Wave two tasked eight 415th TFS and six 416th TFS F-117As to attack chemical and biological warfare facilities, the Republican Guard barracks, one missile facility, an airfield, ammunition stores, Iraq Central Intelligence headquarters, Security Service headquarters, and several highway bridges. Target locations included Baghdad, An Nasiriyah, Fallujah, Kirkuk, Al Basrah, Tikrit, Salmon Pak, and Karbala. A review of F-117A target taped revealed 17 hits and 7 misses.

January 29
Day 13, Wave Three

The 415th TFS and the 416th TFS repeated the pattern of the first wave by flying four and six sorties, respectively. All 10 F-117As took off as scheduled, but due to an air abort, only 9 jets reached their targets. Objectives for the wave included Rasheed Airfield, chemical and biological warfare facilities at Salmon Pak, Tikrit and Kirkuk, the Abu Ghurayb biological warfare facility, and ammunition bunkers at Karbala, Fallujah and Baghdad. Stealth pilots scored 15 hits and 2 misses.

Day 14, Wave One

The 415th TFS launched the first wave against enemy targets with 10 F-117As. A few hours later, the stealth fighters arrived over their prospective targets only to find most obscured by foul weather. Nevertheless, alternate targeting enabled the pilots to strike heavy blows on highway bridges at Al Kifl, Ar Ramadi; an ammunition depot at Karbala; and a fiber-optics bridge at Al Jumhuriya. Fourteen of 20 bombs found their mark.

Day 14, Wave Two

Thirty-seven minutes after the 415th TFS's departure, the 416th TFS sent the second wave on its way to enemy targets. One aircraft ground aborted. Nine others hit out at ammunition dumps in Karbala and An Nasiriyah; the Taji steel fabrication plant; the presidential grounds at Abu Ghurayb; and the Intelligence Service headquarters and a nuclear research center in Baghdad. Bad weather and weapons system problems limited the squadron's effectiveness to six hits, eight misses, and two no-drops.

January 30
Day 14, Wave Three

The 415th TFS and 416th TFS combined forces in the last wave of the day. The 415th TFS bombed bridges at Al Fifl, An Nasiriyah, and Al Madinah, while the 416th went scoreless against chemical and biological facilities at Salmon Pak and an ammunition depot at Tikrit due to foul weather. Strike reports reflected four hits, five misses, and seven no-drops.

Day 15, Wave One

The squadrons again combined operations for the first combat wave of the night. Four F-117As of the 415th TFS joined with six 416th TFS aircraft to attack bridges at Al Basrah, Saqash, and Ash Shuaybah; the Ash Shuaybah telephone exchange; and the sector operations centers at Ali Al Salem Air Base; and various other communication facilities. Pilots were again plagued by bad weather and managed only 9 hits in 14 attempts.

January 30
Day 15, Wave Two

Just before midnight, 14 F-117As took off to strike bridges at Al Basrah, Saqash, and Tannunah; command and control facilities at Ali Al Salem, Ubaydah Bin Al Jarrah, and Tallil; and communications systems at Al Basrah and Um Qasr. The Stealth pilots struck cleanly on 16 of 28 attempts.

January 31
Day 15, Wave Three

Of 10 scheduled sorties, the 415th TFS lost one due to a ground abort and the 416th TFS lost two due to nonavailability of aircraft. Seven jets launched to bomb chemical and biological facilities at An Nasiriyah, Ad Diwaniyah, Karbala, Habbaniyah, and Fullujah, Salmon Pak, Abu Ghurayb, and Ash Shuaybah. These aircraft achieved 11 hits in 12 tries. Two bombs were not dropped due to inclement weather.

Day 16, Wave One

The wing began alternating between two and three waves per day, sending nine F-117As from the 415th TFS and seven from the 416th TFS on the first wave. Targets included enemy bridges at Al Basrah, Tannumah, Al Madinah, and Saqash; communications systems at As Samawah, Tallil, Ad Diwaniyah, and Al Kuwayt; and ammunition stores at Ash Shuaybah, Ad Diwaniyah, and An Nasiriyah. On the way, the 415th TFS jets aborted, but the other F-117As hit on 23 of 28 tries.

February 1
Day 16, Wave Two

The two squadrons combined operations once again with six aircraft each for the second wave. This wave concentrated on bridges at Al Basrah, Al Qurnah,

Ar Rumaylah, and Al Fifl; communications facilities in Kuwait (telephone switching), Al Amarah, and An Nasiriyah; chemical warfare bunkers at Tallil; ammunition storage facilities at An Nasiriliyah and Ash Shuaybah; and Ubaydah Bin Al Jarrah Airfield. Stealth pilots hit 13 targets on 23 attempts.

Day 17, Wave One
The 37th TFW (Provisional) formed the evening's first combat wave against Iraqi targets with six F-117As from the 415th TFS and four from the 416th TFS. Roughly two and a half hours into the mission, the Stealth Fighters reached their objectives: bridges at Al Basrah, Al Madina, Tannunah, Ar Rumaylah, and An Nasiriyah; communications installations at Jaibah and Tall Af Lahm; ammunitions dumps at Ash Shuayban and An Nasiriyah; and Ubaydah Bin Al Jarrah Airfield. In this strike, Stealth pilots achieved 18 hits and missed only once.

Day 17, Wave Two
This wave concentrated on communications installations at Al Amarah, Al Kut, Az Zawr, Shibah, As Samawah, and Al Ahmadi; military headquarters buildings at Az Zubayr; and airfields at Ahmed Al Jaber and Tallil. Six 415th TFS and seven 416th TFS jets joined in the attacks, scoring 20 hits and 1 miss.

February 2
Day 17, Wave Three
Five F-117As (three 415th TFS and two 416th TFS) attacked Tallil Airfield and ammunition storage facilities at Karbala and Habbaniyah, scoring five hits and two misses.

Day 18, Wave One
Poor weather resulted in only two launches against an ammunition storage depot at Karbala. One of the two air aborted, but the other scored two for two against the depot.

Day 18, Wave Two
The 415th TFS and 416th TFS launched a combined attack (six aircraft from each squadron) against hardened aircraft shelters at Ubaydah Bin Al Jarrah Airfield. Stealth pilots scored 11 hits on 13 attempts. Eleven additional drops were canceled due to bad weather.

February 3
Day 19, Wave One
Each squadron launched eight F-117As against Baghdad telephone exchanges, highway bridges, and the Nuclear Research Center; Al Taqaddum and Mudaysis Airfields; and chemical and biological warfare facilities at Samarra and Abu Ghurayb. Bad weather limited attack results to 17 hits.

February 4
Day 19, Wave Two
The second wave also involved mixed unit operations with six F-117As from each squadron. Stealth pilots attacked chemical warfare bunkers at Samarra and Habbaniyah; a bridge at Ar Ramadi; and unspecified airfield alternate targets. Eight hits, seven misses, and nine no-drops evidenced the poor weather wing pilots faced in most target areas.

Day 20, Wave One
The first wave of four 415th TFS and five 416th TFS jets left before sunset to bomb Iraqi communications (primarily radio and television) sites at Az Zubayr, Al Kuwayt, Ar Raw Datym, Al Jahrah, and An Nasirayah. The pilots successfully dropped 14 bombs on target; 4 others missed.

Day 20, Wave Two
The two squadrons combined forces for strikes against chemical warfare bunkers at Samarra. Additional tasking featured hits on the Ministry of Defense, Air Force, and Intelligence Service headquarters in Baghdad; military-related facilities in North Taji; a biological warfare facility at Abu Ghurayb; and a chemical warfare facility at Habbaniyah. Thirteen jets posted 19 hits and missed 5 targets.

February 5
Day 20, Wave Three
Five 415th TFS and four 416th TFS aircraft joined in a concentrated attack against the chemical and biological warfare research laboratories at Salmon Pak. Independent operations on the part of the 416th TFS squadron featured strikes on the short-range ballistic missile assembly plant in Baghdad and the presidential grounds at Abu Ghurayb. Unilateral 415th TFS strikes pasted the Iraqi Air Force headquarters in Baghdad. Bombing results reflected 16 hits and 4 misses.

Day 21, Wave One
Six 415th TFS and four 416th TFS jets attacked various missile production and launch facilities. Pilots of the 415th TFS struck production targets in Al Maydan and Baghdad while the 416th TFS went after launch sites at Dhinan, Habbiniyn, and Al Taqaddum. Both squadrons mounted attacks on the steel fabrication plant at Taji. Wing aircraft released 17 of 18 bombs (one no-drop) and scored 17 direct hits. One aircraft aborted.

Day 21, Wave Two
For this offensive, Headquarters Central Air Forces tasked the 37th TFW (Provisional) to send 12 F-117As (6 from each squadron) against hardened aircraft shelters on Balad Airfield. Also on the agenda were a telecommunications center at Janub; the Juah and Ahar fiber-optics bridge; a biological warfare facility at Taji; and several key targets in Baghdad, including an ammunition depot, the Ministry of Military Industry, and the headquarters buildings for the Iraqi Intelligence Service, Security Service, and Republican Guard. Stealth pilots hit their targets 18 times in 20 attempts.

February 6
Day 21, Wave Three
Twelve F-117As (6 from each squadron) accomplished this early-morning raid on enemy chemical and biological warfare targets at Salmon Pak and Samarra and ammunition depots at Tikrit and Kirkuk. Pilots racked up 16 direct hits and 5 misses.

Day 22, Wave One
Hardened aircraft shelters, ammunition stores, the fuel farm, and the main runway at Rasheed Airfield and hardened aircraft shelters at Balad SE became the objects of attention on this raid as six pilots of the 416th TFS pilots and

four 415th TFS squadrons crippled yet another cog in the Iraqi war machine. Fifteen direct hits, two misses, and three no-drops for bad weather left a memorable impression on Iraqi airmen at Rasheed.

Day 22, Wave Two
The wing sent 14 jets (8 415th TFS and 6 416th TFS) to attack possible chemical warfare sites at Habbaniyah, communications and presidential facilities in Baghdad. Above the designated targets, the pilots lashed out with uncanny accuracy, hitting 26 of their 27 targets.

February 7
Day 22, Wave Three
For the third wave of the day, the wing flew 10 sorties. Once underway, 4 415th TFS and 6 416th TFS F-117As went after the Baghdad nuclear reactor, the Habbaniyah Airfield, a biological warfare facility at Taji, a Baghdad petroleum refinery, and an ammunition storage depot at Latifiya. The pilots scored 15 hits in 20 attempts.

Day 23, Wave One
Twelve jets (six from each squadron) took off to attack communications sites in Ar Ramadi, Sawaij Ad Dacha, and Kuwait International Airport, the Balad Air Defense Operations Center; the presidential command, control, and communications bunker; the Air Force Air Defense headquarters and Ministry of Industry in Baghdad; the Karbala integrated operations center and radar facility; and the Salmon Pak troposcatter station. At their targets, stealth pilots enjoyed great success bombing 20 targets and achieving direct hits on 18.

Day 23, Wave Two
Another 12 F-117As (6 from each squadron) participated in the day's second wave. This attack converged on the chemical warfare facilities at Samarra where the pilots dropped 22 bombs with calamitous effect; only 3 missed their mark.

Wave Two Milestone Event:
A 416th pilot, Captain Scott Stimpert, achieved a milestone for the 37th TFW (Provisional) as he delivered the 1,000th bomb against Iraq in Operation Desert Storm. Stimpert's mission took him over the Samarra chemical warfare weapons bunkers where he successfully dropped two bombs.

February 8
Day 23, Wave Three
The wing decreased its sortie load to 10 jets for the third wave. For target objectives, the wing again sent a few aircraft to Samarra while others went to Kirkuk to attack an ammunition depot. The squadrons also hit Iraq's K-2 Airfield, a pumping station, a signals intelligence facility at Ar Rutbah, and a radio relay station at Ar Ramadi. Target evaluations revealed a tremendous success—18 hits in 18 attempts: 100 percent efficiency.

Day 24, Wave One
Six pilots and F-117As from each squadron traveled to Tallil Airfield to once again attack various bunkers. At Tallil, the pilots dropped 20 bombs onto their targets. Four bombs missed the mark.

Day 24, Wave Two
Twelve more F-117As, with six again from each unit, participated in the second wave. The pilots headed for their objectives: targets at the Rasheed and Al Taqaddam Airfields; a liquid fuel rocket facility at Shahiyat; and a motor production plant and chemical warfare production factory at Habbaniyah. The results were almost as gratifying as the first wave's outcome with 18 hits in 22 attempts.

February 9
Day 24, Wave Three
For this wave, the wing dropped its mission load to 10 sorties, 4 by 415th TFS pilots and 6 by 416th TFS pilots. All 10 then traveled to Samarra to assault chemical warfare bunkers. This wave achieved the greatest success of the day by knocking out 16 out of 17 targets. Aircraft 790 returned to base and blew a nose wheel tire on landing. Pieces of the tire damaged the left and right E-bay panels and three probes.

Day 25, Wave One
Attacks on the enemy targeted possible chemical warfare production facilities at Habbaniyah; an aircraft engine repair and test factory at Al Taji; communications sites at Balad, Baghdad, and Injanah; and integrated operations centers at Al Amarah and Al Kut. Over the targets, both squadrons (six aircraft of the 415th TFS and four of the 416th TFS) had a good night, registering 11 hits in 17 attempts.

Day 25, Wave Two
About three hours after the first wave took off, the wing launched six 415th TFS, eight 416th TFS, and eight 416th TFS F-117As. The 415th TFS pilots concentrated on various surface-to-air missile sites and the Shab Al Hiri tropospheric center, while the 416th TFS assailed a suspected missile facility at Ash Sharqat, the Ministry of Military Industry in Baghdad and the Al Yusufiyah military facility. At their assigned objectives the pilots executed flawlessly, achieving 24 hits in as many attempts.

February 10
Day 25, Wave Three
The last wave of the day featured 10 F-117As striking ammunition depots at Kirkuk and Qayyarah West and the Qayyarah West Airfield. There were six hits, three misses, and nine no-drops for bad weather. Secretary of Defense Richard B. Cheney and General Colin Powell, chairman of the Joint Chiefs of Staff, visited the 37th TFW (Provisional). Cheney commended the wing for doing a great job and for exceeding all expectations.

Day 26, Wave One
The 415th TFS and 416th TFS squadrons launched four and six F-117A Stealth Fighters, respectively, to bomb Iraqi surface-to-air missile sites, exclusively. Al Taji, Saad, Baghdad, Samarra, and Al Iskandiriyah all felt the destructive power of stealth fighter munitions. Stealth pilots made 18 direct hits in 20 attempts (therefore destroying 18 SA-2 and SA-3 sites).

Day 26, Wave Two
The two Stealth squadrons increased their pressure on Iraq's military in the second wave. Eight F-117As from the 415th TFS launched attacks against the Taji

armored vehicle repair facility, Saddam International Airfield buildings, and the Latifiya liquid propellant plant. Meanwhile six 416th TFS pilots went after the signals intelligence center at Al Taqaddum, hardened shelters on Sadam International Airfield, surface-to-surface missile production facilities at Latifiya, and the Al Haqlaniyah radio relay station. Pilot effectiveness dropped slightly in this wave based on 19 hits and 6 misses.

February 11
Day 26, Wave Three
The 415th TFS and 416th TFS launched four and six F-117As, respectively, toward a different target set. This wave primarily focused on Iraqi communications centers at Salmon Pak, Al Jahrah, Aydawah, Al Basrah, Kuwait and Shaibah, and southern Kuwait, but in addition the jets dropped bombs on a commando camp at Al Jahrah. This wave achieved the night's greatest success with 18 targets hit in 20 attempts.

Day 27, Wave One
The 415th TFS led off with six F-117As, while the 416th TFS followed in take-off sequence with four more jets. Once in the air, the Stealth aircraft winged their way toward the evening's first targets: the airfield and ammunition stores at Qayyarah West and the chemical and biological bunkers at Kirkuk. The pilots registered impressive results with 17 hits in 20 tries.

Day 27, Wave Two
The 416th TFS dispatched nine F-117As to bomb hardened aircraft shelters at Kut Al Havy and Al Jarrah. Additional bombing raids laid waste to the Iraqi Intelligence Services, Ministry of Information, and the Baath Party headquarters. The 415th sent six jets to bomb hardened aircraft shelters at Qalat Salih Airfield and Kut Al Havy. Pilots involved in this registered 23 hits and 4 misses.

February 12
Day 27, Wave Three
Six 415th TFS and four 416th TFS jets worked in concert, bombing hardened aircraft shelters at Saddam International Airfield, the Baghdad Military Intelligence headquarters, the Baath Party headquarters, the Abu Ghurayb command, control, and communications bunker, and the Ministry of Information and Culture. The pilots again demonstrated the effectiveness of the Stealth Fighter by striking 17 targets in 19 tries.

Day 28, Wave One
This wave's objectives included military-related facilities in North Taji, bunkers at the Iraqi Air Force headquarters building, a conference center, radio relay station, and Ministry of Defense building in Baghdad. The 415th TFS handled this tasking independently, scoring 15 direct hits in 16 attempts.

Day 28, Wave Two
A larger wave continued the night's assault against Iraqi targets. Eight 415th TFS and six 416th TFS jets took part in the evening's work. The 415th TFS bombed a fighter direction post/interceptor operations center at Al Kut; various radio, television, and communications centers; and the headquarters for military intelligence and the Iraqi Central Intelligence Agency in Baghdad. Pilots of the 416th TFS delivered weapons on communications centers too, but they also hit the Balad alternate air defense operations center and the Baghdad Command Center Building. Wing pilots hit 22 of 24 attempted targets.

February 13
Day 28, Wave Three
For the last wave of the day, the wing dispatched four 415th TFS and six 416th TFS F-117As to bomb miscellaneous bridges; a missile site in Al Adbaliyah; a command, control, and communications bunker at Al Firdos; and various headquarters buildings in Baghdad. Pilots scored 17 hits in 20.

Day 29, Wave One
Six 415th TFS and four 416th TFS jets went after a military barracks at Al Jahrah, communications facilities at Al Basrah, Ad Darraji, An Naayim, and Al Maqwa, command posts at Hsiu Az Zabi and An Naayim, and a commando camp at Al Matla Umm Al Aish. This achieved 15 direct scores and 4 misses. Saudi officials at King Khalid Air Base approved the wing's request to broadcast armed forces radio and television station programs.

February 14
Day 29, Wave Two
Iraqi military barracks at Dib Dibba and garrisons at Al Abrad; communications sites at Al Qashaniyah, Tall Af Lahm, Hsiu Az Zabi, Dib Dibba, Baghdad, Jenoub, Maiden Square, Shemal, and Al Hillah; and chemical bunkers at Kirkuk were selected as this wave's targets. The 37th committed 14 F-117As (6 from the 415th TFS and 8 from the 416th TFS) to the attack. Over the targets, the pilots precisely dropped 17 bombs and missed 3 others.

Day 29, Wave Three
This night's final wave concentrated on communications sites at Al Hillal, Baghdad, Al Qashanivah, Al Basrah, and Az Zubayr; a SAM radar site at Ash Shuaybah; and the navy headquarters at Al Basrah. The jets delivered 13 hits in 18 tries.

Day 30, Wave One
No rest for the Iraqi military machine this night as the 37th TFW (Provisional) routed 10 F-117A sorties over enemy targets in the first of three waves. The first wave chiefly attacked hardened aircraft shelters at Al Asad and Shayka Mazhar Airfields, along with a surface-to-air missile site at Shayka Mazhar. Stealth pilots struck successfully with 15 hits of 18 attempts.

Day 30, Wave Two
The wing launched 14 F-117As against a possible nuclear facility at Tarmiya, Rasheed Airfield, Karbela and Taji ammunition depots, Dib Dibba command posts, and communications sites at Al Basrah, Tall Al Lahm, and Jarbhan. Pilots scored 22 direct hits in 25 attempts.

February 15
Day 30, Wave Three
Ten more sorties closed out this day of combat for the 37th TFW (Provisional). Four 415th TFS jets bombed communications sites at Al Zubayr, An Nasiriyah, Al Kut, Al Basrah, Ar Rumaylah, and Ad Darraji while six 416th TFS aircraft attacked an assortment of targets, including the military garrison at Al Abraq, a radar facility at Ash Shuaybah, and communications sites at Al Basrah, Al Kut, Al Amara, Qal At Salih, and As Zubayr. Stealth pilots scored 16 hits and 2 misses.

Day 31, Wave One

Six 415th TFS aircraft went after Rasheed's aircraft repair depot, the Salmon Pak chemical/biological facility, a possible Scud missile production facility at Basrah, and six surface-to-air missile sites. The 416th TFS also directed four planes to five missile sites, the Salmon Pak chemical/biological research plant, and the Batra missile production site. Over their appointed targets, the F-117A pilots administered the severest form of punishment—16 hits of explosive destruction. Three bombs missed their mark.

Day 31, Wave Two

The night's second wave worked to prevent a raging firestorm. Headquarters Central Air Forces tasked the wing to negate the trench defensive system that surrounded Iraq's troops in Kuwait. As such, the wing sent six 415th TFS and eight 416th TFS Stealth Fighters to take out distribution points and pump stations that could pump oil into the trenches to create a fiery barrier. Stealth pilots also attacked the Mosul missile research and development facility. Wing pilots scored 24 hits in 27 attempts and destroyed the T-junctions, distribution points, and pump stations needed to build an oily inferno.

February 16
Day 31, Wave Three

The evening's last wave pitched the 415th TFS against a missile research and development facility and a missile production plant at Mosul. Two jets went after suspected missile facilities at Ash Sharqat and the Shahiyat rocket engine test facility. The 416th TFS concentrated on the latter two targets. Stealth pilots attacked their assigned targets with routine precision—14 direct hits in 20 attempts.

Day 32, Wave One

The 37th TFW (Provisional) radically altered its flying schedule this evening. Rather than three waves with intermixed squadron forces, the wing set up a wave of 14 jets from each unit. The 416th TFS took off first to conduct strikes on hardened aircraft shelters at three airfields, Tallil, Al Jarrah, and Kut Al Havy. Two pilots also traveled to Al Basrah to attack the railroad yard there. The other 13 reached their objectives and hit 21 of the 24 targets attempted.

Day 32, Wave Two

The 415th TFS launched its 14 jets some two hours after the 416th TFS's take-off. Four aircraft revisited the Al Basrah railroad yard, while others sought out the tactical direction finding site at Dib Dibba, radio transmitters, receivers, and relays at Al Jahrah, and a repeater station at As Samawah; the Um Qasr military barracks; and missile support facilities at Al Jahrah. This wave delivered 24 precise hits in 27 attempts.

February 17
Day 33, Wave One

For the 33rd day of Operation Desert Storm, Headquarters Central Air Forces tasked the 37 TFW(P) to fly 34 combat missions against Iraq targets. Ten first wave pilots attacked an ammunition depot and a steel fabrication plant at Taji; surface-to-air missile sites at Saad, Baghdad, and Habbaniyah; also chemical/biological warfare research facilities at Salmon Pak. One aircraft air aborted. The remaining 9 jets dropped 14 bombs in poor weather conditions, missing with all but 5.

Day 33, Wave Two

The day's second wave of Stealth Fighters attacked the Salmon Pak chemical/biological warfare research facilities; an arms plant at Al Iskandariyah; Taji's surface-to-surface missile storage plant; a Scud assembly factory at Fallujah; a motor case production plant; and an artillery production plant at Habbiniyah. Stealth pilots demolished 23 of 28 possible targets.

February 18
Day 33, Wave Three

The night's final wave sent 10 more fighters on bombing raids to a Scud plant at Taji, a solid propellant at Latifiya, and a probable Scud assembly plant at Fallujah. One aircraft air aborted, but the remaining nine pilots delivered their bombs scoring 14 direct hits and 4 misses. The Central Air Forces commander, Lieutenant General Charles D. Horner, escorted four U.S. senators to King Khalid Air Base to visit the 37th TFW (Provisional). These visitors included Senators Sam Nunn (D-Georgia), John Warner (R-Virginia), Daniel Inouye (D-Hawaii), and Ted Stevens (R-Alaska).

Day 34, Wave One

Pilots of the 415th TFS and 416th TFS set out at dusk to destroy nuclear research facilities in Baghdad. Upon reaching their target, all four 415th TFS pilots found weather obscuring their primary targets, so they settled for a total of eight direct hits on a road bridge and the Karbala ammunition storage facility. The nuclear research facility proved less deceptive for the 416th TFS pilots as they delivered nine out of ten bombs directly on target. Another 416th TFS aircraft visited the Karbala ammunition storage facility to add two more direct hits to the night's tally.

Day 34, Wave Two

The night's second mission package called for the F-117A Stealth pilots to attack hangars at Baghdad Muthenna Airfield. Fourteen aircraft (eight 415th TFS and six 416th TFS) achieved an impressive hit ratio by putting 26 of 28 bombs on target.

February 19
Day 34, Wave Three

The third wave featured attacks on Al Asad Airfield and an Al Qaim mining facility tunnel. Pilots put 14 of 19 bombs on target.

Day 35, Wave One

The night's first wave concentrated on three familiar targets in Iraq: Baghdad's nuclear research facilities, Karbala's ammunition storage facility, and Latifiya's solid propellant plant. Two F-117As also bombed a suspected biological warfare facility at Latifiya. Stealth pilots scored 28 of 30 attempts on target.

February 20
Day 35, Wave Two

Jalibah Southeast Airfield was the sole target for 10 F-117As in the night's second wave. Bad weather inhibited all 10 sorties, and no bombs were dropped.

Day 36, Wave One

Four pilots of the 415th TFS and six of the 416th TFS attacked strategic railroad bridges in Umm Al Wasum and Al Haqlaniyah, and a superphosphate fertilizer plant in Al Qaim. The 415th TFS took responsibility for targets in Al Qaim, and upon reaching the phosphate and fertilizer facility, four F-117As put eight bombs directly on target. The 416th TFS pilots flew against the bridges in Umm Al Wasum and Al Haqlaniyah and successfully put nine of ten bombs on their targets. Two of the six 416th TFS pilots also visited Al Qaim, but their bombing attempts were unsuccessful.

February 21
Day 36, Wave Two

Targets included an ammunition storage facility in Ad Diwaniyah, an arms plant in Al Iskanderiyah, a rocket mortar test facility in Al Musayyib, an ammunition depot in Habbaniyah. Pilots of the 415th TFS concentrated on the test facility in Al Musayyib and achieved a perfect 12-for-12 bombing score against it. The 416th TFS's pilots took on the balance of the night's work and put 14 of 15 bombs on target.

Day 37, Wave One

Radio relays, bridges, bunkers, and an early warning facility were targets for Stealth pilots on this day. In the first wave the 415th TFS sent six F-117As against chemical facilities at Al Taqaddum Airfield, an early warning site at Al Habbaniyah, and communications facilities at Al Amarah and An Nasiriyah. Meanwhile, four 416th TFS jets targeted an international radio communications transmitter in Baghdad, a biological warfare facility at Taji, and a chemical warfare production facility at Habbaniyah. The 415th TFS pilots put 9 of 10 bombs on target, while the 416th TFS pilots scored with 8 of 8.

Day 37, Wave Two

Fourteen F-117As attacked suspected chemical and biological weapons storage and production facilities in Habbaniyah and Latifiya; fiber optics repeater stations in Karbala, Tallil, and As Samawah; Al Hillal's radio relay station; and the H-2 Airfield chemical bunker. The 415th TFS dropped 11 of 12 bombs on intended targets, while the 416th TFS scored on 13 of 16 attempted strikes.

February 22
Day 37, Wave Three

Targets for this night's final attack included a railroad yard, radio communications equipment, and highway bridges at Tikrit; chemical warfare weapons and ammunition storage bunkers at Qayyarah West and Mosul Airfields; the Scud missile plant at Taji; and an underground nuclear facility. Five fighters from the 415th TFS arrived over the target only to be plagued with weapons guidance and target identification problems. Of the ten munitions expended, only four found the mark. The 416th TFS had a better time of it, putting seven of eight bombs directly on target.

Day 38, Wave One

For wave one of day 38, Headquarters Central Air Forces tasked the wing to concentrate on a suspected research facility in Baghdad, a steel fabrication plant in Taji, and a suspected Scud missile production facility in Latifiya. The 37th TFW (Provisional) sent 10 aircraft—4 415th TFS and 6 416th TFS—to accomplish the task. Upon arriving over Baghdad's research facility, the 4 415th pilots and 1 416th TFS pilot directed 10 bombs to target for a perfect bombing performance. Remaining 416th TFS pilots attacked production facilities in Taji and Latifiya, striking them on 7 of 8 attempts.

Day 38, Wave Two

A nuclear research facility in Baghdad represented ground zero for 14 Stealth fighter pilots in the second wave. The 415th TFS successfully unleashed 8 F-117As toward Baghdad, while the 416th TFS offered 6 jets for the attack. One aircraft air aborted en route to the target, but the remaining 13 pilots reached the nuclear research facility and pounded it with 19 hits. Four weapons missed their target.

February 23
Day 38, Wave Three

Wing pilots pooled their resources once again and attacked the Iraqi Intelligence and Special Operations headquarters in this night's third wave. Ten jets from the 415th TFS and 416th TFS (4 and 6, respectively) were launched as planned to destroy these strategic targets. One aircraft air aborted. The others flew on to Iraq and struck their targets with 15 direct hits. Only one bomb failed to hit the mark.

Day 39, Wave One

On this day, the F-117A strike force began in earnest to pave the way for a coalition ground invasion of Iraq and Kuwait. Just before sunset, the 37th TFW (Provisional) began the massive launch that put 31 jets in the air within 44 minutes. In this first wave, the largest Stealth fighter attack to date, pilots concentrated on six different targets: a Baghdad bomb assembly plant at Cardoen, a chemical warfare site at Samarra, a possible nuclear facility in Tarmiya, an arms plant in Al Iskandariyah, and the special security services and Baath Party regular intelligence services headquarters buildings in Baghdad. En route to these targets, one aircraft air aborted; all of the others advanced to their targets and guided 44 of 53 bombs directly on target.

February 24
Day 39, Wave Two

The day's second wave featured 37th TFW (Provisional) on communications equipment and facilities in Iraq and Kuwait. The wing sent four jets from the 415th TFS and two from the 416th TFS to accomplish the task. All six fighters departed as scheduled and successfully arrived over their targets, only to be thwarted by bad weather. Of the 12 bombs carried by the six F-117As, the pilots dropped only 4. Three bombs hit their targets: radio relay stations at Ar Rumaylah, Az Zubayr, and Al Mufrash. The 24 Stealth pilots returned to base with 8 bombs still in their weapons bays.

Day 40, Wave One

First wave targets for this night included a probable presidential facility in Abu Ghurayb, a possible fuse plant in Al Narawan, and a Samarra chemical warfare storage building. The 37th TFW (Provisional) launched four F-117A Stealth Fighters from the 415th TFS and six from the 416th TFS. After successfully reaching their marks, Stealth pilots struck all three Iraqi targets with 19 of 20 bombs released.

Day 40, Wave Two

The 37th TFW (Provisional) launched 14 Stealth Fighters to revisit the site of a probable presidential complex in Abu Ghurayb, a fuse factory in Al Narawan, the special security services facility in Baghdad, and an ammunition dump at Kirkuk. Second wave pilots easily achieved their goals, delivering 18 of 21 bombs on target.

February 25
Day 40, Wave Three

For wave three, the 37th TFW (Provisional) hit the Abu Ghurayb probable presidential complex and the Baghdad special security services facilities from the previous list again and added the Ab Dalli long-haul radio relay and Al Musayyib rocket motor plant to that list. The 415th TFS sent four fighters to Al Musayyib and Ab Dalli, while six 416th TFS jets struck out at the Abu Ghurayb and Baghdad targets. Weather conditions over Baghdad and Ab Dalli negated bomb release; but stealth pilots successfully dropped eight bombs for direct hits on the Abu Ghurayb target and three out of four on the Al Muss Ayyib objective.

February 26
Day 41

Headquarters Central Air Forces canceled all 34 stealth missions due to poor weather.

Day 42, Wave One

Concentrating on a myriad of targets in Iraq, the wing initiated a 32-turn-32 flying schedule, with each flying squadron contributing 16 aircraft per wave. In the first wave, the 415th TFS managed to launch 14 of 16 aircraft, but unfortunately lost two sorties to aborted air refueling tanker missions. Following several maintenance ground aborts and replacements, the 416th TFS managed to launch 15 of 16 aircraft. Unfortunately, poor weather conditions over Iraq persisted and the wing failed to drop 56 of its 58-bomb payload, and the two that did drop missed.

February 27
Day 42, Wave Two

Poor weather continued to inhibit stealth fighter operations as the 37th TFW (Provisional) took position over a Tarmiya rocket facility, a fuse factory at Narawan, the Al Musayyib rocket motor production works, a terrorist camp at Salmon Pak, the Baath Party Headquarters in Baghdad, the Shahiyat rocket test facility and artillery plant in Habbaniyah, and Baghdad's Muthena Airfield and H-2 Airfield. The wing managed to drop only 8 of the 54 weapons it had brought over target, but all 8 were direct hits.

Day 43, Wave One

Team Stealth got back on track with 10 launched from each fighter squadron and a bomb score of 32-for-32 as they devastated the Baath Party headquarters and the Muthenna Airfield in Baghdad and the Salmon Pak chemical/biological research facility. Weather conditions inhibited the release of three weapons, while mechanical faults prevented the use of two others.

Day 43, Wave Two

For the second wave, the 37th TFW (Provisional) sent 10 (5 aircraft from each squadron) F-117As to destroy a possible missile research, development, and production plant, as well as the rocket motor test facility at Al Musayyib. Stealth pilots achieved 14 hits on 20 attempts at target. At 2235 hours Brig. Gen. Glosson informed Col. Whitley that the war would end within hours.

At 2330 hours, Headquarters Central Air Forces canceled the night's third wave. The headquarters also told Col. Whitley to put future attacks against Iraqi targets on hold, but to stand in case events dictated a renewed assault.

Desert Calm
February 28

At 0015 hours, Headquarters Central Air Forces relayed good news: All operations were suspended to give the Iraqis an opportunity to sign a cease-fire agreement.

APPENDIX 2

Bandit List
Test Pilots

Bandit No.	Pilot	Date
117	Hal Farley	
84	Skip Anderson	
100	Roger Moseley	
	Don Cornell	
	Bob Chedister	
101	Tom Morgenfeld	
102	Jon Beesley	
	Steven A. Green	
103	Bob Riedenauer	
	Tom Darner	
	David Imig	
104	Skip Holm	
105	Dave Ferguson	
106	Paul Watson	
107	William Aten	
	Jim Thomas	
108	Craig Dunn	
109	Dale Irving	
110	Pete Barnes	
111	Tom Abel	
	Ken Grubbs	
112	Ken Linn	
113	Jim Dunn	
114	Paul Tackabury	
	Denny Mangum	

115	Chris Seat	
118	Captain Bill Gray	Dec. 20, 1994
119	Jim Brown	Feb. 15, 1995
120	Lieutenant Colonel C. R. Davis	Aug. 2, 1995

Operational Pilots

Bandit No.	Pilot Name	Date
150	Major Alton C. Whitley	Oct. 15, 1982
151	Major Charlie Harr	Nov. 16, 1982
152	Lieutenant Colonel Jerry Flemming	Dec. 2, 1982
153	Lieutenant Colonel Sandy Sharpe	Jan. 13, 1983
154	Captain Denny Larson	Apr. 10, 1983
	(Brigadier General)	Nov. 25, 1996
155	Captain Brian Wilson	May 6, 1983
156	Captain Dennis Day	June 16, 1983
157	Captain Garry Gee	July 14, 1983
158	Colonel Jim Allen	Sept. 8, 1983
159	Captain Tommy Crawford	Aug. 11, 1983
160	Captain Jett Crouch	Sept. 15, 1983
161	Major Byron Nelson	Oct. 19, 1983
162	Major Robert Williams	Nov. 16, 1983
163	Captain Wayne Mudge	Dec. 14, 1983
164	Captain William Aten	Jan. 10, 1984
	(Lieutenant Colonel)	March 5, 1993
165	Captain Stephen Paulsen	Jan. 31, 1984
166	Captain Dutch Riefler	Feb. 15, 1984
167	Colonel Michael Harris	March 7, 1984
168	Captain Mark Dougherty	March 28, 1984
169	Colonel Milan Zimer	Apr. 4, 1984
170	Captain Michael Gill	May 1, 1984
171	Major Wally Moorhead	May 31, 1984
172	Lieutenant Colonel Dave Jenny	May 30, 1984
173	Lieutenant Colonel Medford C. Bowman	June 29, 1984
174	Colonel Howell Estes	Sept. 11, 1984
175	Captain Glen Johnson	Oct. 23, 1984
176	Major Dick Hoey	Nov. 15, 1984
177	Captain Al Frierson	Dec. 6, 1984
178	Captain Robin E. Scott	Jan. 15, 1985
179	Captain Greg "Curly" Nicholl	Feb. 11, 1985
	(Lieutenant Colonel)	July 8, 1992
180	Captain Mike Merritt	Feb. 26, 1985
	(Lieutenant Colonel)	Aug. 28, 1991
181	Major Richard B. Wade	March 28, 1985
182	Captain Harry E. Greer III	April 10, 1985
183	Captain John Krese	May 3, 1985
184	Lieutenant Colonel John Miller	May 30, 1985
	(Brigadier General)	Sept. 13, 1993
185	Lieutenant Colonel Thomas Goslin	June 20, 1985
186	Captain Teddy V. Hale	June 10, 1985
187	Colonel Thomas Mahan	July 29, 1985
188	Captain Wade McRoberts	Aug. 13, 1985
189	Captain Gary "Gar" Frith	Aug. 27, 1985
	(Major)	Nov. 14, 1991
190	Major Lou Alekna	Sept. 10, 1985
191	Major Don Hansen	Sept. 18, 1985
192	Captain Tim Sims	Oct. 9, 1985
193	Captain Guy Bower	Oct. 17, 1985
194	Captain Brad L. Carlson	Oct. 29, 1985
195	Major Bob Ryals	Nov. 14, 1985
196	Major David Greenlee	Nov. 21, 1985
197	Major Michael D. Farmer	Dec. 11, 1985
198	Major Ross E. Mulhare	Jan. 7, 1986
199	Colonel Michael C. Short	Jan. 14, 1986
200	Major Darryl Leger	Jan. 28, 1986
201	Lieutenant Colonel David McCloud	Feb. 5, 1986
202	Captain David B. Wind	Feb. 25, 1986
203	Captain Robert A. Wesolowski	March 4, 1986
204	Captain Ben G. Brockman Jr.	March 19, 1986
205	Lieutenant Colonel Rodger C. Locher	Apr. 3, 1986
206	Captain Michael R. Cook	Apr. 17, 1986
207	Captain Lawrence R. Lee	May 2, 1986
208	Captain Roderick R. Kallman	May 14, 1986
209	Captain Michael S. Sackley	June 4, 1986
210	Captain Richard W. Glitz	June 17, 1986
211	Major Blaine D. Maw	July 9, 1986
212	Captain Paul J. Madson	July 29, 1986
213	Captain John C. Peterson Jr.	Aug. 14, 1986
214	Major John W. Zink	Aug. 26, 1986
215	Captain David L. Russell	Sept. 5, 1986
216	Captain John L. Hensley	Oct. 8, 1986
217	Captain Michael C. Setnor	Oct. 21, 1986
	(Lieutenant Colonel)	Nov. 14, 1994
218	Colonel Herbert T. Pickering Jr.	Nov. 4, 1986
219	Lieutenant Colonel David T. Holmes	Nov. 5, 1986
220	Major Bernard D. Stubbs	Dec. 2, 1986
221	Captain Karl R. Vonkessel	Dec. 12, 1986
222	Captain Bruce L. Teagarden	Jan. 22, 1987
223	Major Jack W. Shaw	Jan. 29, 1987
224	Captain Bryan R. Wright	March 4, 1987
225	Major Lance V. L. Romer	March 17, 1987
226	Captain Jonathan P. Staniforth	March 20, 1987
227	Captain Daniel W. Jordan III	March 20, 1987
228	Captain Gary H. Maupin	Apr. 16, 1987
229	Captain Craig N. Gourley	Apr. 22, 1987
230	Captain Edmund D. Walker	May 1, 1987
231	Major Michael C. Stewart	May 1, 1987
232	Lieutenant Colonel Arthur P. "Art" Weyermuller	May 27, 1987
	(Colonel)	Sept. 3, 1992
233	Major Paul E. Butalla	June 2, 1987
234	Lieutenant Colonel James W. Teak	June 10, 1987
235	Captain Leonard M. Ritchey	June 17, 1987
236	Major Mark D. McConnell	July 7, 1987

237	Captain John Q. "J. Q." Watton	July 9, 1987
238	Lieutenant Colonel Richard C. Groesch	July 23, 1987
239	Major Dale R. Hanner	Aug. 11, 1987
240	Captain George T. Doran	Aug. 11, 1987
241	Lieutenant Colonel	
	James G. Ferguson	Aug. 24, 1987
242	Captain Robert Yates	Aug. 26, 1987
243	Lieutenant Colonel Keat Griggers	Sept. 9, 1987
244	Captain Samuel Hartmann	Sept. 22, 1987
245	Major Gary M. Sanders	Oct. 8, 1987
246	Captain Randall G. Peterson	Oct. 22, 1987
247	Captain Gary N. Flatt	Nov. 11, 1987
248	Captain Joel M. Horie	Dec. 3, 1987
249	Major David A. Ruddock	Dec. 8, 1987
250	Captain Daniel F. Haggerty	Jan. 13, 1988
251	Colonel Anthony J. Tolin	Feb. 4, 1988
252	Lieutenant Colonel William J. Lake	Feb. 17, 1988
	(Brigadier General)	Aug. 24, 1998
253	Captain Joseph M. Ford	March 11, 1988
254	Major Douglas S. Higgins	March 17, 1988
255	Captain Thomas C. Seckman	March 17, 1988
256	Lieutenant Colonel	
	Donald C. Schramski	Apr. 12, 1988
257	Captain Jon W. Behymer	Apr. 12, 1988
258	Major Charles E. Hicks	May 10, 1988
259	Captain Jerry Leatherman	May 10, 1988
260	Major Samuel R. Hays III	May 10, 1988
261	Captain Gregory A. Feest	May 26, 1988
	(Lieutenant Colonel)	July 7, 1994
262	Captain James J. Villers	June 1, 1988
263	Major Steven R. Charles	June 2, 1988
264	Captain Mark W. Renelt	June 8, 1988
265	Captain Nicholas A. Santangelo	June 28, 1988
266	Major Jerry A. Howalt	June 28, 1988
267	Lieutenant Colonel Robert S. Temkow	June 29, 1988
268	Captain James R. Mastny	Aug. 2, 1988
269	Captain Daniel R. Backus	Aug. 5, 1988
	(Major)	Nov. 16, 1993
270	Captain Scott R. Stimpert	Aug. 8, 1988
271	Colonel Gary A. Voellger	Sept. 1, 1988
272	Captain David R. Brown	Sept. 14, 1988
273	Major Frank A. Holmes	Oct. 11, 1988
274	Captain Robert G. Bledsoe	Oct. 12, 1988
275	Captain Kenneth B. Huff	Oct. 12, 1988
276	Captain Donald R. Chapman	Oct. 14, 1988
277	Major Walter E. Rhoads	Nov. 22, 1988
278	Major Robert D. Eskridge	Nov. 22, 1988
279	Major Steven L. Marquez	Nov. 22, 1988
280	Lieutenant Colonel	
	Charles R. Greer Jr.	Dec. 13, 1988
281	Major George L. Kelman	Dec. 14, 1988
282	Squadron Leader Graham	
	Wardell (RAF)	Dec. 14, 1998
283	Colonel Klaus J. Klause	Jan. 4, 1989
284	Captain Marcel E. Kerdavid	Jan. 4, 1989
285	Lieutenant Colonel	
	Gerald C. Carpenter	Feb. 6, 1989
286	Major Timothy D. Phillips	Feb. 7, 1989
287	Lieutenant Colonel	
	Ralph W. Getchell	Feb. 15, 1989
288	Major Kimble N. Fieldstad	Feb. 15, 1989
289	Major Jon R. Boyd	March 15, 1989
290	Major Lorin C. Long	March 15, 1989
291	Captain Robert L. Warren	March 15, 1989
292	Captain Jeffrey A. Moore	Apr. 11, 1989
293	Captain Philip A. Mahon	Apr. 13, 1989
294	Major Jerry T. Sink	Apr. 18, 1989
	(Lieutenant Colonel)	May 3, 1996
295	Captain Joseph A. Salata	May 2, 1989
	(Major)	Jan. 4, 1996
296	Lieutenant Colonel	
	Lewis S. Weiland	May 2, 1989
297	Major Lee D. Gustin	May 3, 1989
298	Captain Daniel J. "Beaner" Decamp	May 4, 1989
299	Captain Neil H. McCaskill	June 7, 1989
300	Major Alan D. Minnich	June 7, 1989
301	Major Walker B. Bourland	June 8, 1989
302	Captain Dennis K. Baker	June 9, 1989
303	Captain Brain R. Foley	July 6, 1989
304	Major Michael T. Mahar	July 6, 1989
305	Captain Charles D. Link	July 6, 1989
306	Captain Philip W. McDaniel	July 17, 1989
307	Captain Mark J. Lindstoem	July 28, 1989
308	Lieutenant Colonel Robert J. Maher	Aug. 1, 1989
309	Captain Michael E. Mckinney	Aug. 1, 1989
310	Captain Gregg K. Verser	Aug. 1, 1989
311	Major Miles S. Pound	Aug. 24, 1989
312	Major Rodney L. Shrader	Aug. 29, 1989
313	Major Leonard C. Broline	Aug. 30, 1989
314	Lieutenant Colonel Barry E. Horne	Aug. 31, 1989
315	Major Robert R. Saroski	Oct. 3, 1989
316	Captain Richard "R. C." Cline	Oct. 5, 1989
317	Captain David W. Francis	Oct. 12, 1989
318	Captain Wesley E. Cockman	Oct. 25, 1989
319	Captain Andrew Nichols	Oct. 26, 1989
	(Major)	Nov. 14, 1994
320	Captain Michael D. Riehl	Nov. 1, 1989
321	Captain Robert B. Donaldson	Nov. 27, 1989
322	Captain John F. Savidge	Nov. 28, 1989
323	Captain Michael W. Mahon	Nov. 29, 1989
324	Captain Russell W. Travis	Jan. 4, 1990
325	Captain Paul T. "Psycho" Dolson	Jan. 25, 1990
326	Major Mark W. Leeson	Feb. 13, 1990
327	Captain Terence J. "Flo" Foley	Feb. 14, 1990

328	Major Steven C. Edgar	Feb. 15, 1990	
329	Lieutenant Colonel Gregory T. Gonyea	March 20, 1990	
330	Major Wesley T. Wyrick	March 20, 1990	
331	Major Joseph R. Bouley	March 22, 1990	
332	Captain Louis McDonald	Apr. 25, 1990	
333	Major Clare G. Whitescarver	Apr. 25, 1990	
334	Captain Steven E. Troyer	May 1, 1990	
335	Captain Kevin A. Tarrant	May 1, 1990	
336	Major Charles G. Treadway (Lieutenant Colonel)	May 29, 1990 Nov. 4, 1997	
337	Captain Raymond J. Lynott	May 30, 1990	
338	Captain Darrell P. Zelko (Major)	May 30, 1990 May 29, 1997	
339	Captain John W. Hesterman	June 21, 1990	
340	Major John Steve "Lefty" Farnham	June 21, 1990	
341	Captain Lee J. Archambault	July 27, 1990	
342	Captain Stephen W. "Chappie" Chappel	July 26, 1990	
343	Major Michael Christensen	July 26, 1990	
344	Colonel Robert C. Huff	Sept. 11, 1990	
345	Lieutenant Colonel Bruce E. Kreidler	Sept. 20, 1990	
346	Major Donald P. J. Higgins	Sept. 20, 1990	
347	Captain John C. "Pete" Peterson	Sept. 20, 1990	
348	Captain Matthew E. Byrd	Oct. 16, 1990	
349	Major Lee E. Huson	Oct. 16, 1990	
350	Captain Andrew W. Papp (Major)	Jan. 10, 1991 March 26, 1996	
351	Captain Greg L. Sembower	Jan. 10, 1991	
352	Captain Richard L. "Rick" Wright Jr. (Major)	Jan. 11, 1991 Oct. 15, 1996	
353	Major Thomas D. "TDY" Young	Feb. 26, 1991	
354	Squadron Leader Chris Topham (RAF)	Feb. 27, 1991	
355	Captain Skeeter Kohntopp	March 21, 1991	
356	Captain Lee Conn	March 21, 1991	
357	Captain Tony Seely	Apr. 18, 1991	
358	Captain Thomas P. "Bulldog" Shoaf	Apr. 18, 1991	
359	Major Dave Brown	Apr. 23, 1991	
360	Captain Raymond A. Bivans	May 6, 1991	
361	Major Douglas N. Campbell	May 7, 1991	
362	Captain Tim Veeder	June 4, 1991	
363	Captain Frank "Vooter" Cavuoti	June 4, 1991	
364	Captain Angelo "Scooby" Eiland (Major)	June 5, 1991	
365	Captain Tony "Lazer" Lazarski	June 5, 1991	
366	Major Mike Daniels	July 9, 1991	
367	Captain Scot S. Soto	July 9, 1991	
368	Captain Mark A. Pope	July 9, 1991	
369	Captain Mark S. Engeman	July 10, 1991	
370	Colonel Raleigh T. "Tom" Harrington	July 18, 1991	
371	Major John D. MacKay	Aug. 6, 1991	
372	Captain John Massee	Aug. 7, 1991	
373	Captain Michael R. Kelley	Aug. 7, 1991	
374	Major James P. Joyce	Aug. 28, 1991	
375	Captain Dave M. "Hendo" Henderson	Aug. 28, 1991	
376	Captain James M. "Leekster" Leek	Aug. 29, 1991	
377	Captain Douglas E. "Cout" Couture	Oct. 2, 1991	
378	Captain David M. Wooden	Oct. 2, 1991	
379	Major James R. Phillips	Oct. 2, 1991	
380	Major Thomas D. "Tinker" Bell	Nov. 14, 1991	
381	Captain Barry D. "Jekyl" Brannon	Nov. 14, 1991	
382	Captain Jeff W. Robinson	Nov. 14, 1991	
383	Major Richard A. Dunham	Dec. 18, 1991	
384	Major James P. Hunt	Dec. 18, 1991	
385	Captain Tony R. "Dawg" Senna	Dec. 19, 1991	
386	Major David A. Adair	Jan. 8, 1992	
387	Captain Michael G. Hesley	Feb. 5, 1992	
388	Captain John P. Regan	Feb. 5, 1992	
389	Captain J. S. Salton	Feb. 5, 1992	
390	Captain Jonathan Bachman	Feb. 18, 1992	
391	Captain Michael J. Hilton	March 11, 1992	
392	Captain Mathew P. McKeon	March 11, 1992	
393	Captain John L. "JMor" Moring	March 11, 1992	
394	Captain John D. "Dave" Silvia	March 12, 1992	
395	Captain Jack G. Mayo	Apr. 15, 1992	
396	Captain George P. Biondi	Apr. 15, 1992	
397	Captain John G. Jerakis	Apr. 15, 1992	
398	Captain Zane F. Morris	Apr. 16, 1992	
399	Brigadier General Lloyd "Fig" Newton	Apr. 25, 1992	
400	Lieutenant Colonel Robert K. Marple	May 20, 1992	
401	Captain Charles E. "Chuck" Osteen	May 20, 1992	
402	Captain John B. Mills	May 20, 1992	
403	Captain Robert "Bobcat" Concannon	July 8, 1992	
404	Captain Mark "Drink" Drinkard	July 9, 1992	
405	Captain Marcus "Coop" Cooper	July 9, 1992	
406	Captain Charlie "Tuna" Hainline	July 10, 1992	
407	Captain Richard J. "Rich" Steckbeck	Nov. 4, 1992	
408	Captain Shayne H. "Shotgun" Doering	Nov. 4, 1992	
409	Captain J. Hugh "Huge" Burns	Nov. 4, 1992	
410	Captain Glenn C. Baugher (Major)	Nov. 4, 1992 Dec. 13, 1996	
411	Captain Joseph M. "Haiji" Skaja Jr.	Nov. 5, 1992	
412	Captain Michael E. Newman	Dec. 2, 1992	
413	Captain John B. "Snake" Pechiney	Dec. 2, 1992	
414	Captain Brian N. "Rotor" Willett	Dec. 2, 1992	
415	Captain Kevin "K. C." Smith	Dec. 2, 1992	
416	Captain Gregory A. Eckfeld	Dec. 9, 1992	
417	Captain William Berg	Jan. 7, 1993	
418	Captain Michael Leclair	Jan. 7, 1993	
419	Captain Parrish Olmstead	Jan. 7, 1993	

420	Captain Dwayne "Bags" Taylor	Jan. 7, 1993
421	Captain David Bromwell	Jan. 11, 1993
422	Captain Peter C. Hunt	Apr. 7, 1993
423	Captain Lawrence G. Alicz	Apr. 7, 1993
424	Captain Braden P. Delauder	Apr. 7, 1993
425	Captain Damian J. McCarthy	May 21, 1993
426	Captain Jacob N. Shepherd	May 21, 1993
427	Captain Kevin L. Smith	May 21, 1993
428	Captain Michael W. Richey	Aug. 17, 1993
429	Captain David Stischer	Aug. 18, 1993
430	Captain William T. Davidson	Aug. 18, 1993
431	Captain Russell C. Howard	Aug. 18, 1993
432	Major Pitt M. Merryman	Nov. 16, 1993
433	Captain Gregg Nesemeier III	Nov. 16, 1993
434	Captain Christopher R. Williams	Nov. 16, 1993
435	Major Dave Schemel	Jan. 11, 1994
436	Squadron Leader Ian Wood (RAF)	Jan. 11, 1994
437	Captain Bryan K. "B. K." Knight	Jan. 11, 1994
438	Captain Philip A. Smith	Jan. 11, 1994
439	Captain Kenneth J. Vantiger	Feb. 15, 1994
440	Captain Joseph H. Kopacz	Feb. 15, 1994
441	Captain Russell A. Vieira	Feb. 15, 1994
442	Lieutenant Colonel William Crabbe	Apr. 6, 1994
443	Captain John Ostromecky	Apr. 6, 1994
444	Captain Rem Edwards	Apr. 6, 1994
445	Thomas J. Palmer	June 14, 1994
446	Captain Francis M. Brown	June 14, 1994
447	Captain Todd J. Flesch	June 14, 1994
448	Captain James A. Marks Jr.	June 15, 1994
449	Lieutenant Colonel Roy Y. Sikes	July 19, 1994
450	Captain Gregory P. Butler	July 19, 1994
451	Captain Hoyt D. Whetstone	July 19, 1994
452	Lieutenant Colonel Kurt A. Cichowski	Aug. 23, 1994
453	Lieutenant Colonel Michael S. Roller	Aug. 23, 1994
454	Major Gary R. Woltering	Aug. 23, 1994
455	Major Daniel S. Gruber	Aug. 24, 1994
456	Colonel John Rosa	Sept. 14, 1994
457	Lieutenant Colonel David L. Brown	Sept. 14, 1994
458	Major Randy Eckley	Nov. 1994
459	Captain Greg Dean	Dec. 16, 1994
460	Captain Jack Forsythe	Dec. 16, 1994
461	Captain Ken Levens	Dec. 16, 1994
462	Major Douglas Stewart (Lieutenant Colonel)	Feb. 15, 1995
463	Captain Joe Rush	Feb. 15, 1995
464	Navy Lieutenant David Bobdell	March 14, 1995
465	Colonel Bruce Carlson	Apr. 14, 1995
466	Captain Kirk Horton	May 16, 1995
467	Captain Charles Langlais	May 16, 1995
468	Captain Charles Maxwell	May 25, 1995
469	Captain Jon Fanning	June 15, 1995
470	Captain Marc Reese	June 15, 1995
471	Captain Steve Kokora	June 15, 1995
472	Major Gene O'Nale	Aug. 2, 1995
473	Lieutenant Colonel Kevin Smith	Oct. 12, 1995
474	Captain Chris Babbidge	Nov. 8, 1995
475	Captain Ken Dwelle	Nov. 8, 1995
476	Captain Dan Ourada	Nov. 8, 1995
477	Captain Jim Less	Nov. 8, 1995
478	Captain Tom McCloskey	Jan. 4, 1996
479	Captain Greg Pantle	Jan. 4, 1996
480	Captain Jim Ward	Jan. 4, 1996
481	Squadron Leader Mark C. Sutton	Feb. 21, 1996
482	Captain Bruce Brown	Feb. 21, 1996
483	Captain Anthony K. Terrell	Feb. 21, 1996
484	Captain William L. Stallings III	Feb. 21, 1996
485	Captain Mark A. Draper	March 26, 1996
486	Captain Ellwood P. Hinman IV	March 26, 1996
487	Captain David F. Toomey III	March 26, 1996
488	Lieutenant Colonel Gregory A. Alston	March 26, 1996
489	Captain Paul Cook	May 3, 1996
490	Captain Jack Stuart	May 3, 1996
491	Captain Ward Juedeman	May 3, 1996
492	Captain Stamp Walden	May 3, 1996
493	Captain Mike Mangus	June 12, 1996
494	Captain Juan Gaud	June 12, 1996
495	Captain Randy Parker	June 12, 1996
496	Lieutenant Colonel John M. Gibbons	July 19, 1996
497	Major Mark R. Perusse	July 19, 1996
498	Captain Thomas L. Rempfer	July 19, 1996
499	Major P. Mason "Mace" Carpenter	July 19, 1996
500	Captain Joe Slupski	Oct. 15, 1996
501	Captain Dave Shipley	Oct. 15, 1996
502	Major Mike Wagner	Oct. 15, 1996
503	Major Rich Baumann	Nov. 15, 1996
504	Major Ron Evenson	Nov. 15, 1996
505	Major Jack Hayes	Nov. 15, 1996
506	Major Byron Kappes	Nov. 15, 1996
507	Major Mark Little	Nov. 15, 1996
508	Captain Anthony J. Dennison III	Dec. 16, 1996
509	Captain Kenneth D. Frollini	Dec. 16, 1996
510	Captain Andrew E. Lager	Dec. 16, 1996
511	Major Andy Lasher	March 20, 1997
512	Captain John Markle	March 20, 1997
513	Captain Douglas Watkins	March 20, 1997
514	Captain George Krajnak	March 20, 1997
515	Major Steve Guzek	Apr. 20, 1997
516	Lieutenant Colonel Fred Zeitz	Apr. 22, 1997
517	Major Lee Wyatt	Apr. 22, 1997
518	Captain Laurence Rice	May 29, 1997

519	Major Kevin Sullivan	May 29, 1997
520	Captain Dean Wright	May 29, 1997
521	Captain Colin Miller	June 25, 1997
522	Major Paul Amidon	June 25, 1997
523	Major Bill Debenedictis	June 25, 1997
524	Major Ed Terry	June 25, 1997
525	Major Frank "Buck" Rogers	Aug. 5, 1997
526	Captain David Sullivan	Aug. 5, 1997
527	Captain Kenneth Tatum	Aug. 5, 1997
528	Captain Thad T. Darger	Aug. 6, 1997
529	Lieutenant Colonel John Snider	Oct. 22, 1997
530	Major Matthew Erichsen	Nov. 4, 1997
531	Lieutenant Colonel Jim Brown	Dec. 15, 1997
532	Lieutenant Colonel Joe Corso	Dec. 15, 1997
533	Major Paul Fazenbaker	Dec. 15, 1997
534	Major David Moore	Dec. 15, 1997
535	Navy Lieutenant Greg Friedman	Jan. 22, 1998
536	Major Bob Hood	Jan. 22, 1998
537	Lieutenant Colonel Sam Johnson	Jan. 22, 1998
538	Major Scott Phillips	Jan. 22, 1998
539	Major Bruce Summers	Apr. 3, 1998
540	Squadron Leader Alistair Monkman	Apr. 3, 1998
541	Captain Lawrence Guichard	May 12, 1998
542	Major David Rabe	May 12, 1998
543	Major Mark Jenner	May 12, 1998
544	Major Phil Delillo	June 30, 1998
545	Major Brad O'Connor	June 30, 1998
546	Lieutenant Colonel John Gytri	June 30, 1998

APPENDIX 3:

F-117 Commanders

Date Command Started

4450th Tactical Group
Colonel Robert A. Jackson	October 15, 1979
Colonel James A. Allen	May 17, 1982
Colonel Howell M. Estes III	June 15, 1984
Colonel Michael W. Harris	December 6, 1985
Colonel Michael C. Short	April 3, 1987
Colonel Anthony J. Tolin	August 10, 1988

4450th Test Squadron
Major William C. Hepler	July 15, 1981
Major Gerald B. Fleming	September 18, 1981
Lieutenant Colonel Ervin C. Sharpe Jr.	July 21, 1983
Lieutenant Colonel John F. Miller	June 1, 1985
Lieutenant Colonel David T. Holmes	January 16, 1987
Lieutenant Colonel William J. Lake	February 5, 1988

4451st Test Squadron
Lieutenant Colonel Wallace C. Weekes	April 13, 1983

Lieutenant Colonel Medford C. Bowman	June 1, 1985
Lieutenant Colonel Robert E. Bruce	July 24, 1986
Lieutenant Colonel John W. Zink	July 15, 1988

4452nd Test Squadron
Lieutenant Colonel Alton C. Whitley Jr.	ca. September 1982
Major Dennis R. Larsen	June 1, 1985
Major Robert D. Williams	August 22, 1986
Lieutenant Colonel Arthur P. Meyermuller	January 7, 1987
Lieutenant Colonel James G. Ferguson	August 14, 1987
Lieutenant Colonel Keat Griggers	June 3, 1988

4453rd Test and Evaluation Squadron
Lieutenant Colonel Roger C. Locher	October 4, 1985
Lieutenant Colonel Arthur P. Meyermuller	August 14, 1987
Lieutenant Colonel Gerald C. Carpenter	May 5, 1989

49th Fighter Wing
Brigadier General Lloyd W. Newton	November 15, 1991
Brigadier General John F. Miller	July 8, 1993
Brigadier General Bruce Carlson	February 10, 1995
Brigadier General Dennis R. Larsen	August 23, 1996
Brigadier General William J. Lake	June 15, 1998

Vice Commanders
Colonel Allan R. Guarino	February 4, 1992
Colonel Robert C. Huff	April 9, 1993
Colonel James W. Bailey III	June 1, 1994
Colonel Frank W. Clawson	June 28, 1996
Colonel Andrew S. Dichter	July 15, 1998

415th Fighter Squadron (inactivated July 1, 1993)
Lieutenant Colonel Bruce E. Keider	July 8, 1992
Lieutenant Colonel William G. Aten III	February 25, 1993

416th Fighter Squadron (inactivated July 1, 1993)
Lieutenant Colonel Michael T. Merritt	May 13, 1992

417th Fighter Squadron (inactivated December 2, 1993)
Lieutenant Colonel John S. Farnham	June 15, 1992

7th Fighter Squadron
Lieutenant Colonel James Phillips Jr.	June 24, 1993
Lieutenant Colonel Gregory M. Nicholl	November 9, 1994
Lieutenant Colonel Richard A. Dunham II	October 7, 1996
Lieutenant Colonel Andrew W. Papp	February 27, 1998

8th Fighter Squadron
Lieutenant Colonel James P. Hunt	January 29, 1993
Lieutenant Colonel Michael P. Setnor	February 10, 1995
Lieutenant Colonel Michael S. Roller	June 14, 1996
Lieutenant Colonel Gary R. Woltering	June 27, 1997

9th Fighter Squadron
Lieutenant Colonel William G. Aten III   February 25, 1993
Lieutenant Colonel William C. Crabbe III   July 8, 1994
Lieutenant Colonel Gregory A. Feest   June 8, 1995
Lieutenant Colonel Joseph A. Salata   June 13, 1997

37th Fighter Wing
Colonel Anthony J. Tolin   August 10, 1988
Colonel Alton C. Whitley   August 17, 1990

415th Fighter Squadron
Lieutenant Colonel William J. Lake   October 5, 1989
Lieutenant Colonel Ralph J. Getchell   November 3, 1989
Lieutenant Colonel Bruce E. Keider   June 7, 1990

416th Fighter Squadron
Lieutenant Colonel Gerald C. Carpenter   October 5, 1989
Lieutenant Colonel Gregory T. Gonyea   August 10, 1990
Lieutenant Colonel Michael T. Merritt   December 31, 1991

417th Fighter Squadron
Lieutenant Colonel Keat Griggers   October 5, 1989
Lieutenant Colonel Robert J Maher   March 23, 1990
Lieutenant Colonel Barry E. Horne   May 10, 1991
Lieutenant Colonel John S. Farnham   June 11, 1992

APPENDIX 4

Program Milestones

1975	April	Lockheed begins research on the Hopeless Diamond.
	June	Echo 1 computer program is developed by Denys Overholser and Bill Schroeder.
	June	First series of tests on the two one-third-scale wooden models of Hopeless Diamond begin.
	July	Lockheed Aircraft Development Corporation (LADC) wins competition.
	Sept.	Quarter-scale model of Have Blue is built.
	Nov.	Lockheed and Northrop awarded contracts of $1.5 million to conduct phase 1 of XST program.
	Dec.	Have Blue RCS model tested at the Grey Butte microwave measurement facility.
1976	Jan.	Second series of model tests at Grey Butte verify design refinements have further reduced RCS.
	March	Lockheed model transported by truck to RATSCAT for testing.
	April	LADC receives go-ahead to build two Have Blue demonstrators.
1977	Sept. 1	Lockheed Machinists strike begins, lasting four months.
	Oct. 17	HB1001 completes final assembly stage and begins ground tests.
	Nov. 4	Initial engine runs conducted at night at Burbank facility.
	Nov. 16	HB1001 airlifted via C-5 from Burbank to Area 51.
	Dec. 1	First flight of Have Blue, HB1001, begins just after 7 A.M.; Bill Park is the pilot.
1978	Jan. 17	Engine selection for F-117 begins.
	May 4	HB1001 crashes; pilot Bill Park ejects but is badly injured; 36 test sorties completed.
	July 20	HB1002 first flight, pilot Ken Dyson.
	Aug. 9	First in flight RCS measurements.
	Aug.	Testing quarter-scale F-117 model.
	Sept.	F-117 proposal submitted.
	Nov. 1	Receive F-117 production authorization.
	Nov. 16	Full-scale engineering development contract awarded for 5 FSD and 15 production aircraft.
1979	July 11	HB1002 crashes; pilot Ken Dyson ejects safely; 52 test sorties completed.
	Oct. 15	4450th Tactical Group activated.
	Oct.	Colonel Bob Jackson begins crew selection procedure.
	Nov.	Assembly of the first full-scale development F-117 (s/n 780) begins.
1980	April	First production engine delivered.
	July	Original planned first flight date of Aircraft 780. The aircraft numbers represent the month and year.
	Aug. 2	First engine run.
	Oct.	FSD Aircraft 781 for performance and 782 for avionics testing begin assembly.
	Dec. 22	First exhaust nozzle failure experienced.
1981	Feb. 12	Improved exhaust nozzle fitted.
	June 18	First flight of FSD F-117, s/n 780 conducted by Hal Farley.
	July 4	First flight of s/n 781 conducted by Dave Ferguson.
	Nov. 18	First air refueling carried out (s/n 780).
	Dec. 18	First flight of s/n 782, conducted by Tom Morgenfeld.
	Dec. (end)	First fully coated RAM flight (s/n 781).
1982	Jan. 23	First RCS test sortie carried out (s/n 781), conducted by Lieutenant Colonel Roger Moseley.
	March 3	First Tactical Air Command flight (s/n 782).
	March 22	First night flight takes place.

	Apr. 10	First flight of s/n 784, conducted by Bob Riedenauer.
	Apr. 20	Aircraft 785 written off during takeoff following maintenance error. Pilot Bob Riedenauer survived but is badly injured.
	July 7	First flight of s/n 783, conducted by Tom Morgenfeld.
	July 15	Flight of first production aircraft s/n 786, conducted by Hal Farley.
	July 7	First weapons release test conducted s/n 781.
	Oct. 15	Major Al Whitley becomes first operational pilot to fly the F-117.
1983	Sept.	Configuration update 1 started.
1984	Oct.	Navy evaluation of F-117.
1985	July	Configuration update 2 started.
	Sept. 25	Aircraft 781 suffers rudder loss.
1986	June 11	Aircraft 818 becomes the first F-117 to have its BX199 radar absorbent coating applied by robotic spray.
	July 11	Aircraft 792 crashes near Bakersfield, California. The pilot, Major Ross E. Mulhare, is killed.
	Sept.	Ten thousand flying hours achieved.
	Dec. 3	First drag link failure suffered (s/n 815).
1987	April	Ten thousand flights completed.
	Oct. 14	Aircraft 815 crashes at a Nellis gunnery range. Pilot Major Michael C. Stewart is killed.
	Oct. 20	A 4450th A-7D crashes into a hotel near Indianapolis airport. Pilot Major Bruce L. Teagarden ejects safely; however, nine are killed on the ground.
1988	Nov. 10	Assistant Defense Secretary J. Daniel Howard reveals photo of F-117 during a Pentagon press conference.
	Nov.	Senior Trend becomes GBU-27 certified.
	Dec. 1	Aircraft 831 undertakes first post-OCIP flight.
1989	March 18	Aircraft 790 became first aircraft to receive tank five modification.
	May 18	First 600-hour inspection conducted.
	May 25	First composite rudder installation complete, s/n 784.
	June 23	First dual lead acid battery kit installed, s/n 831.
	July 18	First composite rudder flight, s/n 784.
	Aug.	Fatigue aircraft, s/n 777, placed in temporary storage.
	Dec. 20	Two F-117s become first to be used in combat during Operation Just Cause.
1990	Apr. 21	First declassified photos released of the F-117.
	July 12	Last production F-117 is delivered.
	Aug. 21	First 18 F-117s arrive at King Khalid AFB, Saudi Arabia.
1991	Jan. 17	Greg Feest drops the first bomb from aircraft, signaling the start of Desert Storm.
	Feb. 28	End of Desert Storm.
	July 17	Aircraft 781 transfers to Wright-Patterson Air Force Base museum. It had accumulated 522 flying hours.
1992	May 16	Aircraft 780 mounted for display at Nellis Air Force Base. Its last flight was in the summer of 1985, and it had accumulated 308 flying hours.
1994	Nov.	Sixty thousand flights completed.
	Dec.	One hundred thousand flying hours achieved.

APPENDIX 5

Individual Aircraft Histories

Tail No.	First Flight	Pilot	AF Delivery	Remarks
Lot 1				
780	June 18, 1981	Hal Farley	N/A	First air refueling Nov. 18, 1981 Last flight 30/6 or 1/7 1985 (308 hours)
781 (Performance)	Sept. 24, 1981	Dave Ferguson	N/A	First fully coated flight 30.12.81 or 01.01.82 First Weapons release July 7, 1982 Rudder Loss Sept. 25, 1985 500 KEAS door open Feb. 1987 July 17, 1991 to WPAFB Museum (522 hours)

782 (Avionics)	Dec. 18, 1981	Tom Morgenfeld	N/A	First TAC flight March 3, 1982 Dec. 17, 1982, first auto weapon separation March 22, 1988, achieved 500 flight hours June 12, 1991, temporary storage July 1992, began DARPA IR coating evaluations
783 (RCS)	July 7, 1982	Tom Morgenfeld		June 1983 signature tests begin Sept. 1984 Navy evaluation begin Feb. 1985 radar antenna tested Apr. 1986 night vision goggles Aug. 1986 achieved 32 flights in one month Feb. 1987 600 flight hours March 1989 turned over to USAF (830 flight hours) March 1990 900 flight hours Aug. 31, 1992, LO antenna May 1993 painted gray
784 IRADS	Apr. 10, 1982	Bob Riedenauer	N/A	First IRAD laser fire May 1982 Sept. 20, 1983 temporary storage Nov. 1984 move to Burbank for radar mod Aug. 8, 1985, first radar flight Jan. 9, 1986, remove radar install WSC/WB1 Oct. 2, 1986, WSC/WB1 mod complete June 1987 dual door completes 500 KEAS Jan. 1988 completes 300 flight hours May 25, 1989, first composite rudder inst. complete July 18, 1989, first composite rudder flight July 1990 complete 600 flight hours June 19, 1991, drops CBU-102

Lot 2

785	Apr. 20, 1982	Bob Riedenauer	June 16, 1982	Aircraft crashed on takeoff, Bob Riedenauer survived but was badly injured
786	July 15, 1982	Hal Farley	Sept. 2, 1982	Config. update 1, March 21, 1984 Config. update 3, Oct. 13, 1986 Config. update 4, Feb. 1, 1990 Config. update 5, June 28, 1993 24 combat missions in the Gulf War
787	July 20, 1982	Hal Farley	Aug. 23, 1982	Config. update 1, Oct. 9, 1984 Config. update 3, March 19, 1987 Config. update 4, Feb. 8, 1988 Config. update 5, June 11, 1992
788	Sept. 8, 1982	Tom Morgenfeld	Oct. 22, 1982	Config. update 1, Sept. 4, 1984 Config. update 3, Nov. 19, 1986 Config. update 5, Oct. 25, 1990
789	Oct. 27, 1982	Hal Farley	Nov. 17, 1982	Config. update 1, Nov. 27, 1984 Config. update 3, April 17, 1987 Config. update 4, March 29, 1990

				Config. update 5, May 28, 1993 31 combat missions
790	Nov. 11, 1982	Skip Holm	Dec. 11, 1982	Config. update 1, March 22, 1985 Config. update 3, Feb. 6, 1987 Config. update 4, Feb. 9, 1989 Config. update 5, Nov. 3, 1992 30 combat missions
791	Nov. 22, 1982	Skip Holm	Dec. 13, 1982	Config. update 1, Oct. 24, 1983 Config. update 2, Jan. 15, 1985 Config. update 4, March 16, 1989 Config. update 5, Jan. 8, 1993 33 combat missions

Lot 3

792	Dec. 9, 1982	Skip Holm	Dec. 22, 1982	Config. update 1, Feb. 8, 1985 Delivered to 4450th TG, Tonopah On Jan. 2, 1986 this a/c became the first F-117 to undergo a 300-hour inspection Crashed July 11, 1986, pilot Major Ross E. Mulhare killed
793	Jan. 20, 1983	Skip Holm	Feb. 1, 1983	Config. update 1, June 12, 1984 Config. update 3, Aug. 12, 1987 Config. update 4, March 1, 1990 Config. update 5, March 5, 1993 33 combat missions Crashed Sept. 14, 1997, Pilot Major Bryan Knight ejected safely
794	March 4, 1983	Skip Holm	Apr. 15, 1983	Config. update 1, May 15, 1985 Config. update 3, Jan. 5, 1987 Config. update 4, Nov. 30, 1989 Config. update 5, Apr. 2, 1993 35 combat missions
795	June 9, 1983	Hal Farley	Sept. 9, 1983	Config. update 1, June 11, 1985 Config. update 3, May 22, 1987 Config. update 4, Apr. 26, 1990 Config. update 5, May 17, 1994
796	June 23, 1983	Tom Morgenfeld	Aug. 4, 1983	Config. update 1, July 19, 1985 Config. update 3, June 29, 1987 Config. update 4, May 14, 1990 Config. update 5, June 16, 1994 29 combat missions
797	Aug. 3, 1983	Tom Morgenfeld	Aug. 31, 1983	Config. update 2, Aug. 29, 1985 Config. update 4, Sept. 7, 1989 Config. update 5, Oct. 5, 1992 8 combat missions
798	Aug. 25, 1983	Dave Ferguson	Oct. 3, 1983	Config. update 2, Oct. 2, 1985 Config. update 4, May 11, 1989 Config. update 5, 5 Feb. 1993

In Sept. 1990, this aircraft became the first F-117 to undertake a 1,200-hour inspection
34 combat missions

Lot 4

799	Sept. 22, 1983	Dave Ferguson	Oct. 28, 1983	Config. update 2, Jan. 17, 1986

Config. update 4, Oct. 26, 1989
Config. update 5, Dec. 20, 1993
21 combat missions

| 800 | Nov. 10, 1983 | Hal Farley | Dec. 7, 1983 | Config. update 2, Feb. 17, 1986 |

Config. update 4, July 6, 1989
Config. update 5, July 28, 1993
On Dec. 22, 1987 this aircraft became first F-117 to undertake a 600-hour inspection, and in July 1989 it underwent the first 900-hour inspection

| 801 | Dec. 21, 1983 | Tom Morgenfeld | Feb. 15, 1984 | Config. update 2, March 25, 1986 |

Config. update 4, June 8, 1989
38 combat missions
Crashed Aug. 4, 1992
Pilot Captain John B. Mills ejected safely

| 802 | Mar. 7, 1984 | Dave Ferguson | Apr. 6, 1984 | Config. update 2, May 4, 1986 |

Config. update 4, Aug. 5, 1989
Config. update 5, Sept. 4, 1992
19 combat missions

| 803 | May 8, 1984 | Hal Farley | June 22, 1984 | Config. update 2, June 5, 1986 |

Config. update 4, July 28, 1988
Config. update 5, Apr. 29, 1993
33 combat missions

| 804 | May 25, 1984 | Dave Ferguson | June 20, 1984 | Config. update 3, Aug. 11, 1986 |

Config. update 5, July 20, 1990

| 805 | July 5, 1984 | Tom Morgenfeld | Aug. 3, 1984 | Config. update 3, Sept. 15, 1986 |

Config. update 5, June 21, 1990

| 806 | Aug. 20, 1984 | Dave Ferguson | Sept. 12, 1984 | Config. update 3, July 7, 1986 |

Config. update 4, Oct. 5, 1989
Config. update 5, July 14, 1994
39 combat missions. Lost on the night of March 27-28, 1999, 40 miles from Belgrade while participating in Operation Allied Force. Pilot Rescued. Details remain classified at time of printing

Lot 5

| 807 | Sept. 13, 1984 | Dave Ferguson | Nov. 28, 1984 | Config. update 3+, Sept. 10, 1987 |

Config. update 5, June 21, 1991
14 combat missions

| 808 | Oct. 29, 1984 | Dave Ferguson | Dec. 20, 1984 | Config. update 3+, Oct. 16, 1987 |

Config. update 5, Sept. 20, 1991
37 combat missions

809	Jan. 3, 1985	Dave Ferguson	Apr. 16, 1985	Config. update 3+, Nov. 25, 1987 Config. update 5, Dec. 20, 1990 Config. update 5+, March 28, 1995
810	Jan. 18, 1985	Dave Ferguson	Feb. 14, 1985	Config. update 4, May 12, 1988 Config. update 5, Jan. 22, 1992 26 combat missions

Lot 6

811	March 8, 1985	Tom Morgenfeld	March 29, 1985	Config. update 4, Oct. 24, 1988 Config. update 5, March 18, 1992 33 combat missions
812	May 1, 1985	Dave Ferguson	June 12, 1985	Config. update 4, Jan. 4, 1990 Config. update 5, Dec. 12, 1991 42 combat missions

Lot 7

813	June 7, 1985	Hal Farley	July 10, 1985	Config. update 4, Dec. 8, 1988 Config. update 5, May 13, 1992 35 combat missions
814	July 26, 1985	Hal Farley	Sept. 5, 1985	Config. update 4, Jan. 19, 1989 Config. update 5, Apr. 19, 1994 34 combat missions
815	Sept. 13, 1985	Hal Farley	Oct. 31, 1985	Crashed Oct. 14, 1987; pilot Major Michael C. Stewart killed.
816	Oct. 30, 1985	Tom Morgenfeld	Dec. 20, 1985	Config. update 4, Jan. 8, 1988 Config. update 5, Dec. 3, 1992 39 combat missions
817	Jan. 9, 1986	Dave Ferguson	Feb. 28, 1986	Config. update 4, Apr. 5, 1988 Config. update 5, March 22, 1994 18 combat missions
818	Feb. 11, 1986	Hal Farley	May 22, 1986	Config. update 4, June 16, 1988 Config. update 5, Aug. 25, 1993 38 combat missions
819	Apr. 14, 1986	Dave Ferguson	Apr. 24, 1986	Config. update 4, July 16, 1988 Config. update 5, Sept. 23, 1993 On June 11, 1986, this aircraft became the first to receive a coating of RAM via robotic spray 30 combat missions
820	May 2, 1986	Dave Ferguson	June 19, 1986	Config. update 5, Jan. 31, 1991 Config. update 5+, March 2, 1995

Lot 8

821	June 20, 1986	Tom Morgenfeld	Aug. 1, 1986	Config. update 5, Apr. 25, 1991 32 combat missions

822	Aug. 18, 1986	Dave Ferguson	Sept. 18, 1986	Config. update 5, Aug. 16, 1990
823	Oct. 7, 1986	Dave Ferguson	Dec. 4, 1986	Config. update 5, May 31, 1991
824	Nov. 13, 1986	Dave Ferguson	Dec. 17, 1986	Config. update 5, Nov. 21, 1990 Config. update 5+ Dec. 8, 1994
825	Jan. 29, 1987	Tom Morgenfeld	March 25, 1987	Config. update 5, July 24, 1991 33 combat missions
826	March 2, 1987	Dave Ferguson	March 25, 1987	Config. update 5, March 28, 1991 29 combat missions
827	Apr. 7, 1987	Hal Farley	May 18, 1987	Config. update 5, Sept. 19, 1990 Config. update 5+, Jan. 17, 1995
828	May 15, 1987	Dave Ferguson	June 17, 1987	Config. update 5, Feb. 28, 1991

Lot 9

829	July 10, 1987	Hal Farley	Nov. 27, 1987	Config. update 5, Oct. 21, 1993 23 combat missions
830	Sept. 3, 1987	Hal Farley	Nov. 27, 1987	Config. update 5, Sept. 18, 1991 31 combat missions
831	Oct. 20, 1987	Tom Morgenfeld	Nov. 27, 1987	This aircraft was chosen to undertake the first F-117 Offensive Capability Improvement Program (OCIP), making its first OCIP flight on Dec. 1, 1988, and went on to become the "testbed" aircraft of the fleet.
832	Dec. 10, 1987	Tom Morgenfeld	Feb. 11, 1988	Config. update 5, Nov. 18, 1993 30 combat missions
833	Feb. 19, 1988	Dave Ferguson	May 25, 1988	Config. update 5, Jan. 26, 1994 30 combat missions
834	Apr. 29, 1988	Tom Morgenfeld	May 27, 1988	Config. update 5, Feb. 22, 1994 34 combat missions
835	June 30, 1988	Tom Morgenfeld	Aug. 15, 1988	Config. update 5, Nov. 13, 1991 26 combat missions
836	Sept. 21, 1988	Tom Morgenfeld	Oct. 19, 1988	Config. update 5, Feb. 19, 1992 39 combat missions

Lot 10

837	Dec. 8, 1988	Hal Farley	Feb. 22, 1989	Config. update 5, July 10, 1992 31 combat missions
838	March 17, 1989	Hal Farley	May 24, 1989	Config. update 5, Apr. 14, 1992 36 combat missions
839	June 14, 1989	Hal Farley	Aug. 14, 1989	Config. update 5, Oct. 16, 1991 39 combat missions

840	Sept. 12, 1989	Jim Thomas	Nov. 1, 1989	Config. update 5, Aug. 7, 1992
				Config. update 5+, Nov. 4, 1994
				32 combat missions

Lot 11

841	Dec. 7, 1989	Jim Thomas	March 8, 1990	Config. update 5, Sept. 9, 1994
				On March 8, 1990, this aircraft received the first production composite rudder.
				18 combat missions

842	March 13, 1990	Jim Thomas	March 28, 1990	Config. update 5, Aug. 11, 1994
				33 combat missions

843	May 11, 1990	Hal Farley	June 27, 1990	On July 12, 1990 this aircraft took part in a final delivery ceremony for the F-117
				Config. update 5, Oct. 7, 1994
				33 combat missions

Lot 10+ (insurance spares fus/wings)				Fuselage Apr. 5, 1990
				Right wing May 15, 1990
				Left wing June 8, 1990
				Right wing June 29, 1990
				Left wing Aug. 9, 1990

APPENDIX 6

Flight Test Summary

Sortie Breakdown by Mission Type, CTF Aircraft
Test flights from June 18, 1981, to January 1, 1998

Mission Type	Hours	Sorties
A/C upgrade	11.0	8
Acoustics	96.9	82
Avionics	1420.7	990
Delivery	0.5	1
FCF	80.3	79
Flutter	291.5	194
Loads	69.6	62
Low-obs	661.1	359
Misc.	406.1	366
PFQ	418.9	314
PROFS/TRNG	551.4	418
Systems	341.2	211
Test Support	272.9	245
Weapons	1,271.8	1,306
Total	**5,893.9**	**4,635**

Sortie Breakdown by Mission Type, CTF Aircraft
Test flights of Aircraft 780 from June 18, 1981, to January 1, 1998

Mission Type	Hours	Sorties
Acoustics	10.7	8
Avionics	14.6	11
FCF	0.8	1
Flutter	38.7	22
Loads	22.8	14
Misc.	0.9	1
PFQ	100.1	77
PROFS/TRNG	2.8	3
Total	**191.4**	**137**

Last Flight April 11, 1985. Present location Static Display at Nellis Air Force Base, Nevada.

Sortie Breakdown by Mission Type, CTF Aircraft
Test flights of Aircraft 781 from June 18, 1981, to January 1, 1998

Mission Type	Hours	Sorties
Acoustics	19.7	19
Avionics	3.5	2
FCF	12.3	15
Flutter	120.4	92
Loads	30.0	35
Misc.	7.0	6
PFQ	213.8	151
PROFS/TRNG	3.0	3
Weapons	112.6	114
Total	522.3	437

Last flight July 17, 1991. Present location Air Museum Wright-Patterson Air Force Base, Ohio.

Sortie Breakdown by Mission Type, CTF Aircraft
Test flights of Aircraft 782 from June 18, 1981, to January 1, 1998

Mission Type	Hours	Sorties
Acoustics	17.4	14
Avionics	261.8	205
FCF	17.0	18
Low-obs	2.7	2
Misc.	15.5	14
PFQ	49.2	39
PROFS/TRNG	129.4	99
Systems	118.3	74
Test Support	11.0	8
Weapons	222.1	246
TOTAL	844.4	719

Sortie Breakdown by Mission Type, CTF Aircraft
Test flights of Aircraft 783 from June 18, 1981, to January 1, 1998

Mission Type	Hours	Sorties
A/C upgrade	8.4	5
Acoustics	1.1	1
Avionics	172.7	133
FCF	15.3	16
Low-obs	524.3	269
Misc.	344.0	305
PFQ	20.1	18
PROFS/TRNG	165.0	121
Systems	37.8	25
Test Support	136.2	124
Weapons	180.7	220
Total	1,605.6	1,237

Sortie Breakdown by Mission Type, CTF Aircraft
Test flights of Aircraft 784 from June 18, 1981, to January 1, 1998

Mission Type	Hours	Sorties
A/C upgrade	2.6	3
Acoustics	28.8	24
Avionics	402.3	286
FCF	19.3	16
Flutter	132.4	80
Loads	16.8	13
Low-obs	70.6	47
Misc.	10.4	14
PFQ	21.5	20
PROFS/TRNG	122.2	93
Systems	99.9	61
Test Support	39.1	39
Weapons	458.5	469
Total	1,424.4	1,165

Sortie Breakdown by Mission Type, CTF Aircraft
Test flights of Aircraft 831 from June 18, 1981, to January 1, 1998

Mission Type	Hours	Sorties
Acoustics	19.2	16
Avionics	565.8	353
Delivery	0.5	1
FCF	15.6	13
Low-obs	63.5	41
Misc.	28.3	26
PFQ	14.2	9
PROFS/TRNG	129.0	99
Systems	85.2	51
Test Support	86.6	74
Weapons	297.9	257
Total	1,305.8	940

APPENDIX 7:

Glossary

AAA	Anti-Aircraft Artillery
ABDR	Advanced Battle Damage Repair
ADF	Automatic Direction Finder
AFFTC	Air Force Flight Test Center
AFSC	Air Force Systems Command
ALCM	Air Launched Cruise Missile
AMAD	Airframe Mounted Accessory Drive
AMPS	Automated Mission Planning System
APU	Auxiliary Power Unit
AR	Air Refueling
ARCP	Air Refueling Control Point
ASTRA	Air Staff Training Program
ATF	Advanced Tactical Fighter
ATA	Advanced Technology Aircraft
AWACS	Airborne Warning and Control System
BOQ	Bachelors Officers Quarters
BSAX	Battlefield Surveillance Aircraft, Experimental
CAP	Combat Air Patrol
CAS	Chief of Air Staff
CENTCOM	Central Command
CG	Center of Gravity
CIA	Central Intelligence Agency
CMDI	Color Multifunctional Display Indicators
CMFD	Color Multifunction Display
CMS	Chief Master Sergeant
COMINT	Communications Intelligence
CTF	Combined Test Force
DARPA	Defense Advanced Research Projects Agency
DLIR	Downward-Looking Infrared
DO	Director of Operations
EAOB	Electronic Air Order of Battle
ECM	Electronic Counter Measures
ECS	Environmental Control System
ELINT	Electronic Intelligence
EMD	Engineering, Manufacturing, and Development
EPU	Emergency Power Unit
FADEC	Full Authority Digital Engine Control
FBW	Fly-By-Wire
FCF	Functional Check Flight

FES	Flutter Excitation System
FLIR	Forward-Looking Infrared
FMS	Flight Management System
FPA	Flight Path Accelerator
FS	Fighter Squadron
FSD	Full-Scale Development
FW	Fighter Wing
FWS	Fighter Weapons Squadron
GCI	Ground-Controlled Intercept
GFE	Government-Furnished Equipment
GPS	Global Positioning System
HAC	House Appropriations Committee
HARM	High-Speed Antiradiation Missiles
HAS	Hardened Aircraft Shelters
HASC	House Armed Services Committee
HSI	Horizontal Situation Indicator
HUD	Heads-Up Display
IES	Inertial Exciter System
IFR	Instrument Flight Rules
ILS	Instrument Landing System
INS	Inertial Navigation System
IOC	Initial Operational Capability
IOC	Intercept Operation Center
IP	Instructor Pilot
IR	Infrared
IRADS	Infrared Acquisition and Designation System
IRRCA	Integrated Real-time Information in the Cockpit/Real-time Information Out of the Cockpit
KVA	Kilovolt Amps
LANTIRN	Low Altitude Navigation and Targeting Infrared for Night
LGB	Laser-Guided Bomb
LIOC	Limited Initial Operational Capability
MDI	Multifunction Display Indicators
MDPS	Mission Data Planning System
MMLE	Modified Maximum Likelihood Estimator
MOD	Ministry of Defence
NAS	Naval Air Station
NATO	North Atlantic Treaty Organization
NBC	Nuclear, Biological, or Chemical
OCIP	Offensive Capability Improvement Program

ORI	Operational Readiness Inspection
OT&E	Operational Test and Evaluation
PAARS	Pilot-Activated Automatic Recovery System
PGM	Precision-Guided Munitions
PTO	Power Take-Off
RAF	Royal Air Force
RAM	Radar Absorbing/Attenuating Material
RAS	Radar Absorbing Structure
RATSCAT	Radar Target Scatter
RCS	Radar Cross-Section
RLG	Ring Laser Gyro
RNIP	Ring Laser Gyro Navigation Improvement Program
RTU	Replacement Training Unit
RSS	Relaxed Static Stability
SAC	Senate Appropriations Committee
SAC	Strategic Air Command
SAM	Surface-to-Air Missile
SAR	Special Access Required
SASC	Senate Armed Services Committee
SEAD	Suppression of Enemy Air Defenses
SOC	Sector Operations Center
SPEAR	Strike Projection Evaluation and Anti-Air Research
SPO	Special Project Office
SPO	System Program Officer
TAC	Tactical Air Command
TALD	Tactical Air-Launched Decoys
TDM	Transportable Data Module
TFG	Tactical Fighter Group
TFTS	Tactical Fighter Training Squadron
TFW	Tactical Fighter Wing
TG	Tactical Group
TLAM	Tomahawk Land-Attack Missiles
TOT	Time Over Target
TTO	Tactical Technology Office
UFC	Unified Fuel Control
VFR	Visual Flight Rules
VLO	Very Low Observable
WBI	Weapons Bay Improvement
WSC	Weapon Systems Computer
WSCS	Weapon Systems Computational Subsystem

index